AUTHORITY FAILS
IN ENGLAND

Christine Flourish

Endorsement Letters

Authority Fails in England is a book by Christine, who has tried to share her knowledge, skills and experience in a nurturing capacity as a childminder. I recommend this book for all parents, teachers, and even kids to read and appreciate the influence of the social, economic, cultural, environmental, religious, and political factors in developing a healthy society.

Coming from South Asian origin with the taboo of divorce, never in my life had I dreamed of being a single parent with two kids to succeed in a foreign country. I had a decent job as a Staff Nurse in NHS and worked in the critical care unit, a job that I absolutely loved. However, juggling between work and family life without any support from my other half required a lot of hard work. I accepted life as it was, thinking it was normal for women to put in extra efforts. But at one point, I decided to part ways with my husband, who, although a good son, never grew to be a responsible adult as a husband or father. Getting divorced after eight years of marriage was difficult. I had no idea how I would manage with two kids on my own in a foreign country.

That's when I met Christine while searching for a childminder close to school for a breakfast club and school drop off while I take my six months old to a nursery, which was pretty expensive. I switched over to the day shift after eight years of night shift to suit the changing demands of life. I owe my heartfelt gratitude to this lady who helped me at the right time when I felt I could not continue with the job and manage the kids alone. While I was arranging for my mom to come over here to support me and look after the kids, it was Christine who stood by me, a stranger who very soon became like a family from a different continent. She encouraged me with examples of ladies who have succeeded in their life being single parents. I honestly did not have any hope, but I was ready to strive to pull through with the support of my family, friends and my childminder.

Life could have been worse, but the perseverance, love, faith and support of my family, friends and Christine helped me overcome all the obstacles. While facing financial difficulties with no support from my other half, I decided to work hard when my mom was there to support me and save money for a deposit to buy a house. Which I did within a year.

My job timing was between half seven in the morning and three-thirty in the afternoon and occasional weekend shifts and nights. These were not family-friendly shifts as I had to work five days a week to meet the bills. Then I began working 30 hours and agency shifts to earn extra money to pay the bills and meet childcare expenses. Although the government covered 70% of childcare expenses, the rest were paid by me. Throughout my struggles, I just passed one day at a time. I also grew close to God in faith, and Christine, who was also practising Christian, was good with timely support with biblical verses. I had to change my job to a 9 to 5 job. I regretted every day when I went there to work in a different capacity, but I just needed a job to feed my family. When my father's health deteriorated, he needed someone to help him at home. That's when my mom thought I should get married to help me and my kids live happily.

After being convinced for five years, I got married for the second time. This marriage was, however, shortlived. As he walked away within 16 months, I felt betrayed and confused. Although initially supportive, he got stressed with time as kids needed more attention from me. My new job and masters study at the university asked for time too. Being a single mom was difficult, but now completing the course and working was another level of challenge which I successfully achieved.

It is important to have government policies to support when the family support system is minimal or if they are immigrants and others who are not lucky to have anyone. The politics and bureaucracy at work do not help parents, indirectly impacting the kid's growth and development. It is very important for working women to have affordable childcare options and for the employer to consider the working hours without discrimination for the working single parents at least. I believe my success is because of my strong faith in God and hard work to achieve my goals. I believe I have set an example for my kids of how to persevere the goal against all odds and the importance of hope and faith in life.

I have seen many people who fail to thrive or lose their focus due to compromises in life. I am sure there is a great influence of environment in the child's development, but equally the person's perseverance and sacrifices matter too. Above all, a strong faith to rely on when there is no one to support or seek help because people are selfish and judgmental.

Kids have their own challenges in society with little support. There have been many occasions where I had to explain to them that this is our life and we must accept it as it is. There was a time I got a volunteer psychologist to come and spend some time with kids as they just saw me and the childminder. I guess the government should voluntarily get both parents to contribute to kids' upbringing if they are working and more help available to raise a healthy family. I wish kids get supported at school and some socialising place to play safely with friends to develop them socially.

I hope *Authority Fails in England* provides hope to people and much needed support to the struggling single parents. My best wishes to my friend Christine to achieve great success in her new endeavour.

Jashmin Maria. Msc ANP.

***

I'm honoured to be asked to endorse *"Authority Fails in England"* by Ms Christine Flourish. It's gratifying to know that young people from Minority Ethnic backgrounds are contributing to their communities by their literary contributions.

As the first Mayor of Crewe, from a minority ethnic background, I am aware of the obstacles, real or imagined, that we all face, but we must overcome these and give our best to the communities where we reside.

I hope this book will resonate with all who read it.

Congratulations to Christine for taking on this work. This book should be the first of many!

Irene Faseyi,
Mayor of Crewe, 2013 to 2014

***

There is no better time than this to have a practical book on Parenting and Child Development.

Christine's love for children development is overwhelmingly depicted in this book. Right from working and caring for children and now directly with them, she has developed firsthand experience with child development. This book thus goes beyond the theoretical aspect of the subject. It is indeed a must-read book for all parents, carers, support workers and lovers of children.

As a Certified Accountant and being aware of the importance of analysing information in a more easily understandable way, this is exactly what Christine has done exceptionally well in this book. This book studies the relationship between a parent and child, highlighting key areas which the reader can easily understand and apply. I therefore highly recommend this book.

Pastor Geoffrey Kwakye-Donkor
(Snr Pastor-Goodnews Assemblies of God-

Manchester UK)

***

As a parent of 3 kids in different age groups, I am facing several challenges on a daily basis like any other caring parents of similar ages. *Authority Fails in England* gives parents guidance in an easy-to-understand way, helping them comprehend the psychological development the children are going through and the reasons behind their behaviours. Christine has in her book established an effective guideline for parenting in a very professional way. I truly believe her book is going to help parents to be able to assess their own relationship with their children.

I strongly recommend this book to every responsible parent.

Dr Alex Hashemi
Dental surgeon

Dedication

I dedicate this book to my loving late mother, Sophia.

I also dedicate this book to all the parents and caregivers present worldwide, particularly those struggling with the many challenges of parenting. May this book be the source of guidance for you all.

Acknowledgment

I would like to acknowledge with gratitude the support and love of my family members. This book wouldn't have been possible without the inspiration of my late mother,
Sophia.

TABLE OF CONTENTS

About the Author

I have always loved children, ever since I was a child myself. I used to babysit my little cousin when I was only eight years old. I remember my love for children never subsided. In fact, I carried on with it and cherished being around children.

When I was 14 years old, I was a Sunday school teacher. Every Saturday before Sunday, I would ask different parents and caregivers if they could allow me to take their children to Sunday school. I used to take about five children with me to Sunday school. I never knew that was my field where I'm called.

I was an Ofsted registered childminder and a qualified Early Years Practitioner in Manchester, England. I started running after-school clubs as a manager. I worked with ten different parents of different nationalities, including Indians, Somalis, British, Philippines, Nigerians, South Africans, Zimbabweans, Ghanaians, Jamaicans, and Sri Lankans. Most of them were university students studying to be health care professionals or were already health care experts and parents who run their own businesses.

Working with all these amazing children and their parents for eight long years taught me a lot about parenting and how it differs from everyone's perspective and culture. However, besides everything, there was one thing in common amongst the people of the above-mentioned nationalities. It was boundaries and authority.

In my early years, I have worked with several agency settings all around northwest England. In the meantime, I carried on to work in primary schools and high schools. With all this experience, I have a great insight into how so many things work in different Education environments in England. It is so amazing working as an agency staff member in different settings. You learn and see so much happening around you that you can bring change into it. There is an African saying which goes something like this – "The one making the line sees it straight, but the one behind sees all that is not straight."

I spent almost 12 hours or less with the majority of these children from age six months. A time came when the babies used to call me mummy due to the amount of time I spent with them. However, doing all this, I had my nephew and nieces alongside me since they were one year and two and a half years old who are now 11 and 13 years old. In all, I have got 20 years of working with children in my entire life.

I moved due to a change in my career. I thought I needed a change, but who knows, you can never run away from your passion. I started getting slow in the business, so I decided to get back to working with children.

I'm an inventor, motivational speaker at Youth Conference and in high schools, and the founder of Kristal Education Academy and hold a degree in Childhood and Youth Psychology. I volunteer on the streets supporting children and young people, which has been and continues to be a great experience. I worked in high school as a SENCO with children with behavioural problems and autism, which has inspired me with my studies and all the related experiences.

Since I've worked with and around children almost my entire life, I thought about writing this book called *Authority Fails in England* and highlight some of my concerns regarding pupils' upbringing and future. I hope you will enjoy reading this book as much as I enjoyed writing it.

Preface

Parents and caregivers present across the globe would agree with me when I say that parenting is no piece of cake. Although fun at times, this responsibility is surely laden with its own challenges. The way parents raise their children eventually decides the kind of people those kids would grow up to be.

I decided to write *Authority Fails in England* because I noticed that childhood is in crisis as parents, caregivers, and politicians have failed the children at every level.

My biggest inspiration for this book comes from my late mother. She did a very good job with us and raised us. Besides being a great mother, she was an inspirational teacher who was often visited and thanked by her former students for being their guiding light. I really wish for every parent to incorporate some of the ideas from this book.

While writing *Authority Fails in England,* I made sure to carry out proper research to back up the story.

Through intensive research and hard work of eight long months, I was finally able to put my thoughts to paper. I hope my readers will find the answers to what they wish for. Furthermore, I hope this book becomes a source of guidance for parents and caregivers worldwide.

Page Blank Intentionally.

Introduction

I was born into a big family. Throughout my childhood and as far as I can recall, my mother played the role of both my father and mother. She was very strict yet loving, kind, and generous to her children as well as others. She was not only a teacher but also a role model in her community. That's why I believe we all have a certain standard of responsibility to play when it comes to being teachers. Sophia's children live their lives in principles that have led the older to be very successful and responsible adults in the communities.

No one would deny the fact that every home needs rules for children to abide by them and for parents to be role models. While growing up, we had various rules and reward systems that had a great impact on our lives. Staying next to mum and help her prepare dinner earned you extra delicious desserts. But, in case you were not at home while the dinner was being prepared, there were two possible consequences that you might end up facing. Number 1, there will be no dessert, or number 2, you would have to cook your meal from scratch, even if the meal was almost ready. These were the rules for the boys in their twenties at that time. In all these principles, the best thing that has helped and come out of it for them as well as me is knowing how to make very delicious foods.

In terms of our mum being a role model, she barely had any friends; *we* were her friends. After dinner every evening, I remember we had a story and comedy time, after which we would have a very good laugh about all the jokes and stories shared that evening. Being her friends never meant disrespecting her or being rude towards her, no. We were extremely sympathetic and helpful to her. I remember explicitly how we made sure to obey all the rules. Unlike the kids these days. Parents who have become way too friendly have resulted in the kids taking advantage of their generosity, further becoming rude and disrespectful. Unfortunately, these children show a lack of appreciation, hardly any empathy, and zero gratitude. They think everything is free. Nothing is free in this life. There are rules in every part of each country that all the citizens must follow. When you break the law, you will be punished for your behaviour and not rewarded.

In our day and age, parents, schools, and organisations have been forced to believe that children must get away with everything without any consequences, especially in the United Kingdom. This system is set to fail children. From my little experience of working with children from early years, primary school to secondary schools, I have had the opportunity to observe children closely and analyse how they think, react and interact. There is only one way, a common characteristic of children's behaviour: *I'm always right, and adults are wrong*. Teachers are constantly in fear of any allegations raised by a child that could lead to disciplinary actions. Likewise, with parents and caregivers, any allegations a child makes leads to your child being taken away from you, its parents, to strange organisations that are made responsible for raising your child. It saddens my heart that such children have already been labelled as damaged, dangerous, and unwanted. The sad truth is that children suffer more abuse in institutions than in their homes. Since the system knows a child's background, that's it; the stigma never goes.

In most cases, when the child makes complaints about what's happening in the institutions, nobody takes them seriously because they have already been labelled. The institution lifestyle for them to get at age eighteen to get them out without any principles about the life of good and bad. Remember, everything they did in the institutions was acclaimed, where there was no proper distinction of good or bad as is documented of their challenging lifestyle. Institutions just pamper them, treating them like babies. Yes, children need to be pampered but to overdo it, as is done in the institutions, is entirely unfair for the kid. As a result, after all the extravagant lifestyle the children are given until they reach eighteen and are sent out to the new world of humanity, they find it extremely challenging to adjust to the brave new world. They try to go back to the institutions, and at that point in time, they get a rejoinder from the institutions. The same system will put them in prison for any offences committed. However, when they were younger, they were never told about what the law required from them. How can we explain this?

Everything falls back to the parents to ensure that their children don't have anything up their sleeves in the systemic institutions.

This, however, does not, in any way, support or promote child abuse. It saddens the depths of my heart when parents' lifestyles or actions cause injury or emotional harm to their children, which may or may not result in their deaths. Children are the greatest gift from God that any parents, caregivers, and Institutions can have. They are the next generation to carry on and the future of our nation. I don't want to go into so much confusion of why adults harm their helpless, little souls, who carry their DNAs, or even if they are not relatively connected to them. Is pure wickedness of a man's heart the reason to cause a child pain and harm? No amount of words can describe the evilness such individuals commit. Occasionally I think that the punishment for such people is way too lenient or perhaps not as harsh as it ought to be. There has to be a significantly tougher punishment for child abusers to face.

The lack of respect for authority by children is another main issue that would be focused on in this book. Since there is no discipline at home from parents as the head of the family, the children show no signs of respect for home, school, adults, people in uniform (the police), and various institutions and bodies. The abuse that the police, teachers, institutions, and senior citizens go through at the hands of the children is equally disturbing and disgusting. There was this story of young pupils who attacked an elderly woman on the streets of England with eggs. Another incident tells us that some students waited for their teacher to finish work, and on her way home, they stabbed and killed her. This woman was a year left to her retirement. How horrific is that!

Chapter 1

The Fundamental Pillars for Raising Children

Parenthood is not a piece of cake. Teaching kids what's right and what's wrong, what path should be taken, and what habits must be avoided is even more complex. Parenting requires considering several important aspects related to daily reality, manners, ideals, interaction, and socialization, i.e., the way of connecting with the world and education. **The essential tool with regards to taking care of and "growing" is open communication.**

Note: It is important to educate children with positive values: to be good citizens, responsible, respectful, and good people.

According to the psychologist Adriana Guraieb,

"Answering their [children's] questions and telling them why we have said a certain thing is the best thing. Another advantage is that children, from a young age, learn to develop their reasoning before the events that life presents to them, instead of repeating what they say the father or the mother."[1]

Moreover, keeping channels of communication open helps individuals to develop healthy relationships with their children.

---

[1] https://rb.gy/zut8yp

These relationships are devoid of all kinds of biases and conservativeness. As a result, children feel free to participate actively. A safe space is created where a child understands what is explained to him, and in this way, he will be better open to receive suggestions. He will become more confident in voicing his opinions and better understand his own perspectives.

Note: If the situation becomes complicated, consultation with a psychology specialist is recommended to clarify and develop a way to restore the bond.

Another crucial aspect is to set limits, but oftentimes, it is easier said than done. You have to think about it, raise it, maintain it, and respect what has been said.

That's because it is never a good idea to establish rules that will not be followed. Making rules and following them go well with discipline. In order to have fun, it is essential that we must first study.

"This teaching will serve them for the rest of their lives, and when they enter working life, they will be prepared to fulfill their responsibilities and then allow themselves to have fun and social expansions," explained the specialist.

Parental Beliefs and Responsibilities

Parental beliefs, and beliefs in general, hugely influence the choices made regarding the issues related to a child's behaviour. The way how children are ready to voice themselves depends considerably on their parents' beliefs. It goes without saying that the type of parenting a child receives greatly affects their adult life. Studies show that the way a child is brought up can majorly affect their present as well as future capacity to endure and control their emotions and feelings in society. Furthermore, it can inform their ability for moral judgement or how they carry it out. (Carlo et 2011)

The way in which parents fulfil their role is partly dependent on *their* parents' upbringing. Moreover, it is dependent on the expectations and outlooks of the society they're a part of.

According to the family law, parental responsibility means "all the rights, duties, powers, responsibilities and authority that a parent has in relation to the child."[22]

As for the education law, the department believes that it is mandatory for a 'parent' to consist of:

- Biological parents, married or not.

- Any individual, who even though is not a biological parent, is aware of what parental responsibility for a child/infant or young person is. This person could either be a step-parent, relative, adoptive parent, or guardian.

- A person who cares about a kid or young person, despite neither being a biological parent nor having any parental responsibility.

Authority

Authority takes place with the power to influence the views, outlooks, and behaviours of others. According to Weberian sociology, authority consists of a specific kind of power. The main usage originates from functionalism, which defines authority as "power

---

[2]https://dera.ioe.ac.uk/32123/1/Understanding%20and%20dealing%20with%20issues%20relating%20to%20parental%20responsibility%20-%20GOV.UK.pdf

which is recognized as legitimate and justified by both the powerful and the powerless."[3]

Authority has been divided into the following three categories by Weber:

Weber first discusses **Traditional Authority**.

According to Weber, this type of authority stems from customs, traditions and long-established ways of living, and societal structures. As the name suggests, traditional authority is the power that is passed on from generation to generation. An example of this could be the system of monarchy, where different rulers of the same family continue to rule generation after generation. Throughout history, we see several examples of monarchic rules and traditional authority. For instance, the Mughal family in India or the Tudors in England.

Rational-legal Authority is the second type of authority defined by Weber. This form of authority depends on its validity on established rules and official laws of a country. These sets of rules are mostly written down and can sometimes be very difficult to understand. Rational-legal authority and its power has even been stated in the constitution. Current societies depend largely on legalrational authority. Government representatives who are an example of this type of authority are prevailing worldwide.

The third category discussed by Weber is **Charismatic Authority**. This form of authority mainly focuses on the charisma of an individual or a leader. When a leader asserts that his authority is originated from a "higher power" or something "heavenly," such as God or natural rights, which is clearly greater than the power of both traditional rational-legal authority, supporters instantly accept it.

---

[3] https://psychology.wikia.org/wiki/Functionalism_(sociology)

They agree to follow this supreme form of authority instead of the ones they'd been following till now.

From what has been written for centuries, a thorough authority has been observed. There has been order and diligence in most parts of institutions. Having the right leadership to exercise authority can promote great people who can also support others to become excellent leaders in the future. If nothing is being done to educate our young ones on the importance of showing respect to authority, especially from home as parents/caregivers and teachers, police, politicians, what good will come out of them when they are adults? There will be a great disappointment to the economy and society.

Religious Insights

Religions, such as Islam, Christianity, Sikhism, and Hinduism, practised by several people today across the globe, have always believed God to be the absolute authority. Scriptures and holy books of these religions have thought God to be the all-knowing, who is in control of everything. He is considered to have all the wisdom and knowledge which is far greater than the wisdom of any one individual. The main source of this authority generally includes great power and consideration along with supremacy in the physical as well as spiritual worlds. The one who is viewed as divine or heavenly is often thought of as the one who creates and is, therefore, greater than all other creatures.

As stated in the religious scriptures, divinity demands the final authority for absolute truth and actuality. Moreover, it offers several rules and instructions for the usage of formation. In such a system, authority's question is, *"What is it that God desires from me, and how would I know this?"*

It wouldn't be wrong to say that the answers to such a question in a divine authority reflection vary from person to person and is in accordance with an individual's experience.

The common experience of an individual is nothing more than a religious history. There are multiple methods of knowing the association to divinity, but all these methods look like they require some amount of belief in divinity and observation of perhaps several communication methods.

The Four Authority Structures Included in the Christian Belief Are as Follows

Family; Husband—Wife—Children

Husbands, considered to be the head of the family, have been trusted by God with regards to the guidance of their families. A husband is supposed to love his wife in the same way as he loves himself. Similarly, a wife should be kind and loving. She is to care about her husband and support him in all his endeavours. Together, as parents, they are responsible for educating and training their children. Children, likewise, are to respect their parents and listen to whatever they say.

Government; National Leaders - Local Representatives - Citizens

According to the bible, one must obey the government and view the authorities with respect and admiration. It instructs us to live a life of honesty and honour the citizens of our communities. National leaders and honourable officials have been given the responsibility to pass judgement in case any crime is committed. Furthermore, they have been instructed to honour those people who do well.

Churches; Church Officials—Church Members

Churches and the guidance of church leaders, including the Pope, Archbishops, Bishops, teachers, pastors, and elders, is of the utmost importance for the well-being of the religion itself. Believers should respect the church leaders in the same way that Christ valued and loved the Church and always led a virtuous life.

Business; Employers—Employees

Some of the challenges that employers face on a daily basis include acting with equity and treating employees with respect, imitating their behaviour after God, who is *their* supreme authority. Employees are liable to work well. They are to perform their tasks passionately, without any reserves, because God sees everything. He is aware of our good and bad deeds, rewarding us accordingly.

Christianity is not the only religion that follows definite religious structures. Several other religions prevalent across the globe have authority patterns that their followers abide by. It is also important to remember that many times, although religions have authority structures, they aren't necessarily properly institutionalised. For instance, in Islam, religious experts are given the titles of *Ulema, maulvi, imam, qari, shaikh,* but a lack of definite organisational hierarchy still remains. Despite that, they are respected and obeyed for having authority over others.

Tips and Recommendations for Good Parenting

Acknowledge Good Deeds

Have you ever wondered about how many times a day you get mad at your child? Have you ever noticed the number of times your voice gets louder with hints of aggression and annoyance when you speak with your little ones? You may conclude that you criticize them or speak harshly many more times than you compliment them. Now put yourself in their shoes. What would your feelings be if your own boss treated you in such a negative way, even if he meant well for you? How would you feel if someone constantly bashes you with hurtful words and anger?

The most positive approach is to acknowledge the good deeds of children and to be supportive of them. For example, you can say, "You tidied up your room without being asked, that's great!" or "I was looking at you while you were taking care of your sister, and I am really happy that you were very tolerant." These comments will be far more effective in encouraging long-term good behaviour than continued reprimands or constant lectures.

Make it a point to find something to appreciate every now and then. Give them rewards, such as your love, attention, and hugs. Praise may seem something ordinary, but in essence, it can do wonders and is often gratifying enough. You will soon realize that you are "cultivating" more of the behaviour you would like to see.

You must:

- Reinforce your behaviour as well as speech the love of the family towards the child.

- Set limits and be consistent with discipline

Discipline is necessary for all households. Its chief goal is to enable children to choose acceptable behaviours and learn self-control. Children may test the limits you set, but these limits are imperative for them to become responsible adults. These gestures may seem to be small in value and even unnecessary, but in reality, they possess the power of doing wonders in the long run.

Setting house rules helps children understand your expectations, beliefs and enhance self-control. For instance, some of these rules may include not watching television or going out to play until homework is done and not allowing hitting, insulting, name-calling, or hurtful teasing. I believe that it is essential that you enforce a system: a warning followed by consequences, which could be a penance or loss of privileges. It has been noticed that one of the most common mistakes that several parents make is not following through with consequences. You cannot discipline children for a bad answer one day and ignore the fact the next. Consistency, as a matter of fact, becomes of the utmost importance. You need to finish what you have started. Being consistent teaches the children what you expect and what they are supposed to do.

Parents, as a couple, should:

- **Avoid mutual disqualification in front of the children.**

- **Give children your time and attention.**

It has become difficult for several families to have a meal together in our day and age, let alone spend quality time with one another. However, there is probably nothing kids would like more than that. Make a habit of getting up a few minutes earlier in the morning so you can have breakfast with your children or leave the dishes in the sink and go for a walk after dinner. Children who do not receive the attention they want from their parents often overreact or misbehave because in doing so, they are sure that they will receive their attention.

Many parents find that scheduling time to spend with their children is rewarding. Schedule a "special night" or a "fun day out" each week to spend more time together. You can also let your children help decide how to spend the time. Find other ways to bond. For example, put a note or something special, such as a candy, in the children's bags or lunch boxes.

It has been observed that younger children seem to need more individual attention from their parents in contrast with young adults or teenagers who usually appear to need less of it. Since there are fewer opportunities for parents and teens to spend time together, parents should do their best to be available when their children express a desire to communicate or be a part of family activities. Attending concerts, travelling to new places, playing games, and exploring museums with your teen is a way to convey affection. It also allows you to learn other things about your child and his/her friends that are important. It will enable you to come in contact with that side of your child's personality, which has so far been hidden away, further strengthening the parent-child bond.

Don't feel bad if you are a working parent. Children have a habit of remembering the little things that you do for them, such as making popcorn, playing cards, looking at windows, colouring, or drawing with them.

- Pay attention if the child cries a lot, and if it is in good health. If not, it is time you ask yourself what is happening at home so that the child shows that she is suffering. Then, let her communicate her concerns regarding whatever it is that is bothering her.

Show Flexibility and Be Willing to Change Your Parenting Style

If your child's behaviour often disappoints you, it may be because your expectations are unrealistic. For parents thinking about "what to do" (for example, "My child **should be** using the potty by now"), it may be helpful to read about it or talk to other parents or child development specialists.

The environment around children has an impact on their behaviour; therefore, you can change that behaviour by modifying your environment. If you are constantly saying "no" to your infant, find some way to restructure the environment, so there are fewer things forbidden. This will be less frustrating for both of you.

As your child changes, you will need to modify your parenting style gradually. What is effective for your child today will most likely not be as effective in a year or two. Change is natural, and the only way to accept it is to adapt to it.

Adolescents tend to look for their idols in their peers rather than in their parents. Still, be sure to show them the right way and motivate your adolescent and provide proper discipline while, at the same time, allowing them to become more independent. Don't forget to take advantage of all the moments you have to establish a relationship.

If you have children, you receive many suggestions on how to raise them. Experts, particularly other parents, are always ready to give you unsolicited advice. Tips on parenting, survival guides for parents, dos and don'ts, new things appear every day, almost wherever you go.

It is incorrect to think that there is only one "correct" way of being the perfect parent. Being good parents includes:

- Keeping your children healthy and safe

- Showing affection and listening to them

- Providing order and its consistency

- Determining and enforcing limits

- Spending time with your children

- Monitoring your children's friendships and activities

- Setting the example

- As parents, you must have an open mind during the childhood of your children. One of the reasons behind this kind of behaviour is that children go through several crises regarding growth. There is a possibility that children may experience adaptations to new acquaintances or damaging effects of bullying or verbal abuse. In case the children are not prepared for psychosocial changes, it would almost be impossible for them to understand them, as children are closed and do not speak.

Be the Perfect Role Model

Young children are great observers. They learn immensely about how to act by watching their parents and adults. The smaller they are, the more they imitate it. Before you react aggressively or get angry in front of your child, think about its consequences. Is this how you would want your child to behave or react when angry? Always remember that your children are aware of your moods and behaviour, even when they pretend otherwise. They are keen observers who learn what they see. Studies have shown that children who hit generally imitate the pattern of aggression at home.

Set an example of the qualities you want to cultivate in your children: respect, warmth, honesty, kindness, tolerance, and loyalty. Be generous. Do things for others without expecting retribution. Help those in need. Express your appreciation and praise. More than anything else, treat your children the way you expect other people to treat you, i.e., with love and admiration.

Do not allow abuse of shouting, manifestations of violence, mistreatment of parents, siblings, or colleagues. Teach them that there are other ways to express the discomfort they feel. Screaming at others or misbehaving is not the solution.

Be fully aware that they learn a certain model of behaviour from parents. You have to be extra careful about this since children copy. If an aggressive situation occurs, it is most likely that the child will learn that communication also involves verbal violence.

Try not to look for ways to compensate for the short amount of time they see them with presents or favours to the limits that have previously been established.

Boost Your Child's Self-confidence

Children start to develop, and with time, grow their sense of self as infants when they see themselves through the eyes of their parents. Your children take in your tone of voice, your body language, as well as all your expressions. Your words and actions as a parent impact your self-esteem development more than anything else. Praise for accomplishments, even small ones that may seem insignificant, will make children proud. Allowing them to do things for themselves will make them feel capable and strong and eventually prepare them to become responsible for the years to follow. On the other hand, degrading comments or negative comparisons with other children will make them feel worthless and inferior.

Leading comments or hurtful statements such as "You are dumb! you fool! you idiot!" or "You should learn something from your cousin" are not only demoralising but are also immensely upsetting. Such painful words have the power of causing the same, if not more hurt as physical strikes.

So choose your words carefully and be understanding. Tell your children that they are not the only ones who have made mistakes; a lot of people go astray and that you still love them, even when you don't approve of their behaviour. This is the only way they'll learn and understand the importance of their actions.

- Participate in their activities, whether they are infants, pubescent, or adolescents. Accompanying them to a field, participating in recreational activities that they like does them very well.

Make Communication a Priority

To expect that your child would do everything just because you asked them to is quite unreasonable. They, too, want explanations and deserve to be given proper answers, just like adults. If we don't take the time to explain, children will start to question our values and motivations and whether they have foundations. Parents who explain matters to their children allow them to understand, learn, and even figure out ways without making value judgments. They enable children to view a situation from different perspectives and act accordingly.

Make sure to let out your expectations clearly but politely. If you come across a problem, describe it, express your feelings, and have a discussion with your child to find a solution together. Be sure to mention the consequences.

Along with making suggestions, offer alternatives, and come up with new solutions together. Also, show enthusiasm and willingness while listening to your child's ideas and pay heed to his/her advice. Negotiate. Children who participate in decision-making are more motivated to carry them forward.

When children have wrong behaviour, it is recommended to speak before sanctioning and convey why the parents are upset. After this, a limit or sanction must be put that explains the reasons.

The resoluteness in the explanations has the tendency of transferring confidence to the little ones.

Show That Your Love Is Wholehearted

If you are a parent, it is your responsibility to correct your child's behaviour and guide them in the right direction. However, the way you express your corrective guidance greatly influences the way a child receives it. When confronting your child, avoid blaming, criticizing, or looking for fault; all of this can weaken morale and cause anger and resentment. Instead, strive to educate and encourage, even when you discipline your children. Make sure they know that your love is unconditional even though you want and hope for better next time.

Be Conscious of Your Own Requirements and Limitations as a Parent

Face it: you are not a perfect parent; neither are you a perfect human being. As the head of the family, you must have several strengths but also some weaknesses. Come into contact with your real self. Acknowledge your abilities: "I am loving and dedicated." Promise to work on your weaknesses: "I must be more consistent with discipline." Make sure to have realistic expectations for yourself, your spouse, and also for your children. You do not necessarily have to know all the answers that too instantly - indulge yourself.

Your emphasis should be on making parenting a manageable job. **Focus on the areas that need the most attention rather than trying to tackle everything at once.** Go slow but remain steady. Admit when, and if, you feel worn out. Take time out for yourself and pay attention to the things that will make you feel happy as a person (or as a couple). Go for a walk or dine out at your favourite restaurant for a change of pace.

Focusing on your needs doesn't make you selfish. It simply means that you care about your own well-being, another important value for your children to take as an example to follow. Always remember that in order to take care of your children, it is integral that you first take of yourself.

Psychologist View on Behaviour

Explaining human behaviour and conduct is one of the basic roles of psychology. By using a set of approaches, such as the personality approach, we can succeed in explaining human behaviour in a better way. The personality approach supports the theory that people act the way they do gradually with time, mainly due to a set of constant and lasting inner dispositions (McAvoy, 2012). By using this approach, psychologists say that human behaviour is a creation of one's internal influences.

Unlike the personality approach, other approaches argue that human behaviour is a result of external influences, for instance, imitation. Imitation, or the act of copying, is a form of social learning that tends to change behaviour.

Another approach that shows human behaviour as a creation of external stimuli is through consequences (Toates, 2012).

Let's assess the statement that human behaviour is affected by external behaviour.

Impact of External Factors on Human Behaviour

According to Skinner's theory (1953), a child's behaviour could be changed by reinforcing or strengthening good or desired behaviour. He shifted the focus of his theory from animals to humans by using reinforcement built on the reinforcement of lever-pressing in a Skinner box, also called Operant Conditioning Chamber, using pellets. If reinforcement, as well as punishment, worked properly on animals, then it would surely work on human beings too. Skinner (1971) goes on to claim that the chance of reinforcement being more effective than punishment was noticed. The reinforcement used for animals was food, which was relatively less complicated than the kind of reinforcement used for humans, which was praise and compliment. Skinner (1953) realized every species' tendency to struggle to survive by gaining their basic needs, including food, clothing, and shelter. The pursuit of these basic survival tools acts as a learning source, hence shaping human behaviour (Toates, 2012).

Behaviourist theory makes it clear that a child's behaviour can be altered and improved by using positive reinforcement. A child who draws attention in class by misbehaving is likely to get the teacher's attention but in the form of punishment. This attention given by the teacher works as a reinforcing factor (Toates, 2012). If the reinforcing element – attention, is removed, a drop in undesirable behaviour is noted, consequently endorsing the claim that human behaviour is a result of external influences. Skinner argued that, usually, everything that happens in the world is a consequence or an outcome of the past. This applied not only to human behaviour but was also based on determinism.

The study of Adorno et al. (1950) was further expanded by Milton Rokeach (1960) by using dogmatism as a more common form of authoritarianism. Rokeach, unlike Adorno, thought the authoritarian personality was a product of a distinct cognitive style. He described the cognitive style as the customary way an individual processes information. People who had high dogmatism were narrow-minded. They were less likely to assess different information and were more able to keep conflicting beliefs depending on the power behind the message. Such people were more particular about the source of information instead of its credibility. On the contrary, people with low dogmatism were more flexible and open. They focused more on evaluating information and the message rather than the authority behind the message. To sum it up, Rokeach (1960) viewed dogmatism as a cognitive function (McAvoy, 2012). For that reason, cognitive function is considered to be one of the internal influences of human behaviour.

If, indeed, human behaviour is influenced by external factors, then the theory can shape English pupils' behaviour, such as misbehaving, in various ways. When the system is taken as a Skinner Box, the main issue at hand would be to determine who offers reinforcement. Without determining this, global behaviour change is elusive. Therefore, if interested parties can find a suitable reinforcement practice or policy, external influences would be used to regulate their worst behaviour to be much kinder, sympathetic, and more respectful to others.

False memories as external influences on human behaviour suggest that false memories can be created to alter personality development. For instance, if experiencing domestic violence caused a higher level of aggression in children, then planting a false memory about domestic violence would alter an individual's personality. Various studies that focused on personality as an internal influence of human behaviour, concluded that personality has the ability to stem from external factors, such as one's upbringing. One of the sources of personality is kept in the unconscious, which often results from past experiences and memories. Keeping in mind that memories and experiences can influence one's personality, which in turn influences human behaviour, it can be said that human behaviour is a factor of both internal as well as external influences.

This indicates the importance of authority in our society. If nothing is done about this generation on how children must be taught to respect authority, several problems can arise. By focusing on authority, we could help children to be better adults in society. This reminds me of a story told about two families in the USA. The children of one family had a very good upbringing while the other did not. Children with a good upbringing grew up to be lawyers, teachers, and civil servants, which helped the US economy. But the other children ended up committing many crimes, which cost the government a lot more money because they had no jobs, not contributing anything to the economy.

Chapter 2

Too Much of Attention

The old proverb, "Excess of everything is bad," is what needs to be remembered by all parents, especially when it comes to giving attention to their little ones. **Excess of attention directed towards children is a behaviour that has the tendency of giving rise to various problems.** Since families today have become smaller, there are more chances of parents going overboard regarding the attention they give to their children. Although initially, the problems that stem from giving too much attention remain hidden, gradually, they become more evident. These complications further result in children becoming more attention-addicted.

For many parents, it is difficult to understand the consequences of giving too much attention. In a world where most children are neglected or unloved, it seems odd to suggest that too much attention can be problematic. But what people fail to realize is that too much attention given to children can generate, if not all, then most of the same behaviours that are generally observed in attention-starved youngsters. The child might go out there in the world, expecting everyone to give them the same attention they received from home. When they are in school, they want special attention from teachers and even from their friends, believing that the whole world revolves around them. This can cause severe issues for them that tend to remain with them for the rest of their lives. Other children will start picking on them because they can't give them that attention.

As a result of this, children who have become used to too much attention might join bad groups where they are forced to do the things they don't want to but do them anyway to achieve a sense of belonging and acceptance. The fact that they want to belong somewhere leads them into unhealthy friendships. However, they become so obsessed with themselves that they want people to see them as their parents see them. They create their own world, making other children worship them, leading them to bully others for power. Too much neglect, as well as too much attention, gives rise to dissatisfied children. Such children remain insecure and doubtful throughout their entire lives. **The abandoned child remains unsure of love and affection** since these are the emotions that he has never experienced. On the other hand, **a child who is showered with too much attention gets trapped in a bubble of insecurity.** That's because he constantly fears that this attention will eventually come to an end.

Signs That Indicate We Give Too Much Attention to Our Kids

Before we dig deeper into the effects of giving too much attention to our children, let's first look at some of the signs which indicate that we are giving extra, even unreasonable, attention to our children.

1. Accepting Their Irrational Demands

While listening to and understanding the demands made by your children is advisable, it is not necessary to always accept them too. Children, no matter how smart or intelligent they become, lack the experience which their parents possess. Accepting all their whims indicates that you, as a parent, are going overboard with your attention towards your child. For instance, buying whatever they put their finger on all the time or not stopping them from mistreating other children, so they don't pitch a fit. There are times when parents, through their behaviour, must make it clear that they are the ones in charge.

2. Treating Children as If They Are the Stars of the Family

No one denies the fact that most parents think highly of their children. Some parents go so far by showing their child as the star of the family in gatherings and family gettogethers. **They push them to perform in front of others and keep displaying the many achievements of their children.** By doing that, they bring their child into the spotlight. Soon the kid begins to consider himself as the centre of attention. Problems arise when people around him stop giving the attention that the child has been made used to, or worse, when they shift their attention to someone else, perhaps his sibling or cousin.

Children are worthy of respect and love for who they really are. We do not need to dress them up like little dolls or puppets and put them on display for everyone to praise. Their existence itself should be enough for people to admire them.

3. Cooking Separate Meals for the Kids Every Day

Treating your children with what they like once in a while is understandable, but **always cooking separate meals for them shows that you're paying way too much attention than is required.** Parents who have made it a habit of cooking separate meals or ordering junk food online for their children all the time simply to satisfy them can be problematic in the long run.

4. Giving Up Your Own Rights

Parents who give up their own rights is another aspect less talked about. This includes parents who allow their kids to sleep with them or allow them to make decisions. Parents should also work as a team for the best results that will be beneficial for the child in the long run. Make sure you share information with your partner, other relatives, and teachers when you need help to handle a situation regarding your children. There is no need to pretend that your children don't want to be the authority in the house. Share your problems with other parents who are facing the same issues or know how to tackle such behaviour. These parents often forget the importance of spending some private time with their partners and how fruitful that can be for a healthy marriage. **Remember, turning away from your child to turn towards your spouse in no way means you're ignoring or hurting your child.** It is essential to have an adult-only space. This does not have to happen every day, but whenever it does, it will allow your children to understand the value of other relationships too. **The child will begin to understand that his parents need time for one another too.**

5. Not Stopping Children from Interrupting

If you, as a parent, are allowing your child to interrupt conversations between adults, then it is recommended that you put an end to this behaviour instantly. **Children who are allowed to interrupt will always continue to do so to acquire their parents' undivided attention.** With time, they would become more obstinate and impatient.

- Steps that can be taken to deal with the abovementioned situations

- When your children insist on having their demands fulfilled, try and reason with them. **Tell them the consequences of their actions** and explain to them how things cannot always go according to their wishes.

- If your child interrupts conversations, it is better to **teach them how they can let their presence known without interjecting.** You can show your child how they can either lay one hand on their mother's or father's arm, or on the leg, indicating they need to speak while waiting patiently till the parent is ready to speak. To show the kid you have acknowledged their presence, you can cover your child's hand with your own – a small gesture that is enough to make them know you understand.

- If you find yourself unable to maintain a life of your own and feel like you have to compromise on your own rights all the time, then **make a habit of insisting your child sleep in their own bed.** Moreover, asking them to go to their bed at a reasonable hour (if not early) would also be beneficial for both you and your child.

- **Taking part in similar activities separately would also give them the freedom and independence they should be getting.** For instance, give them a book to go through while you read a grown-up book with your spouse. This would help the child understand that while sometimes mom or dad would read with the kid, there are other times when they will read to themselves. It would enable them to understand a parent's personal space and how to respect it.

- You can also go to your room, along with your partner, and lock the door to stop your child from interrupting the conversation. As a result, the child will learn that it is better not to interrupt and be around the parents than to interrupt and be without them.

What happens when you give extra and unreasonable attention?

Attention Addicted Children

If a child always gets what he wants while the rights of his parents are ignored, the child will become an attention addict. Nothing or no one would ever be able to satisfy his demands. Nothing would ever be enough for a kid like that. He would continue to ask for more.

Soon, parents would become annoyed and would start taking out their anger on the child. In this way, their attention towards the kid continues. This time, however, the attention is somewhat more pessimistic. But since the child is used to getting attention, he would carry on with his stubborn, all-consuming nature.

In case parents try to alter their behaviour, the child who is literally addicted to attention will develop very manipulative manners in an attempt to continue the interaction. **Attention addicted children either end up being extremely demanding and destructive or completely inactive and helpless.** They do whatever suits them the best. As a result of this tumultuous life, the child remains truly dependent, dissatisfied, and displeased since no amount of attention can ever be enough to content him. No matter how much one tries, one would never be able to make an attention-addicted child happy.

Here I must point out that paying attention to children is needed because they cannot prosper without it. But what we must remember is that **overdoing it by not setting limits would only result in chaos.** When we respect our own rights, we, in turn, teach our kids to respect us. Furthermore, we avert the damage that attention-addiction can do to the child as well as his/her family.

I will end this chapter by sharing Thiruvalluvar's famous quote:

"If your child is too quick to anger, it is because you give too much attention to challenging behaviour and you give little attention to good behaviour."

Chapter 3

Postnatal Depression and Child Development

Postpartum psychiatric disorders can categorically be divided into three groups: postpartum blues, postpartum psychosis, and postpartum depression. These three forms vary from one another mainly on the basis of their severity.

Postpartum blues is considered to be a relatively common emotional distress where an individual, particularly the mother, may experience confusion, rapid changes in mood, anxiety, and gloominess. These symptoms that are evident during the first week postpartum, may continue for a few hours to a few days. However, postpartum blues do have the tendency to become more severe, resulting in postpartum psychosis. Postpartum psychosis is relatively serious than postpartum blues. It begins within four weeks postpartum. Some of its symptoms include hallucinations and delusions. When these symptoms continue to deepen and become stronger, postpartum depression begins, which includes fatigue, dysphoric mood, anorexia nervosa, sleep disturbances, insomnia, anxiety, guilt, and suicidal ideation.

Postnatal Depression

Postnatal depression develops after the birth of a child, and it can have drastic mental, physical and emotional effects on women if it is not treated properly. It can start at any point in the first year after giving birth and may develop either suddenly or gradually. Many women feel emotionally distressed or anxious in the first week after childbirth. These feelings can become stronger and more overwhelming until they manifest into physical symptoms that can affect the daily life of the mother and harm the relationship with the baby, other family members, and friends. This condition is often referred to as *"baby blues"* and is a very common part of childbirth and early motherhood. The *"baby blues"* don't last for more than two weeks after giving birth if treated. But, if the symptoms last longer than this or start later, it could lead to postnatal depression.

Postnatal depression can affect any mother, but it is strongly associated with the financial and educational level of the mother. Depressed mothers can sometimes find it very difficult to respond to their infant's cries. The lack of sleep and energy can make them become irritable, and their care can be inconsistent, which can be detrimental to the welfare of the infants.

Termine and Izard (1988) reported that **infants whose mothers looked sad and angry tend to smile less, display sadness and anger expressions, play less and may avert their gaze from others.** The researchers suggested (just as Lavelli and Fogel (2005) did) that these infants avert their gaze as a way of reducing the amount of negative emotion they receive. These findings often lead to strong implications for the development of emotional responsiveness in babies whose mothers might be depressed and show negative affect.

It could make the child feel unhappy and unwanted if the parents carry on denying the child's emotional needs that he/she wants from the mother.

Dealing with a Difficult Child

- Infants may contribute to their mother's depressed state.

- Hyper-active children often cause emotional stress for parents.

- Children who experience abuse and neglect may show signs of typical emotional development in terms of their behaviours and cognitive development. • Supporting parents can enhance the emotional environment of the home by managing their child's behaviour.

- Some children show resilience to adverse environments, and this may be a genetic quality.

- They ignore or refuse to follow instructions from their parents.

- Some children refuse to eat certain foods or wear certain clothes.

Dealing with Difficult Children from the Early Stages

From the age of two, some toddlers begin to abuse mothers and other children by biting, pushing, and kicking them. This comes from a deep-seated need for attention because these toddlers have learned that this is the only way for them to get attention from others around them. Mothers often find it difficult to deal with such aggressive children, which leads to stressful situations.

At times, mothers may choose to avoid public places and gatherings because of their children. It causes isolation and depression as well when staying out of touch with friends and family. This creates a cycle where because the mother is emotionally, physically, and mentally exhausted, she is unable to meet the needs of the child.

When these children get older, they start exhibiting much more severe behaviours such as talking back, insulting, rudeness, violence, etc.

Mother-child Socio-emotional Interactions

In the early months of life, a child's attention and focus are exclusively on the mother; this forms a dyadic system. As the child grows, the interest moves towards other objects around them, which leads to a change in the relationship. Attention is then shared between the child, the mother, and a given object or situation.

Genetics also has a vital role to play in children's emotional development when their behaviour is too complex to handle with their aggressive and oppositional behaviour. Children often imitate or develop feelings and actions through their interactions with their parents. Aggressive and hyperactive behaviour is likely to be developed through genetics.

However, one aspect that severely affects motherchild interactions is maternal depression. Research shows that maternal depression has the power of affecting the pair's capacity to jointly regulate the interaction. That's mainly because of two extreme interactive patterns shown by mothers; intrusiveness or withdrawal. Mothers who are intrusive, i.e., intruding way more than is necessary, show an aggressive affect, disrupting the infant's activity. As a consequence, infants feel anger; some may even begin to avoid the mother in an attempt to limit her intrusiveness and internalize a hostile style of coping.[4]

Withdrawn mothers, on the other hand, are completely opposite. They are not really active and are mostly unresponsive. Such mothers are affectively flat and are not seen supporting the infant's activity. Because of this attitude, the infants fail to cope or self-regulate this negative state. They end up developing passivity, withdrawal, and self-regulatory behaviours. Some common patterns include sucking on the thumb and looking away.[5]

The Signs of a Problematic Child from the Early Stages

Tantrums, (anger) kicking, throwing things around, running away to hide when they are angry, stiffening limbs or arching back, dropping to the floor, shouting, screaming, crying excessively, pushing, and hitting are all signs of problematic children. These findings suggest that the child's cognition might play a role in the behavioural progression of a tantrum – a child might become angry initially when they realise their caregiver is thwarting their wishes, but then the child becomes saddened when they realise that their anger has had no effect, and they will not get their way.

As a child gets older, they acquire a range of adaptive skills that help them to deal with many of the emotional challenges they face. However, some children do not show a decline in tantrums with age, and their behaviour can become problematic. There are different

---

[4] https://pubmed.ncbi.nlm.nih.gov/2925579/
[5] https://www.sciencedirect.com/science/article/abs/pii/S0163638398900248

researches, which indicate that it is possible to identify potential problems as early as two years of age. It is better if the intervention takes place as early as possible, as consistently high levels of aggressive, destructive, and oppositional behaviours are related to the development of problems in later life, such as juvenile delinquency. Early intervention can enhance a child's emotional knowledge and prevent later behavioural issues.

Postnatal Depression and Its Influence on Infants, Preschoolers and School-age Children

The behavioural, as well as cognitive development of infants, preschoolers, and school-age children of postnatally depressed mothers, are adversely affected.

Infants whose mothers experience postnatal depression are said to display patterns of emotional dysregulation, i.e., a poor ability to manage emotional responses. A study conducted by Murray titled *The impact of postnatal depression on infant development* shows that cognitive performance with regards to the "independent existence of objects was worse for infants of 61 postnatally depressed mothers than the infants of 42 non-depressed mothers, even after adjustment for contextual adversity."[6]

Various studies show that depressed mothers are usually less attentive and responsive to the needs of their children. They are not great models for negative mood regulation and solving problems. Many studies have compared the behaviours of depressed and non-depressed mothers. These studies also pay particular attention to the development of the children of these mothers. Most of these studies

---

[6] https://www.ncbi.nlm.nih.gov/pmc/articles/PMC2724169/

conclude that children whose mothers are postnatally depressed grow up to be more passively non-compliant and resisting authority, "with less mature expressions of ageappropriate autonomy." Such children are also most likely to turn down friendly approaches and participate in low-level physical activity. Moreover, these children are less likely to take part in individual creative play than other children.[7]

Several studies conclude that school-age children whose mothers are depressed show impaired adaptive functioning, which includes internalizing as well as externalizing problems. Children of postnatally depressed parents are more prone to psychopathology, including depression, conduct disorders, and anxiety. Studies with no demographic differences between depressed and nondepressed parents have shown a higher risk of psychopathology in children with depressed parents.

The Components of Emotional Knowledge

The following are common components of emotional knowledge in children:

1. **Recognition.** At 3–4 years of age, children begin to be able to recognise and put a name to emotions (e.g., happiness, sadness, fear, anger) in pictures based on expressive cues. This is where the child starts recognizing different moods and behaviours.

2. **External Cause.** By around 3–4 years old, children begin to understand how external causes can affect the emotions of others. For example, a scary situation will develop a feeling of insecurity and cause nervousness. A happy and lively place will change the mood and bring joy to the mind of the child.

---

[7] https://pubmed.ncbi.nlm.nih.gov/10604404/

3. **Desire**. At around 3–5 years of age, children begin to understand that people's desires affect their emotions. A child often insists on buying toys; when this desire is fulfilled, it changes the mood and brings happiness to the child. The child develops the ability to recognize and label basic emotions, i.e., happy, angry, afraid, sad, and children are quite skilled at recognizing basic facial expressions

4. **Belief**. Between 4 and 6 years of age, children begin to understand that a person's beliefs about a situation will affect their emotional reaction to that situation. Children develop the ability to understand the contexts surrounding particular emotions, such as being happy to receive an ice cream or sad for having lost a toy.

5. **Reminder**. Between 3 and 6 years of age, children start to understand that memories of events are linked to emotions. Also, they come to realise that emotional intensity subsides with time.

6. **Regulation**. Children of different ages use different strategies to regulate emotion. Children aged 6–7 are more likely to employ behavioural strategies, whereas children aged eight and older make more use of psychological techniques such as distraction.

7. **Hiding**. Between 4 and 6 years old, children understand that emotions can be hidden; for example, there can be a discrepancy between the real emotion and its expression. Children might hide if they feel scared about something and prefer not to disclose their feeling to elders around.

8. **Mixed**. From approximately eight years of age. Children begin to understand that a person can experience more than one emotion about a given situation. They learn a mixture of feelings, e.g., a

child might feel afraid and thrilled at the same time for taking a ride in an amusement park.

9. **Morality**. From around eight years old, children begin to understand that morally reprehensible acts such as lying and stealing are associated with negative emotions. They tend to adopt such habits at this age, and if not dealt with correctly, these habits become a norm and tend to stay for years even when the child becomes an adult.

Parenting also appears to play an important role, as children who display greater emotional knowledge have emotionally expressive mothers, exhibiting low rates of anger and sadness.

A child's emotional knowledge also plays an integral part in how they are evaluated and accepted by their peers. Preschool children with well-developed prosocial skills, such as an understanding of the emotional states of others, are rated more highly by their peers and their early years' teachers. Research also suggests that the relationships that children build with their peers and with their teachers can support their academic achievement. On the other hand, lack of emotional knowledge can result in aggression and disaffection with learning.

Chapter 4

Children's Rights

The CRC, i.e. the *Convention on the Rights of the Child,* is an agreement between countries joined together to protect minors. All children up to the age of 18 years are entitled to inalienable rights. To think of them as the property of their parents or abandoned charity objects is not only unfair but also unlawful. Every child deserves healthy food with adequate nutrition, non-discrimination, their own identity, protection, education, etc. They should be provided with a healthy, clean, and safe environment with proper care and supervision by their parents or other adults. CRC focuses on giving a quality life to all children rather than a privilege that is enjoyed by a few. All children should grow up in the spirit of peace, dignity, tolerance, freedom, equality, and solidarity. All the countries are responsible for providing these rights by the law of the UN.

Children rely on adults for the nurturing and guidance they need to grow up and move towards independence in their lives. It is the adults' responsibility who nurture them. Still, when primary adult caregivers cannot meet their children's needs, it is up to the State as the primary duty bearer to look for a substitute that is beneficial for the child in the long run.

Education

To think of literacy as a great device by which economically as well as socially side-lined individuals, including adults and youngsters, can lift themselves out of poverty, change their present-day circumstances and participate in society fully as citizens wouldn't be incorrect. According to a report by the Global Education Monitoring in 2016, 61 million children do not have access to primary education, and 758 million grown-ups in the world are illiterate because they never got into school. Education is a fundamental human necessity. Every individual is entitled to free schooling, irrespective of race, gender, nationality, ethnic or social origin, religion or political preference, age, or disability. Every child should be capable of reading, writing, counting, understanding and developing their mental and physical abilities to reach their full potential as adults. In the early years, the teachers build up the foundation for future evolution, providing a strong base for lifelong learning and abilities, including cognitive and social progress.

In developing and developed countries, children do not have access to basic education because of inequalities in sex, health, and cultural identity. They find themselves on the margins of the education system and do not benefit from learning in a manner that is vital to their intellectual and social development. Factors linked to poverty, such as unemployment, illness, and parents' illiteracy, increase the risk of non-schooling and a child's drop-out rate for children.

Undeniably, those who come from disadvantaged backgrounds are forced to abandon their studies due to familial pressure to work and provide support for their families.

Over 32 million young minds remain uneducated in Sub-Saharan Africa. Central and Eastern Asia and the Pacific are also severely affected by this problem, with more than 27 million unschooled children. More than 50% receive teachings for less than two years in certain countries, such as Somalia and Burkina Faso. The lack of schooling and poor education has drastic effects on the population and the productivity of the country. The children leave school without having acquired the basics skills they need to become a contributing member of society, which significantly impedes their well-being.

Healthy Food

Children must be able to benefit from a balanced diet to develop healthily. All the meals must be nutritionally filling and contribute to their physical and intellectual development. Balanced meals are predicated correctly between necessary proportions of nutrients, carbohydrates, proteins, lipids, minerals, vitamins, fibre, water, etc. In this way, malnutrition can be avoided along with other problems linked to either excessive eating or dietary insufficiencies. Healthy food leads to strong and healthy bodies; therefore, children must grow in a safe, clean environment to become fit and fine. They must be provided three meals a day, along with clean drinking water and a sanitary environment with proper toilet facilities.

Identity

From the beginning, every individual has the right to have an identity as it asserts their existence in society. It gives recognition of their individuality and differentiates them from their peers. Every child must be officially recognized as a human being and preserve their identity, including their nationality, name, and family relations, without unlawful interference. An individual will hold obligations specific to their status (woman, man, child, handicapped, refugee, etc.). Parents must declare the name, surname, and date of birth of a new born to the authorities in charge. Through this, the State officially recognizes the child's identity and their existence, formalizing its status in the eyes of the law. Recording the names through the Registration of Births and Deaths helps in establishing filiations, which links to the blood relations of the father and mother.

This identity will also entitle them to judicial protection via their parents and the State. They will then benefit from minors' protection programs of the country that will safeguard their rights and prevent exploitation.

Furthermore, the delinquent child will benefit from minors' sentences, a program adapted to their age, maturity, and awareness. As a result, these young offenders will not encounter certain sentences. The judgement against them won't be too harsh (for instance: the death penalty); rather, they would be judged in accordance with their age. It goes without saying that a child without an identity of his own will remain unseen by the public, somewhere in the background of society. Such a child would not be able to take advantage of the protection and safety that social services, vital to their growth, have to offer.

Therefore, states should help children regain any aspect of their identity that has been taken away from them illegally.

Right to Protection

First of all, protection must be ensured initially by the parents and the community surrounding them and then by the states. Well-being cannot be obtained in the same way because every child is a unique human with specific needs. Countries must establish a protection system, including laws, policies, procedures, and practices that are intended to prevent and fight against various problems of mistreatment, violence, and discrimination that can damage a child's wellbeing. The governments set up this protection system by ratifying the primary principles of international standards of protecting children's rights and then implementing them in their legislation. It is integral that they must also guarantee care to special child profiles, including disabled and refugees, and arrange for adequate as well as long-lasting solutions.

A secure and caring environment brings safety. Each child deserves to be protected from all forms of violence, physical or mental exploitation, and slavery. It helps develop a healthy and peaceful life everywhere in the world. Our human rights were written down for the first time in 1945 in a document called *"The Universal Declaration of Human Rights."* Governments across the world realized that there was a need to give special attention to children's rights.

In the year 1989, governments implemented the *United Nations Convention on the Rights of the Child,* which is popularly known as CRC. This convention guides governments and all citizens, young and old, on what human rights mean and what should be done so that youngsters can enjoy and benefit from them. The governments have signed the *Convention on the Rights of the Child* to provide these to every child in their country. Governments have passed new laws to make sure that people respect them. From parents to educators and caregivers to children themselves, everyone in society needs to help enforce and protect these rights.

All children, big or small, living in a village or city, anywhere in the world, are unique in many different ways. These are all connected and are all equally important. These young minds deserve the right to:

- live and grow,
- eat healthy food,
- drink clean water,
- go to school,
- cared for by their parents or guardians,
- have a name,
- belong to a country,
- share their ideas,
- practice their religion,
- treated fairly by everyone,
- not to be enslaved, or exploited,
- not to be forced to do work that harms,
- should have the right to play and rest,
- should be in the care of responsible adults and caregivers.

Despite the strong rhetoric, many young people throughout the world continue to be marginalized. Today, children and youth are still subject to danger in various forms such as slavery, prostitution, pornography, torture, racism, sexism, and being forced to serve in armed conflicts. Poverty and inequality remain prevalent across the globe.

Chapter 5

Negative Influences Fantasy for the Children

It wouldn't be wrong to say that most of us have grown up reading, listening to, and even enjoying children's fairy tales while being mesmerised by their unique characters and astonishing events. This culture of telling fairy tales to children, particularly within 1 to 10 years of age, is even deemed necessary by most people. That's because most people believe that fairy tales, rich with fantasies, myths, and magical creatures, help in enhancing children's imagination and confidence. Moreover, they believe that such stories teach kids what is right and wrong, what path to take, and what should be avoided. However, recent studies have raised several questions about whether these fairy tales with supernatural and often unrealistic settings **may influence children negatively, resulting in lower confidence and an unrealistic sense of reality.** Let's take a look at some of the reasons why we believe fairy tales are negatively influencing children.

1. Creating an Imaginary World That Doesn't Exist

Fairy tales are known for their happy endings. Everything works out just fine in the end. The "bad people" of the story are defeated badly while the good characters enjoy their moments of 'happily ever after.' But one might notice how this clichéd ending negatively affects children considering the fact that this is not always how reality works. **Setting unrealistic expectations of life and being certain of the idea that everything will work out perfectly can often be misleading for young children** who are, at that stage, not aware of the many complexities of life. When faced with disappointments, children may not know how to deal with setbacks. Fairy tales create a world that most of us are not aware of, a world that generally does not exist.

The goal should be to prepare children for what lies ahead in life. Reality, we all would agree, can be a bit messy, disappointing, and to some extent, even gloomy, and these are some of the factors that are missing from our fairy tales.

Children who always read about the 'perfect, happy endings' unconsciously look and wait for those endings for themselves too. In case they don't meet such beautiful endings themselves, they remain dissatisfied throughout their lives.

2. Unrealistic Beauty Standards

No one would deny the fact that Disney princesses are always beautiful, slim, and mostly white. Although recently, these beauty standards are being challenged and even somewhat changed, **a serious lack of racial and physical diversity has been noticed** amongst the mainstream fairy tales.

For children, who come across such stories for the first time, such limiting beauty standards can be extremely damaging. In most cases, these stories represent the idea that beauty, as well as happiness, is tantamount to thinness.

3. The Stereotypical Association of Physical Features with Good and Bad

Another noteworthy problem with fairy tales is that they are tremendously shallow, conveying the message of how only attractive people can succeed in finding love, happiness, and prosperity while those who do not fit into the beauty standards fixed by society are not considered to be beautiful. In fact, they are portrayed as evil, worthy of living miserable lives.

A scholarly article titled *The Pervasiveness and*

Persistence of the Feminine Beauty Ideal in Children's Fairy Tales written by Lori Baker-Sperry and Liz Grauerholz points out several issues with fairy tales amongst which physical appearance is highlighted. According to it, **"31% of all stories associate beauty with goodness, and 17 per cent associate ugliness with evil."**[8]

Let's quickly analyse Cinderella and get a better understanding of this argument. Cinderella, a gorgeous kind girl, is forced to live with her stepmother and two stepsisters, who are not only "ugly" but are also cruel and hard-hearted. The story concludes with Cinderella marrying a handsome prince who has fallen in love with the girl after dancing with her at a ball just once. On the other hand, Cinderella's stepmother and stepsisters continue an unsatisfying life. We can see how this same idea is repeated in other fairy tales, such as the Little

---

[8] https://lis721fairytales.weebly.com/negative-effects.html

Mermaid, where the anti-hero is physically unattractive. The central character is a pretty, skinny girl with beautiful eyes and shiny red hair.

Focusing on one's physical features and associating beauty with goodness and ugliness with evil has the tendency of lowering the self-esteem of young girls. It forces children to be shallow and judge others by how they look. As a result, children start focusing more on looks and less on other people's personalities and characters. The way people are on the inside then becomes of less value to children, and all they start focusing on is people's appearances.

4. Gender Stereotyping

Gender stereotyping refers to the practice of assigning certain qualities, characteristics, or traits to a woman or man only on the basis of their belonging to the social group of women or men. Fairy tales show an alarming state of gender stereotyping. Several tales show how women are only capable of being attractive to men. They show how women are only passive damsels who have no knowledge of their surroundings and are solely dependent on men who are there to protect them. These stories show women as if they have no voice of their own.

Moreover, female characters are seen as submissive, busy with household chores. For instance, if we look at Cinderella, Snow White, and Belle, we will notice how the main characters are bound to the home. Cinderella is seen cleaning and mopping the whole house. Snow White caters to the needs of the seven male dwarves by cooking and cleaning for them. Belle can save her father from the Beast's trap only by becoming a housemaid.

Most fairy tales show that women feel the need to change themselves and their mannerisms just to please men and be acceptable to them. This has stopped women from becoming empowered or think for themselves. **Such stories negatively influence young minds, particularly girls, who begin to view themselves as passive beings, inferior to men.**

Research shows that during the eighteenth and nineteenth centuries, several stories were written for the sole purpose of teaching young girls to become "domesticated, respectable, and attractive to a marriage partner and to teach boys and girls appropriate gendered values and attitudes."[9]

An article titled *Children's Reflections on Gender Equality in Fairy Tales: A Rwanda Case Study* written by Pierre Canisius Ruterana discusses the gender roles in children's books, particularly fairy tales. He writes:

"In fairy tales male characters have been portrayed as being strong, potent, and powerful, with mastery themes such as cleverness and adventure, whereas female characters were portrayed as impotent, weak, passive, naïve, even sweet, with second sex themes such as beauty, gentility, domesticity, marriage, emotions, motherhood, and so on."

Such narratives negatively influence younger minds, especially girls, who are then forced to live similar lives. Women must be accepted and appreciated for who they really are. They must be given space to explore themselves and choose their future without any restriction. To attach unrealistic expectations from them is unfair and unethical that needs to stop at once.

---

[9] https://lis721fairytales.weebly.com/negative-effects.html

The Kind of Stories We Need to Write Today

Luckily, fairy tales that are being written today and the more developed forms of the old classics have introduced narratives and characters that are different from the clichéd ones. For instance, the female characters in Frozen, Mulan and Moana portray a more feminist society where women are in charge of their own lives. Here, the female characters are loved for who they are and for being independent, lively, and active.

To sum it up, some of the features that need to be incorporated in today's fairy tales are:

- **Creating more realistic settings** that do not necessarily show the traditional 'happy endings.' Fairy tales need to properly show how society is actually run.

- **Marriage is not and should not be the ultimate reward in fairy tales.** If stories are a depiction of reality, we need to show how marriage is not the ultimate goal of an individual's life and that there are other equally if not more meaningful aspects to life.

- There **should be racial and social diversity** within the characters of fairy tales.

- Characters, particularly **women, do not need to have glossy hair, a thin waist and white skin to portray goodness** or virtuousness.

- Showing **women as independent characters** who do not always depend on men is essential. A woman does not need to be saved by a charming prince on a white horse to live her life to its fullest.

- **Breaking gender stereotypes** and showing that cooking and cleaning are skills that both men and women can carry out must be focused on.

- **Looks shouldn't be at the centre of defining the character** of an individual. It's time that we focus on a character's inner rather than outer beauty, as is done in stories like Shrek and Beauty and the Beast.

Storytellers across the globe need to consider the above-mentioned points while writing fairy tales. What is essential to understand is that children, particularly young girls, who read about independent, strong women and become familiar with such characters will become confident in finding their true worth. It teaches its readers that there isn't a particular law, or rule, that commands you to act or look a specific way. It benefits both boys and girls in understanding the many complexities or layers of life, which further prepares them for what lies ahead. They begin to understand how not everything is black or white and the fact that many characters or situations in life can be grey. They'll become more open to one's character rather than his or her physical features because, by the end of the day, it's who you are from within that makes all the difference. Giving children stories that are relatively modern, or have characters that are different from their stereotypical role, teaches children that they can do and be whoever they want to be.

Chapter 6

Unfold Behaviour and English Children

Throughout the years that children live with their parents, they are under a constant radar and are continuously observed for their behaviour. This is one of the reasons why most students only live a fake life while they are with their parents. Since they always have it in their minds that their parents denied them from doing many things, they take any medium that comes their way or the little bit of freedom they have to unfold some new habits in them, which might not necessarily be positive. Most times, this is influenced by one's peer group. That is, whenever children are privileged to go out of their parent's house to meet and play with friends, they end up getting influenced negatively by different kinds of bad habits such as smoking, drinking too hard or taking drugs.

Physical Assault Directed Towards Teachers by the Students

Hitting, punching, shoving, spitting at, or kicking teachers are all different forms of physical attack. A recent survey shows that about one in four teachers is physically assaulted by students at least once every week. A study from the NASUWT teaching union shows that

about three in ten teachers (29%) have been physically attacked, i.e., punched, hit, kicked, and about two in five teachers (39%) have been pushed or shoved by students.[10]

Several other physical attacks, such as spitting (7%) and head-butting (3%), have been directed at over 4,900 teachers, the survey reveals.

According to one teacher, they have been pushed and shoved by students, spraining their thumb one time and striking their head on a radiator as a result of being punched repeatedly. An earlier rugby player stated they felt more protected and secured against physical and verbal violence on the pitch than they felt when they were within the four boundaries of their school.

Taking a Look at the Statistics

In 2018,[11] **about nine out of ten teachers reported being targeted for physical as well as verbal abuse by pupils.** Because of this, more than half of the teachers have started thinking of quitting their work.

About 24% of the teachers are facing a physical assault from their students at least once every week or even more than that. 4% of teachers stated that they are experiencing such instances of violence almost every day.

According to the survey, three out of four teachers do not feel they have enough resources or funding to satisfy the behavioural needs of the students, they teach at present. These results come after the National Education Union (NEU) notified that local systems do not

---

[10] https://www.independent.co.uk/news/education/educationnews/teachers-pupils-violence-classroom-behaviour-nasuwt-teachingunion-a8877776.html

[11] https://www.independent.co.uk/news/education/educationnews/teachers-pupils-violence-classroom-behaviour-nasuwt-teachingunion-a8877776.html

have enough wealth to afford satisfactory resources for Special Educational Needs (SEN) facility in schools.

Several members of the NEU voiced their worries about the effect of zero-tolerance methods to discipline in schools on weak, defenceless pupils at one of their conferences held in Liverpool.

NASUWT's latest survey[12] shows that several teachers do not feel safe in schools mainly because of the poor behaviour of students. **About 49% of the teachers say that physical or verbal violence is a part of their system,** and the teachers should expect such occurrences.

An article posted by the Independent titled: *Nearly one in four teachers physically attacked by pupils at least once a week, survey suggests,*[13] spoke with several teachers, both former and those working currently, and recorded their experiences regarding bad behaviour by pupils. Their responses are as follows:

A former teacher states, "Having taught for almost 40 years I have witnessed a demonstrable and seemingly unstoppable deterioration in pupil behaviour."

Another teacher said: "My school has become a frightening place over the last few years. I often try to only go on the corridors at times when I expect them to be quiet, as I simply assume I will be stampeded, pushed or sworn at." One of the teachers showed her concern by saying that they are seeing a higher number of younger kids who are being more physically as well as verbally abusive to staff.

---

[12] https://www.independent.co.uk/topic/nasuwt?CMP=ILCrefresh
[13] https://www.independent.co.uk/news/education/educationnews/teachers-pupils-violence-classroom-behaviour-nasuwt-teachingunion-a8877776.html

NASUWT's general secretary named Chris Keates, said that teachers shouldn't go to work with the expectation that they will get physically or verbally harmed. However, this survey indicates that quite a lot of teachers are, unfortunately, experiencing such instances almost every other day.

The indiscipline of pupils adds up to the worries of teachers who have already been burdened with their workload. **Pupil indiscipline is also leading to retention crises.** The fact that employers are unable to do their legal duties of providing care and protection to their employees is simply objectionable.

In our day and age, the school system is torn apart with poor as well as unacceptable employment procedures that end up putting teachers at serious risk, eventually forcing them out of their occupations. We all can unanimously agree that teachers are responsible for providing one of the most vital public services, and keeping that in mind, it wouldn't be wrong to say that they deserve better.

A Department for Education's representative believes that **teachers, as well as the school staff, should feel safe while coming to their jobs**. Physical or verbal abuse is totally unacceptable and should completely be eradicated.

School officials and authorities must come together, under the same umbrella, and strive to get rid of this inhumane culture at once. Authorities must come up with effective measures and try to tackle these incidents with utmost proficiency.

Accounts of Personal Experiences

As a teacher assistant, I have had the opportunity to work in different school environments. I have witnessed and experienced verbal abuse on multiple occasions. Honestly, it is disgusting and disgraceful to see how young people can show such appalling behaviour to someone who is there to help them be educated. Unfortunately, swearing, treating teachers poorly, and spitting on their faces is nothing to some of the students. Misbehaving under the garb of "fun" is not new for such students. They have the indecency of humiliating and insulting you in front of anyone.

Foreign teachers go through the worst in the hands of some of these students. Supply teachers can't get much classroom work done because those students who are constantly causing disruption make it even worse. I remember the time when an Asian teacher came as a supply. The students mocked him and humiliated him in front of the class to the point where he just had to work out of the class and left to go home. Some students have attacked supply teachers physically. The sad thing is that it is always the supply teachers who get sacked while the students never face any consequences. This has carried on for many years and gives these students more power to display such behaviour.

In some cases, some students refuse to go to lessons. They don't show any interest in whatever is going on in the schools. They end up roaming around the school doing nothing for someone to be going after, pleading with them to attend their lessons.

I wish parents, caregivers, and educational authorities must see what happens in the schools. Ofsted must be made aware of what goes on in the schools regarding students' behaviours instead of always going for inspection to intimidate the headteachers and staff members. They have no idea the exact worries they cause when it is time for school inspections. Just showing up with a list of instructions does not solve problems teachers face in everyday lives. The schools have to put up a perfect show to make them believe that everything is going alright, but in truth, it is not. Ofsted is alone interested in many things that do not include the welfare of staff members – something that needs to be addressed at once. Furthermore, extra support should be in place.

I remember when I was a registered childminder and had an Ofsted inspection. Two people came out of whom one was so intimidating it was difficult to communicate. With all that stress that I underwent, he kept bombarding me with questions. I gathered some courage and told them what I was going through at that time, making things very clear and easy for them to understand. In the end, we had a good conclusion about handling matters.

The point which must be stressed is that schools where pupils scream vulgarities, physically or verbally assault their teachers, swear and threaten the staff face severe disturbance each day. Furthermore, I believe that inappropriate parenting and the pressure on schools for not rusticating such students further worsens the situation.

It seems as if the Department for Education and Ofsted is unaware of the degree of classroom disorder. They believe that pupil behaviour in 99.7 per cent of schools is pleasing. An educationist named Professor Terry Haydn at the University of East Anglia refers to international data that teachers present in England are facing more difficult pupil behaviour than in several other rival nations.

His study shows results from the Organisation for Economic Co-operation and Development, which is known for administering the world's most extensive education survey called PISA. OECD members comprise several wealthy nations of the world.

According to his report: *"Some data from PISA research … suggests that teachers in England may be teaching in more difficult contexts than their counterparts elsewhere."*

Testaments from teachers show the real state of behaviour in most schools. One of the teachers stated: *"It is a condition of working at this school that you have to face serious disruption on a daily basis, pupils screaming obscenities, refusing to comply with requests to stop appalling behaviour, threatening, spitting, swearing. You feel wretched for the poor kids who would like to learn."*

The current situation of pupil misbehaviour needs to be acknowledged, addressed, and corrected right away. This isn't something that can, or should, be brushed under the carpet. The future of our nation depends on the kind of children we raise today. Hence, immediate action must be taken at the earliest because this is the only way forward.

Teaching 'British Values' in Schools and its Consequences

The bad habits and negative complaints based on the English students can be traced to the problems with teaching 'British values' in schools.

The head of Ofsted, named Amanda Spielman, states that **"British values are being "actively perverted" by** religious extremists."[14]

Recently, in one of her speeches, she pointed out that extremists, by using schools, are:

- Narrowing down young people's perspectives

- Isolating and separating

- To some extent, brainwashing gullible minds

Although Spielman's speech has faced harsh criticism for its lack of evidence and for targeting Muslim children in British schools, one wonders what these "British values" are that she refers to. Does it include arranging formal balls, showing support to the Queen, or meeting for tea drinking?

The government describes major "British values" as **democracy, individual freedom, the rule of law, common respect and acceptance of people with diverse faiths and beliefs.** Since the year 2014, educators in English schools must support the above-mentioned British values and their advancement is checked by the Office for Standards in Education, Children's Services and Skills.

The initiative was a response by then secretary of state for education, Michael Gove, going along the famous "Trojan Horse

---

[14] https://www.pressenza.com/2018/02/problem-teachingbritish-values-school/

Affair", where it was claimed that Islamists were planning on taking over state schools that were situated all over Birmingham. However, despite a number of investigations, no proof was found to confirm the allegation of conspiracy.

The Common British Values

Considering the fact that Britain does not have a written constitution, these rudimentary public values had to be acknowledged once again. The identification of government of specific values as "British" is the result of official choices – with the diction derived from the Prevent anti-extremist plan.

The British values have neither been talked over by parliament nor the masses. These values are both broad as well as imprecise, resulting in several people signing up for them. This evades more clear-cut definitions that might create debate and disagreement.

A few education experts from UCL and the University of Bristol's departments of Law and Education claimed at a recent event that **declaring specific values as "national values" is nothing more than an extension of state power,** as the state pursues to handle the growing diversity. Furthermore, they highlighted the significance of bearing in mind the context of the promotion of such values.

Black Lives Matter

The recent events of discrimination and prejudice directed towards racially marginalized groups worldwide, particularly in the West, have once again highlighted the many atrocities faced by people of colour regularly. These incidents make one question the upbringing of those individuals who think of themselves as superior, better than others, solely on the basis of the colour of their skin. The injustices directed towards minorities and the abuse aimed at them indicate how difficult it has become for us to accept the existence of others. To accept people for who they are and not judge them on the basis of the race they belong to is something that children should be taught from a young age.

Diversity, which should have been embraced and supported, has unfortunately become an issue even in schools and universities. **According to a BBC News report, the proportion of black and Asian students in London is the highest, making up 17% and 25% each.**[15] With the proportion of black students increasing in various schools, the discrimination against them seems to be growing as well. **A recent survey released by the YMCA reports that 95% of young black people share how they have "heard and witnessed the use of racist language at school."**[16]

The 19-year-old Adele Tondu, a YMCA's BAME youth advisory group member, shares how she herself has experienced discrimination at school on multiple occasions. While stating that the school that she went to was predominantly white, she says, "I had racial language used towards me multiple times when I was at school.

---

[15] https://www.bbc.com/news/education-44226434
[16] https://www.ymca.org.uk/wpcontent/uploads/2020/10/ymca-young-and-black.pdf

I remember in year 7, it was few days into school, I got called a monkey by one of the boys. I told the teachers. He got a detention, but nothing else happened."[17]

It is shocking that young people growing up in the UK are getting more violent, abusive, aggressive, and intolerable with each passing day. It is essential that we pay heed to young black peoples' concerns and, most importantly, focus on our children's upbringing so that the atrocities that George Floyd and Breonna Taylor experienced are not faced by anyone else in the future.

Systemic Racism in Police and Forces

But then again, systemic racism is not restricted to academic institutes only. Rather, it has existed and is becoming more rampant in the police, military forces, juvenile courts, and justice departments with each passing day. CNN's poll regarding institutionalized racism points out that people of colour are twice as likely as white people to state that the police have not treated them with respect in Britain.[18]

According to an article posted by the Independent in June 2020, **racism is not just alive but also thriving in the British policing system.**[19] When an inquiry regarding the treatment of black and other ethnic minority groups within the forces was held, MPs were told the many truths that often, if not always, remain in the background. A retired experienced police officer named Nick Glynn shared how he was attacked with a "racial slur" just before he left the

---

[17] https://www.theguardian.com/world/2020/oct/29/mostblack-british-children-report-experiencing-racism-at-school

[18] https://edition.cnn.com/interactive/2020/06/europe/britainracism-cnn-poll-gbr-intl/

[19] https://www.independent.co.uk/news/uk/home-news/ukpolice-racism-blm-floyd-home-affairs-a9570956.html

department in 2015. He went on to say that "racism is alive and kicking in policing… These things are happening on a daily basis…"

Let's look at the study titled *Dangerous associations: Joint enterprise, gangs and racism* published by Patrick Williams and Becky Clarke in 2016. In the study, gang databases and prosecutions in the cities of London and Manchester were examined. Young black and several other people belonging to the minority ethnic groups frequently appeared in gang databases despite not being responsible for the most severe violence in their neighbourhoods. Three-fourths of the black prisoners stated that the prosecution declared that they belonged to a 'gang,' compared to only 39 per cent of prisoners who were white.

Black Inferiority

People of colour have always been looked down upon. Many 18th-century leaders, both political and intellectual, considered blacks to be naturally inferior, maintaining the stance that they were only suited for slavery.[20] This attitude towards people of colour and them being intellectually inferior is still dominant in several institutes. In most settings, black people are paid and recognized less, offered temporary jobs, and almost always remain in the background, despite their abilities and hard work.

The truth is that discrimination is still rooted and continues to grow. A 2016 report by the Equality and Human Rights Commission revealed that **black graduates were typically paid 23.1% less than equally qualified white employees in Britain.**[21] The chances of black workers being in insecure employment systems such as temporary

---

[20] https://www.britannica.com/topic/race-human/Building-themyth-of-Black-inferiority

[21] https://www.equalityhumanrights.com/en/ourwork/news/widespread-inequality-risks-increasing-race-tensionswarns-commission

jobs or contractual commissions are also high. Studies tell that people of colour are mostly the targets of misconduct.

According to the report, "You are more than twice as likely to be murdered if you are black in England and Wales." On being accused of a crime, blacks are three times more likely to be put on trial and sentenced than their white counterparts.[22]

While working in one of the high support SEND students, a topic was discussed that left me thinking for days.

A teacher asked the students to raise their hand if they think the government should acknowledge the black and Asian people who took part in world war two. To my disbelief, none of the children raised their hands. The teacher asked why they said it was not important. I was really disappointed to find year seven thinks people don't deserve many recommendations based on their cultures or kin colour. This is a disgrace. Everyone dies, everyone gets sick, we all take the same medications and breathe the same air. There is no difference in being black, Asian, Chinese, or English, and that alone is the absolute truth, period. Furthermore, more efforts should be made on educating children based on race in our schools. It must be part of the curriculum in schools.

---

[22] https://www.theguardian.com/commentisfree/2016/oct/30/what-itmeans-to-be-black-in-britain-today

Stereotypical Behaviour Towards Black Pupils and How It Hinders Their Productivity

Racial discrimination is more like a disease that seems to be spreading across the nation, seeping through each crack and corner. It is present in institutes, police forces, offices, and neighbourhoods. The Guardian's article titled *Black pupils 'are routinely marked down by teachers'* reveals biases directed at young black children by their teachers. They talk about how black children regularly receive less marks from their teachers, who involuntarily stereotype them.[23]

When researchers studied the Stats marks given to hundreds of children at age 11 and compared them with the teachers' assessments made within the classroom as well as in other tests, their results were eye-opening. The study reports that black students perform better in external exams than in those conducted by teachers, over and over again. The report also shows that low expectations from children are harming their prospects. The co-author of this report, Simon Burgess, says, "What is worrying is that if students do not feel that a teacher appreciates them or understands them, then they are not going to try so hard." According to his study, these differences stem from stereotyping and are rampant in areas where the ratio of black children is less.

Black Caribbean Underachievement

Simon Burgess's opinion reminds us of Bernard Coard's book *How the West Indian Child is Made Educationally Sub-normal in the British School System*, published in 1971. In his book, Coard explained the

---

[23] https://www.theguardian.com/education/2010/apr/04/satsmarking-race-stereotypes

many stereotypes that have been wrongly attached to Black pupils. To believe that children of colour are somehow "educationally subnormal" only results in damaging pupils' motivation. Furthermore, the low expectations of teachers affect the self-confidence of black children. This eventually results in sentencing them to a life of underachievement.

Black Caribbean Underachievement in Schools in England by Feyisa Demie and Christabel McLean is another essential book. It discusses the many causes and consequences of racism at school and how badly it influences ethnic minority pupils, particularly the AfroCaribbeans. The underachievement of Afro-Caribbean pupils has been a continued problem facing the national policymakers in the schools of Britain for several years. The national research of the last four decades shows that the achievements of Black Caribbean heritage pupils continually fall behind the usual accomplishment of their counterparts. Moreover, the gap is rising at the end of primary as well as secondary education.

The underachievement of ethnic minority pupils isn't a new issue. In fact, it has been at the forefront since the 1980s. We know this because of the studies and reports conducted on the issue in those years. This problem was first officially acknowledged by The Rampton Report in 1981 and was later confirmed in 1985 by The Swann Report. This report concluded that:

"There is no doubt that Black Caribbean children, as a group, and on average, are underachieving, both by comparison with their school fellows in the White majority, as well as in terms of their potential. Notwithstanding that some are doing well" (Swann 1985: 81).

What these two reports claimed is now being confirmed with substantial data. In 2014, National Statistics DFE SFR conducted a survey called *Permanent and Fixed Period Exclusions in England: 2012/2013*.[24] The report's data showed:

- The Afro-Caribbean pupils are three times more likely to be excluded forever from their school in comparison with their white counterparts.

- Out of all black Caribbean men, only 16% go on to University.

- The black Caribbean individuals are almost eight times as likely to be searched and inquired by the police than the whites.

- Of all black Caribbean men, 15% are unemployed, in contrast with 5% of White British counterparts.

- Black Caribbean individuals living in poverty are 30%.

- The British national prison population includes 10% black individuals.

The Reasons for the Underachievement of Black Caribbean Pupils

We now understand that Black Caribbean pupils lag behind their white counterparts in most cases, but what could possibly be the reasons behind their underachievement? According to Feyisa Demie, some of the factors that have been considered to be the main cause of this issue are:

---

[24]https://www.lambeth.gov.uk/rsu/sites/www.lambeth.gov.uk.rsu/files/black_caribbean_underachievement_in_schools_in_england_2017.pdf

- ➢ Low expectations of teachers

- ➢ Poor leadership of head-teachers on equality problems

- ➢ Exclusions

- ➢ Stereotyping

Low Expectations of Teachers & Poor Leadership:

Among all the above-mentioned reasons, low teachers' expectations have been especially discussed by most researchers. They believe this to be the primary factor of low accomplishment amongst Black children. In his book, *The White British-Black Caribbean achievement gap: Tests, tiers and teacher expectations,* Steve Strand talks about the same issue in detail. He explains how Black Caribbean students are methodically under-represented not only on entry but also on higher education levels relative to their White British counterparts. He went on to say that, as a matter of fact, this has contributed to attainment gaps. Strand concludes that racism within institutions and teachers' low expectations are some of the major reasons why black children failed to enter top-tier examinations.

Maylor puts it correctly, "(teachers') conscious or unconscious stereotypes and assumptions about minority groups can impact negatively on pupils' achievements" (Maylor 2009).

Exclusions:

Before we dive into the details of exclusions and how black pupils have to experience them at school, we must first understand what exclusion basically is. Exclusion is an act of leaving something or someone out, sometimes unconsciously but most of the time on purpose. In other terms, when you do not include someone in whatever it is that you intend to do, you have excluded that person.

Some acts of exclusion for racism include making coloured pupils sit at one table, not giving them the chance to participate in class, or thinking of them as not being smart.

Recent research shows that exclusion for racism has unfortunately become a part of various academic institutes and seems to be becoming more significant. In his article titled *Exclusions for racism in primary schools in England up more than 40%*, Frankie McCamley sheds light on the incidents of racism that coloured pupils face at school. In particular, he talks about a nine-year-old kid named Nai'm, who faced five incidents of racist abuse at his primary school within a year.

Official figures show that exclusions for racism at primary schools in England are over 40% within a decade, with the highest rise in the North West.

According to the analysis of BBC News[25]:

- o In the academic year of 2006-07, there were 350 temporary exclusions for racism from various primary schools.

- o In 2017-18, this figure saw a rise of 40% as there were 496 temporary exclusions for racism.

- o If we look at the North West, there were 36 temporary exclusions during 2006-07, a figure that went up to 76 exclusions within 2017-18

---

[25] https://www.bbc.com/news/education-50331687

Stereotyping:

Stereotyping is a very basic and active way in which racism is spread. Thus, there is a majority of depictions or representations of these groups within limited kinds, e.g., sports, entertainment, crime, etc. Stereotypes are mainly one-dimensional. They only focus on particular features, often used to characterize whole crowds of people. This results in a situation where people begin to make assumptions about others solely on the basis of the common stereotypes, making them behave in a way they wouldn't have otherwise.

It wouldn't be wrong to say that even the police have started viewing people of colour In a different light because of these stereotypes. They have started suspecting the Black

Caribbean of crimes they haven't even committed.

Sometimes several extreme measures are also taken against the blacks, solely on the basis of their skin colour. The police are likely to stop black people more and interrogate them than whites. **The stop and search ratio between whites and blacks is 1:3.6,** which is quite alarming. However, the ratio **between whites and Asians is 1:1.2.**[26]

Racism Faced by Asian Schoolchildren in Britain

Racist remarks and sneers directed at Black Caribbean pupils are not restricted to that group alone. In fact, racism towards other minority groups that are inhabiting England, such as South Asians, Hispanics, and Chinese, is also very much present and seems to be

---

[26]https://www.lambeth.gov.uk/rsu/sites/www.lambeth.gov.uk.rsu/files/black_car ibbean_underachievement_in_schools_in_england_2017.pdf

spreading like wildfire. Several kinds of research have been conducted that prove these claims.

For instance, Asians of different ethnic groups and following different religions were surveyed in the year 2010 by Mike Eslea and Kafeela Mukhtar. Both the researchers devised a questionnaire and surveyed 243 Hindu, Indian Muslim, and Pakistani children. While some of these children attended temples, others went to mosques in the Preston as well as the Bolton area of Lancashire. These children were questioned about their experiences regarding school bullying. Moreover, they were asked as to who bullied them and also in what way.

When the results of the survey came in, it revealed that bullying was prevalent. About 57% of boys and 43% of girls had been bullied in that particular school term.[27] It was also made clear that children belonging to all three ethnic groups had to go through this behaviour equally. While some were bullied because of the language they spoke, others were made fun of because of the way they dressed or due to their religious beliefs.

The bullies of these children were not only whites but even members of other minority groups. However, on the whole, the ratio of white bullies was relatively greater.

Dr. Zubaida Haque, the deputy director of the Runnymede Trust, rightly believes that racism within schools is a reflection of the attitudes prevalent outside the classroom[28]. **It all comes down to one thing – disciplining children from a young age.** That is the only solution to achieving a peaceful, tolerant society, state, and world at

---

[27] https://www.tandfonline.com/doi/abs/10.1080/001318800363845?journalCode=rere20
[28] https://www.bbc.com/news/education-50331687

large. Kindness, patience, and tolerance are some of the proper values that must, at all costs, be preached and practised.

How to Promote Proper Values

Keeping in mind the conciseness of the present-day policy rules, teachers have substantial liberty for deciding how to support and promote these values.

Several teachers rely on the Union Jack themed presentations, confusing British values with the popularly known British symbols or stereotypes. Teaching common values is a more profound task that goes beyond the popular British signs and symbols.

Britain's colonial history and its history of racial superiority may well affect how minority groups receive talk of "our" values. Due to this reason, teachers, who are responsible for teaching students coming from different backgrounds, often talk about the universally established values in an effort to level out the possibly nationalistic notion of "British" values.

Likewise, many schools often adopt British values into prevailing school practices, for instance, learning about democracy and equality through the school council. Many schools go further than that, with advanced inventiveness that emphasises worldwide interconnections as well as human rights.

Liberal Values

It wouldn't be wrong to say that discussion with students regarding basic British values is restricted. That's mainly because of:

- Busy, occupied school timetable.

- Some teachers who are justifiably distrustful of possibly controversial issues.

These values are trifling values for schools to encourage. After all, research indicates that young people are already supporting liberal values, particularly those from ethnic minorities. However, if schools wish to motivate youngsters, teaching must go beyond stereotypes, signs and symbols.

Instead of broad allegations of extremists weakening as well as challenging "our" values, schools must be motivated to improve political literacy in the younger generation. One basic step that needs to be taken into consideration is educating and training teachers along with giving them the time and resources they need to develop safe spaces for debate with students as part of an extensive programme of citizenship education.

This is of great significance because, in the end, the most basic of British values is that schools create a readiness in their pupils to participate in essential moral questions through rational as well as widespread dialogue to boost sincere commitment towards important democratic values.

Where Are Pupils the Best Behaved?

In the rest of the countries, the number of wellbehaved students is higher than those in the UK. Pupils across the globe are relatively more behaved and respectful of the authority. According to a study conducted by the Organisation for Economic Co-operation and Development, OECD's Programme for International Student Assessment (PISA), the students of Japan are the best behaved.[29] The report further mentions the top 10 countries where students behave properly. These countries include:

---

[29] https://vancouversun.com/news/staff-blogs/high-schoolstudents-are-well-behaved-especially-in-japan

- Japan

- Kazakhstan

- Shanghai-China

- Hong Kong-China

- Romania

- South Korea

- Azerbaijan

- Thailand

- Albania

- Russian Federation.

Classroom discipline is and should be integral for all schools at all levels. When classrooms fail to maintain disciple, they become less conducive to learning. That's because, in such scenarios, teachers spend most of their time trying to create the order before they get the chance to begin teaching.

The report continues to state that "Interruptions in the classroom disrupt students' concentration on, and their engagement in, their lessons. Results from PISA 2009 show that disciplinary climate is strongly associated with student performance. Students who report that their reading lessons are often interrupted perform less well than students who reported that there are few or no interruptions in class."

Mental Health of Children Amidst the COVID-19 Pandemic

The Covid-19 pandemic has taken a heavy toll on millions of people. **While it has harmed people physically, financially, and emotionally, it has also seriously impacted people's mental health.** The fear of the unknown, followed by severe anxiety, and panic attacks, has drastically changed the outlooks of people.

Considering the world's current situation, the WHO Regional Director for Europe, Dr Hans Henri P. Kluge believes that we must try to fight this battle together and face this crisis as individuals, family members, friends and colleagues. How we react to this crisis and our willpower is of utmost importance. The only way forward out of this pandemic is through patience and dedication while being optimistic and hopeful that we will surely come out of it stronger and better.

WHO acknowledges the mental health issues that have stemmed because of the pandemic. The organization takes the power of the crisis on people's mental health earnestly and observes the condition along with national consultants while briefing and guiding the governments and the public.

Dr Hans Kluge believes:

"With the disruptive effects of COVID-19 – including social distancing – currently dominating our daily lives, it is important that we check on each other, call and video chat, and are mindful of and sensitive to the unique mental health needs of those we care for. Our anxiety and fears should be acknowledged and not be ignored, but better understood and addressed by individuals, communities and governments."[30]

The Influence of the COVID-19 Calamity on Children's Mental Health

Covid-19 has deteriorated not only adults' mental health but even that of children. The disruption caused due to the pandemic greatly affects children who tend to face similar anxieties and worries as that faced by their elders. The fact that children worldwide have been restricted to their homes because of the closure of the schools has decreased their opportunities to spend quality time with their friends or have a laugh or two. Fear of death and fear of a relative's death, along with the gloominess that follows, are some of the issues that can seriously burden children.

According to WHO, "Being at home can place some children at increased risk of, or increased exposure to, child protection incidents or make them witness to interpersonal violence if their home is not a safe place."[31] This is something that is deeply disturbing.

Despite children being perceptive to change, they may find these changes hard to comprehend, and as a result, young as well as older children may show bad temper and annoyance. Children may feel that they need to be nearer to their parents and demand more from them. As a result, some parents or guardians may feel they are under an unjustified burden themselves.

Other serious issues that children are going through during this time are the complexities associated with the online world. Children have been extremely exposed to so many things that can actually be detrimental to their young minds. This may include online bullying,

---

[30] https://bit.ly/2M80iGP
[31] https://bit.ly/3638q2C

grooming, radicalism, incidents of cyber-crime, and many other related problems.

To tackle situations such as these, parents must make sure to:

- give young children the love and attention that is important for them

- help them acknowledge and resolve their doubts

- be honest with their young ones

- explain to them what is happening in words that *they* can understand

- make them understand what Covid-19 is and the precautions that one must take to encounter it

- help children look for ways to voice their opinions through innovative activities

- try providing some kind of structure in the day. This can be attained through forming routines, mainly if they aren't going to school any longer.

Don't forget that children learn what they see. How you tackle this situation is ultimately going to help them understand their role. That's why parents also need to be backed in handling their own stressors to be exceptional models for their kids.

Mental health along with psychosocial care services should be introduced and made active and efficient. Moreover, child security services must adjust to guarantee that the attention is still offered to those children who need it the most.

The Lighter Side: Covid-19 has Sparked More Appreciation for Teachers

The lack of respect for teachers from their students and the parents of those children seems to be getting less with each passing day. That's because today, people, particularly parents who have been made responsible for taking on the role of the teachers, have understood the many complexities faced by the teachers in trying to teach, educate and guide the younger generation. Teaching has never been an easy job because it requires immense patience, wisdom, and willpower. This aspect, which had been taken for granted by most children and parents, is now finally tailing off. They now know the importance of the role teachers have in their children's lives.

Covid-19 has opened the eyes of many parents as many have been forced into home-schooling while side by side working full-time jobs. A survey including 2,000 parents conducted by OnePoll and Osmo shows an increase in the public's appreciation for teachers' work. According to the poll:

"80% have newfound respect for teachers; 77% believe that teachers should be paid more; 69% believe being a teacher is harder than their current job, and 53% will take a greater interest in their child's education after the stay-athome mandate concludes."[32]

However, the question is, will this change give teachers a say in teaching and their working conditions once the dust settles down?

---

[32] https://apnews.com/press-release/businesswire/d7d10eb8c3cb4ee1bb757abf3a2c5421

Professor Tony Gallagher, known as one of the world's leading academic specialists currently teaching at Queen's University, wishes that the teachers' plaudits might have the power to transform the outlook of the education system. He says, "I suspect when we come out of this, there is going to be a lot of re-evaluation. Even the very concept of essential workers, who are often in very low paid, transient jobs turn out to be essential workers because we need them to keep things going."[33]

There is a higher chance that this crisis may provide an important opportunity for school systems to make this appreciation for teachers, in theory, become a reality. The truth is that teachers will always work harder to make sure that students are taught well. Their efforts, which both children and parents are now understanding, must also be acknowledged by policymakers who are in power to make their working conditions better and provide them with the necessary resources. While the pandemic has destroyed millions of lives and crushed several dreams, this can surely be seen as a light at the end of the tunnel.

---

[33] https://www.qub.ac.uk/coronavirus/analysiscommentary/coronavirus-new-appreciation-of-teachers/

Chapter 7

How to Enforce Discipline from an Early Stage

It's the task of every parent to educate, train and discipline their children so as to guide them in the right direction, towards the perfect way that eventually leads to their greater future lest they end up being bad by acquiring ill habits. Sadly, many people struggle with how to enforce discipline on their children in their early years. This has affected a great many children from an early age and has actually misled them as they end up cultivating several bad characteristics and habits. This fault can be traced to the way their parents disciplined them from a young age.

The Best Ways to Discipline Your Children Effectively

If you, too, believe that your child has refused to obey and listen to you despite your constant requests, then it is time to take some action and adopt a few measures to discipline them. But remember, disciplining kids is not as easy as it sounds. Although a gradual process, it is by no means a smooth ride. Which is why I have come up with a list of dos and don'ts that each parent must practise.

Below I will be talking about different ways to discipline your children and their effects on them.

1. **Communicating:** Telling children what is right for them is of utmost importance in the long run. The information that you share with them is equally important to *how* you share it. The tone of your voice, as well as the manner in which you speak, needs to be proper.

2. **Listening to Their Side of Story:** Listening is as important for a parent as talking. Give your child the chance to voice out his opinions or concerns. If they have been accused of misbehaving by a third person, hear them speak their side of the story. If you notice them being jealous or resentful regarding a particular person or situation, ask them what is bothering them.

3. **Explaining Good/Bad Behaviour by Giving Examples and Consequences:** Talking with your child and explaining matters to them by giving examples that they could relate to would have a massive impact on them. Although this may take some time and a lot of patience, it will help little minds understand big lessons. Similarly, explaining the consequences of their actions is also advisable. For instance, if they do not tidy up their room, they won't be allowed to go out and play.

4. **Setting Limits:** It is integral to have certain welldefined rules that your children must follow. These rules may include the number of hours they can play or the number of sugary foods they consume in a day. Make sure to explain the rules that you've set in words that are easily understood by your child.

5. **Practising What You Preach:** Teaching your children lessons regarding honesty, integrity, hard work, and virtuousness that you yourself are not adhering to can often be misleading for a child. Hence, practise what you preach.

6. **Positive Reinforcement:** Children, like adults, need little positive reinforcement every now and then. When you see them performing a good act on their own, acknowledge it, and tell them how proud you are of them. Your reinforcement can be in the form of:

   - Giving a quick high five
   - Praising them
   - Patting them on the back
   - Sharing their good deed with others in front of your child
   - Hugging them or giving a thumbs up
   - Buying them a little treat

7. **Giving Attention:** One of the most influential tools for disciplining children is attention. Paying attention to the needs, concerns, queries of your child and coming up with solutions together strengthens the child-parent bond.

8. **Redirecting Bad Behaviour:** There are times when children misbehave simply because they don't have anything else to do. In times such as these, it is essential to look for activities that help distract them.

9. **Be Prepared for your Child's Misbehaviour:** Children sometimes get cranky and show mood swings that are quite unexpected. In such cases, it is better to make them participate in activities that are interesting as well as catchy.

10. **When to Not Respond:** As long as your kid is not meddling with something that is physically or emotionally harmful, ignoring their bad behaviour sometimes can be a useful way of putting a halt to it. For instance, if your child drops food on purpose and keeps on doing it, he/she will soon have nothing left to eat. If your child throws a toy that eventually breaks, they will have nothing to play with. Soon he/she will understand the consequences of their actions on their own.

Hitting Children or Bombarding Them with Harsh Words Is Wrong

Teaching good behaviour is not the same as punishing bad behaviour. While the former is needed, the latter must be avoided at all costs. According to research, hitting, spanking, or punishing a child physically do not work well in correcting a child's behaviour. The same can be said regarding verbally abusing or shouting at a child, making them feel worthless or insignificant. Extreme physical or verbal punishments are not only ineffective but can also be severely damaging for a child's physical as well as mental health conditions, specifically in the long run.

That's why one must be watchful of the following main aspects integral to the upbringing of children:

1. Discipline is Not Synonymous with Punishment

Many people confuse discipline with punishment. Disciplining your child involves a whole lot of attention using methods that are age-appropriate and effective.

Discipline includes actively engaging children to alter their characters for their own betterment. On the other hand, punishing kids is ineffective as well as illogical, which has the tendency of seriously affecting children.

Paediatrician Edward Gaydos once said, "With discipline, we are teaching our children self-control and restraint. Punishment is a direct, pointed penalty or a loss of privilege that serves as retribution."[34]

Discipline, although more effective, requires a little more work than punishment and a lot of patience. Just don't forget that good things take time.

2. Look for Chances for Praise

It's essential to pay closer attention to the activities your child is participating in or how they are behaving. According to Dr. Gaydos, making an effort to note when your kid is energetically busy in being good and complimenting him/her on their good behaviour is advisable.

Taking out the time to listen to what your kids have to say and then agree with them when suitable is important. If you disagree, tell them so, along with an explanation as to why you disagree.

Parents who are there for their children and show understanding towards them succeed in being tremendous role models. Communication is always the answer.

---

[34] https://health.clevelandclinic.org/discipline-5-dos-anddonts-when-your-kids-wont-listen/

3. Being Consistent with the Limits You've Set

Setting limits will not yield fruitful results if the factor of consistency is absent from the equation. Setting limits but not sticking to them is like setting the alarm but not getting up on the set time. Remember, the very reason we set limits is so that we follow through with them. In case your child fails to follow it, he/she will then expect a consequence. But all of this must be anticipated by the child; nothing about it should be new or alarming, worthy of negotiations.

4. Threatening Children is NOT Acceptable

Dr. Gaydos once said, "Warning children, 'You better be good,' is too broad and general a message."[35]

To assume that a child knows what we want them to do or how we want them to behave instead of explaining what we expect in advance will lead to disturbance.

Moreover, to set unrealistic limits for children that are impossible for them to achieve is also problematic.

5. Be a Parent, Not a Pal

Some people may find it appealing to treat their children as if they're best friends. Nevertheless, children need you as a parent to educate and guide them with each passing day. Teaching your child and disciplining them will encourage them to be confident as they go through their lives.

---

[35] https://health.clevelandclinic.org/discipline-5-dos-and-dontswhen-your-kids-wont-listen/

"With discipline, we're not passive observers, we're actively involved as teachers," states Dr. Gaydos. "It's an ongoing process and requires work."

Disciplining your child may at times feel like too much work but remember, your patience and hard work will eventually result in confident individuals with good morals.

Note: Learn from Mistakes — Even If They're Your Own

The way children take time to develop and grow, there are chances that you, as a parent, may experience something similar. There will be times when you would feel frustrated and exhausted; remember that such emotions are natural. But what you need to do is learn how to handle yourself when you undergo such moods. Some of the things that you can do to relax yourself include:

- Ensure your child is in safe hands, then take out some

- "me time."

- Take a nap

- Read a book

- Light scented candles to calm your nerves

- Call or meet a friend

- Watch a movie

- Go out for a walk

- Take a long, warm bath

Once you start feeling like yourself again, go to your kid, hug them, and start over.

In case you have failed to handle a situation properly the first time, don't fret over it. Go over the situation in your head and see how you could have dealt with the situation differently. Once you figure it out, try not to do it the next time. If you say something to your child in the heat of the moment that you later realize you shouldn't have said, apologize to them and assure them that in the future, you'll handle the situation in a better way. But make sure to keep up with your promise because remember, how you act is what your child will learn.

Useful Disciplining Tips in Accordance with Children's Age

Babies	<ul><li>Infants mainly learn by observing what you do or how you behave. Therefore, try to set good examples of behaviour you want to see in your child.</li><li>Using positive words to teach your baby will do wonders. For example, when you tell them, *"It's time to go to bed,"* instead of, *"Do not stay up late."*</li><li>Limit the usage of the word "no." Use it only for the most critical issues, like security. Putting away dangerous objects or keeping them out of reach for your baby can help you use "no" less.</li><li>Diverting your baby's mind and replacing unsafe objects with those that are acceptable to play with is effective at this age.</li></ul>

	• Children, including infants, need constant discipline. Therefore, speak with your spouse and family members, and come with a basic set of rules that everyone follows.
Toddlers	• This is the time your child begins to see whether and to what extent you react to his actions. During this time, it is best to compliment them for their good behaviour and avoid the ones you do not want them to adopt. • Tantrums in toddlers are frequent since this is the time they try to master skills that they aren't familiar with. Expect their tantrums and try to redirect their attention to something else. Make sure that they are timely fed and have taken their naps to lessen the tantrums. • Teach your child how hitting, biting or using bad language is not acceptable. Make sure you never spank your toddler or yell at them. If you do that, they are bound to learn that behaviour too. • Follow through the limits that you've set. Try not to take sides when and if your children contradict or argue over something. For example, if the argument is because of some toy, try to just put it away.
Pres-school Age	• Children, at this stage, are still trying to figure out the consequences of their actions and how things work. They will continue to test the limits of their parents, mainly to learn appropriate behaviour.

	• Start assigning little tasks to preschoolers. Such as asking them to put away their toys or tidying up their bed. Once they do it, praise them. • Give your child the chance to make choices among suitable alternatives. • Ask your child to treat others the way they want to be treated by others. • Explain to your child that to feel mad at times is understandable but hurting others or breaking things is out of the question. Teach them how to deal with anger or negative emotions in a positive way, such as through conversation.
Grade School-age Children	• At this stage, your child starts to understand the right and wrong way. Try talking to them about difficult situations, the good and bad options that they have. Also, talk about what might happen next, i.e., depending on what decision they make or what path they choose. • Tell them what you expect from them or what would happen if family rules are not followed. • Maintain a balance of freedom and responsibility, rewarding them with privileges on following good behaviour. • Do not hit, spank or shout and do not let anyone from the family do that too.

	• Make sure to teach how to respect others. • Model this behaviour too.
Adolescents& Teens	• As your child cultivates and starts making decisions, you must balance your unconditional love with well-defined rules and limits. • Show them with your affection through your actions. Make sure they know they have your attention and support. • Put an effort in getting to know their personal lives, who their friends are, and what they like. Teach them about respectful relations and friendships. • Recognize your teen's hard work, accomplishments, and triumphs in their actions. Compliment them on not using drugs or alcohol. Be a good role model by not using any of these substances.

Theories of Human Development

The development of the human mind and body has been the centre of focus for several renowned psychologists for centuries. From the cognitive abilities and physical skills of a human being to their emotional intelligence, various theories have been introduced, several of which have been backed by supporting evidence and controlled experiments.

Some of the leading developmental and emotional theories have been discussed below.

1. The Seven Basic Human Emotions

In psychology, it is believed that human emotions are a function of evolution that have empowered us to unravel problems, guard ourselves as well as our families, continue to live on despite desperate circumstances and procreate.

The role of emotions in lifestyle also influences:

➢ the manner in which we learn and understand things

➢ the goals that we set for ourselves

➢ interact with each other

➢ rank daily tasks

➢ the way we perceive ourselves as individuals

The point to which we undergo an emotion can also cause a mind-body experience. Seven emotions that are considered to be the foundation are:

- **Anger:** Anger is such a powerful emotion that it can be recognised by your facial expression, your gestures, and body language. When one is angry, his eyebrows are pulled down involuntarily, while upper, as well as lower eyelids, are pulled up. The margins of lips rolled in also indicates one's frustration. Even their lips may become tightened, and the tone of their voice ranges from severe irritation to utter frustration. When anger is left unchecked, a person may find it problematic to make sensible decisions. Anger can even disturb one's physical health.[36]

---

[36] https://www.ncbi.nlm.nih.gov/pmc/articles/PMC3019061/

- **Fear:** Fear is a controlling emotion that has the tendency of playing an important role when it comes to survival. When one faces danger and is met with fear, they automatically go through the fight or flight response. When one is afraid, their muscles become stiff, along with an increased heart rate and respiration. They become more alert, preparing their body to either run from the threat or stand persistent and fight the danger.[37]

- **Disgust:** The sense of disgust can arise due to a couple of things, such as a disagreeable taste, sight, or an unpleasant smell, including blood, infection, death, or bad hygiene. According to researchers, disgust can also originate as a reaction to various foods that might be dangerous.[38] Eyebrows pulled down, and nose wrinkled are some of the typical reactions that show disgust.

- **Sadness:** Sadness is one of the emotions that is, in most cases, short-lived. If an individual experiences it for prolonged periods of time, it may lead to depression, which is rather more severe. Sadness is indicated by feelings of dissatisfaction, sorrow, hopelessness, and indifference. When people are sad, their inner corners of eyebrows often get raised, and lip corners pulled down.

- **Happiness:** Happiness is often described as an agreeable emotion characterized by feelings of satisfaction, ecstasy, fulfilment, and a sense of security. Happiness shines through one's demeanour. When one is happy, he smiles, laughs, and is more relaxed, spreading positivity wherever he goes.

---

[37]https://journals.lww.com/hrpjournal/Fulltext/2015/07000/Fear_and_the_Defense_Cascade__Clinical.3.aspx

[38] https://www.verywellmind.com/an-overview-of-the-typesof-emotions-4163976#citation-7

- **Surprise:** The emotional state of surprise can originate from any positive, negative, unpleasant, or shocking event. The emotion of surprise is often, if not always, short-lived – a few seconds at the most. When one is surprised, both eyebrows, as well as eyelids, pull up, mouth hangs open, and pupils dilate.

- **Contempt:** Although the emotion of contempt can overlap with anger and distrust, the facial expression is unique. Eyes remain neutral while the lip corner pulls up and back on one side.

2. Plutchik's Wheel of Emotions

One of the most prominent psychologists, Robert Plutchik, depicted emotions through a colour wheel. The eight sectors of Putchik's wheel of emotions are designed to the point that there are **eight primary emotions: anger, anticipation, joy, trust, fear, surprise, sadness, and disgust.**

- Joy is the opposite of sadness. Physiology: Connect vs withdraw

- Fear is the opposite of anger. Physiology: Get small and conceal vs get big and loud

- Anticipation is the opposite of surprise. Physiology: Examine closely vs jump back

- Disgust is the opposite of trust. Physiology: Reject vs embrace

Emotional Combination: Just like colours can be mixed to form different tints and tones, emotions, too, can be joined to give rise to different feelings. The emotions that are colourless signify an emotion that's a blend of the two basic emotions. For instance, anticipation, together with joy, give rise to optimism. Joy, when blends with trust, becomes love.

It goes without saying that emotions are often complex. To learn to understand when a sense is really a mixture of two or more distinct feelings may be a helpful skill in the long run.

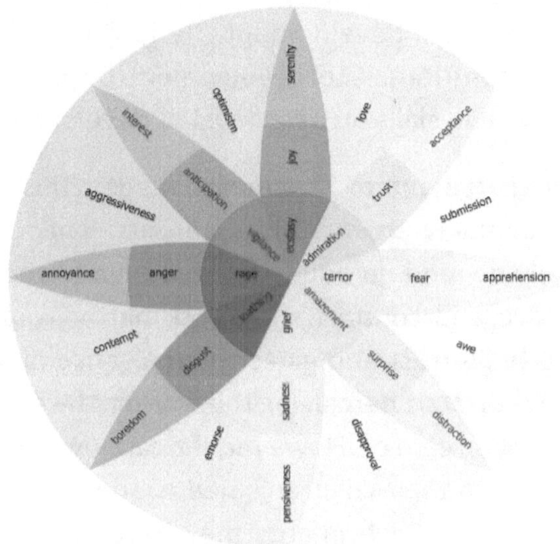

Image source: ResearchGate

3. Erikson's Theory

The kind of person your child grows up to be hugely depends on how you treat them when they are little. Several psychologists have thoroughly studied the life and development of human beings. One of them is Erik Erikson, who introduced the famous Erikson's Theory.

Erik Erikson was a famous German-American developmental psychologist as well as a psychoanalyst who contributed greatly to psychology. One of his most celebrated contributions was the introduction of Erikson's Theory. Basing the theory on Freud's debatable study of psychosexual development, Erikson took it one step further. He modified it as a psychosocial concept, developing it into eight stages.

The Eight Stages of Psychosocial Development

Freud's psychosexual theory became the basis of Erikson's eight stages of psychosocial development. He further elaborated on how ego positively contributes to development by mastering attitudes, outlooks, ideas, and skills on each level of development.

- **Trust vs Mistrust (0 to 12 months of age):** This is the age where infants habitually trust adults, parents, and caregivers. They completely depend on adults to feed them, keep them safe and secure, love and comfort them, no matter what. This enables babies to build trust and gives them a sense of security. At this point, children start perceiving the world to be a safe space where they'll be taken care of. However, if a caregiver remains aloof and fails to cater to their children's needs, the caregiver-infant bond may get tainted. Such infants may experience feelings of fear, anxiety, and mistrust and end up seeing the world as a harmful place. They may also struggle to build healthy trust relationships when they grow up.

- **Autonomy vs Shame/Doubt (from age 1 – 3):** Children's ability to learn about the environment is at its peak at this level. They try to take control of the objective environment. At stage two, they wish to make friends, socialise with other children, and even learn how to comfort another child in case they fall or get upset. A toddler's main duty is to resolve the issue of autonomy vs shame and doubt by working to develop independence. Their confidence is built by learning how to choose between two things. For instance, their favourite colours of clothing, or what food to eat, or their favourite toy to play with. When a toddler is deprived of these small yet significant things, it might affect their self-esteem in the future, leading to anxiety, low self-esteem, or shame.

- **Initiative vs Guilt (from age 3 – 6):** Children at this age begin to initiate play through social interaction, for instance, role play. During this role play, children learn how to take control of different made-up situations, maintaining leadership. For example, one can ask them to act as a parent, say a mother or father, while the parent pretends to be the child, asking them to help take care of "their kids." When children are given this role to play, they instantly step up, holding the reins of the matter. This further helps them to be achievers,   having self-control, and   becoming confident in whatever they do. On the other hand, when kids are not given this opportunity to show their role-play role, it can lead them to self-pity and self-loathing in the future.

- **Industry vs Inferiority**: (from 6 – 12): Children, at this age, would show signs of Industry vs Inferiority. This is the time when they start to become competitive with other peers. They wish to see who excels in a team, schoolwork, family lifestyle, and other social activities. They understand the concepts of accomplishment and superiority. In case they do not learn how to interact positively with other children, their future relationships will see serious issues, eventually leading the individual to an inferiority complex into adolescence.

- **Identity vs Role Confusion (age 12 – 18):** Erikson stated that an adolescent's main mission is attempting to develop a sense of self. They struggle to know who they are in essence, what they want to achieve in life, where do they see themselves in the future. They are bent on trying new possibilities, exploring, and discovering their "adult" selves during this stage. Those who successfully understand what they want or who they are, develop a strong sense of identity. They remain true to their missions and are not swayed by any problems. In case adolescents are indifferent, or if they are forced to live their lives in accordance with their parents' wishes, they may end up developing a weak sense of self. This is when confusion hits them. As a result of this confusion, they will become unsure of their sense of self, their future, and what they can achieve. This is when they begin questioning themselves, and as they grow older, they struggle with finding their true selves.

- **Intimacy vs Isolation (20s through early 40s):** Once we succeed in developing a sense of self, we move on to the next, more crucial step; sharing our lives with others. In case the initial-stage issues have not been resolved, an individual may struggle in developing and maintaining relationships. When positive self-concept is not developed in the adolescents' stage, adults may end up feeling lonely and may also face emotional isolation.

- **Generativity vs Stagnation (from age 40s – 60s):** This stage is also known as middle adulthood. Generativity is when individuals begin volunteering to work for others through different activities, including supporting or raising children. At this stage, middle adults play a huge role in the lives of others, particularly those present near them. However, those adults who are unable to meet up to this standard feel stagnant in life. They feel as if they have nothing to show for. But those who have influence in other people's lives keep on exploring and developing.

- **Integrity vs Despair (from the mid-60s to the end of life):** Erikson added that, in this stage, we begin to learn and develop more. Late adulthood is the time of reflection and looking back on our lives. At this point, people look at all the decisions they've made and whether or not their life was a success or a failure. People who achieve more have a sense of integrity at this point. They are naturally proud of their success. If adults have not been able to achieve anything, they may start questioning themselves and wonder how they could have done things differently. Such individuals feel as if they've wasted their lives and time. This causes a lot of regrets, anger, bitterness, depression, along with disappointment.

Development and growth are major factors in the lives of humans, animals, plants, especially childhood. Without change and development, the universe will fail to progress at every level. Children's development is a significant part of maturity. When they are well nurtured, they'll be aware of expanding their emotions socially, physically, and cognitively. They would not only be able to communicate effectively but will also grow up to be happy individuals. Erikson's developmental stages are very alarming for development in all human beings to reflect on.

4. Theory of Multiple Intelligences by Howard Gardner

When we hear the term intelligence, the first thing that pops into our mind is the IQ test and how well one does in this test. Intelligence is thought of as cerebral potential that can be measured. It is also often associated with the capacity that we, as individuals, are born with. However, lately, other theories regarding human intelligence have come to the forefront.

The book *Frames of Mind: The Theory of Multiple Intelligences* written by Howard Gardner in 1983, first viewed intelligence in a different light. **Howard Gardner explained how each person has different sorts of intelligences.**

Based on eight different "intelligences" representing talents, personality traits, and skills, this theory gave rise to a lot of criticism too. Many psychologists, as well as educators, were not pleased with it. Several critics believed Gardner's approach was too extensive. Despite the theory's scarcity of supporting data, some teachers still use Gardner's theory in classrooms.

Gardner introduced eight intelligences. However, he has hinted at the possibility of adding one more intelligence called "existentialist intelligence."

- **Visual-Spatial Intelligence:** Some people with great visual-spatial intelligence have an enhanced ability to visualize things. Such people often become artists, architects, and engineers as they excel in directions and devising maps, charts, and pictures.

- **Linguistic-Verbal Intelligence:** As the name suggests, verbally intelligent people are good with words, both written as well as spoken. These people tend to become: writers, reporters, lawyers, and teachers.

- **Mathematical Intelligence:** People who are good at logical-mathematical intelligence are incredible at rational thinking, investigating problems, and identifying patterns. Mathematically intelligent people often become scientists, mathematicians, accountants, and programming engineers.

- **Bodily-Kinesthetic Intelligence:** Those individuals who possess this intelligence excel at physical control and bodily movements. Their motor skills are sharp, allowing them to participate in dancing and sports and become actors or athletes.

- **Musical Intelligence:** People with sharper musical intelligence are relatively better with patterns, forms, sounds, and composition of music. They excel at the structures and rhythms of music, so they often become musicians, singers, music teachers, and composers.

- **Interpersonal Intelligence:** Interaction and socialization skills of interpersonally intelligent people are greater than others. Such people understand those around them in a much better way, which is why their career choices include sales, politics, and philosophy.

- **Naturalistic Intelligence:** Naturalistically intelligent people are good with nature. They are often attracted to exploring new places rich in nature and pay more attention to different species present in the environment. Career choices for these individuals include biologists, gardeners, and farmers.

5. The ABCDE Method by Dr. Martin Seligman

Optimism is an approach displaying a conviction or hope that the result of a particular struggle, or results in general, will turn out to be pleasant and positive. When you believe that things would come together by the end of the day and everything will be alright, you'll be reflecting optimism.

Many experts believe that optimism, although partially hereditary, may get influenced by childhood experiences. This includes how children are brought up by their parents, their lifestyle, values, and financial strength.

Dr. Martin Seligman takes this theory one step ahead. He believes in the possibility of learning skills that would enable an individual to become more optimistic. Optimism can be learned, especially by those with higher pessimistic levels.

But how would one know whether or not he/she acquires optimism? Seligman introduced a test regarding learned optimism. He created this test to enable people to figure out how optimistic or pessimistic they are.

Seligman's method to learn optimism is grounded upon the approaches of Aaron Beck and Albert Ellis. Both methods, Beck's cognitive-behavioural procedures and Ellis's behavioural therapy, revolve around recognizing the fundamental views and feelings that affect behaviours and then effectively challenging those thoughts.

Seligman's learned optimism method is known as **ABCDE**.

Adversity: All of us have faced several hardships at one point or another in our lives. These adversities can be with regards to our relationships, an event we were looking forward to that didn't go as planned, or perhaps a lost opportunity.

Belief: How do you feel when faced with an adversity? What are the thoughts that would run into your mind?

Most of us would start doubting our capabilities, accompanying it with a whole lot of self-criticism and selfloathe. We might hear ourselves think, *"I would never be able to accomplish my goal,"* or *"Why do I even try, knowing I'm no good at anything."* Or something like, *"I'm really bad at public speaking. I always make a mess of it,"* *"I really ought not to do it again because I'll just be as bad."*

Consequence: The thoughts that cross your mind in step two would decide whether or not you can lead yourself in the right direction. Did your thought processes lead to fruitful outcomes, or did they stop you from achieving your aims?

In case of negative beliefs, you turn down opportunities to speak and end up letting your fear get the better of you.

Disputation: Disputation is arguing with yourself and doubting your beliefs. How useful is holding on to a negative belief or put into perspective your belief?

Energization: How do you feel once you've challenged your own beliefs? What are the emotions you'd undergo once you reach your goals and attain the objective you'd been aspiring to achieve? You'd agree that you may feel more energized and driven when you tick all the items on your to-do list.

Screaming at Your Children Is Not the Solution

Parents shouting at their kids is becoming the norm in most households these days. Shouting soon becomes a bad habit that most parents are unable to let go of. Research shows that **shouting is one of the eight discipline strategies that can bring more harm than solace and has the tendency of making behaviour problems worse.**[39] Moreover, **shouting gives rise to more shouting,** and that can never be good for your child. Remember, the more you scream at your kids, the more they become indifferent, eventually tuning you out.

One of the basic problems of shouting is that children do not learn how to manage their behaviour through this mode of expression. **If a kid hits his sibling and is then screamed at for his action, he will only learn more violence and hatred.**

The only way to counteract hatred is through peace. When we explain to children the consequences of their actions in a peaceful manner, they understand things in a better way.

---

[39] https://srcd.onlinelibrary.wiley.com/doi/abs/10.1111/cdev.12143

Some ways of disciplining without screaming at them include:

- **Establish clear-cut rules from the start**. Let your child know the actions that are not and will never be accepted beforehand. These may include hitting other kids, harming birds and animals, leaving home without informing and so on. This would enable you to avoid shouting.

- **In case a rule is broken, show your disapproval by communicating and explaining politely** but DO NOT SCREAM. Remember, they are just kids who will eventually learn your side of perspective, and that shouting would only make matters worse.

- **Making kids aware of the consequences, in case they break the rules, ahead of time is also recommended.** Make sure they know that you'll use time-out and take away some of their privileges.

- **Nothing works for kids as much as Positive Reinforcement.** If they face negative consequences when they break the rules, they must experience positive reinforcement for doing something good. The more you appreciate them and reward them for good behaviour, the more they'll want to adopt positive performance.

- Positive reinforcement can be in the form of saying **positive words, complimenting or rewarding** them with little presents or treats.

- If you ever find yourself screaming at your children, try to look for the reasons that make you want to shout at them. **If you're shouting because you yourself are angry or frustrated, learn ways to calm yourself** and work on your anger management strategies.

- If you find yourself shouting because your kid doesn't pay attention to what you're saying the first time, **look for new ways to gain your child's attention.**

- Take some time to **clear your head** instead of screaming at your children.

- **Giving a warning with "when ... then" statements** usually works well. It is also an effective way of disciplining your child that does not require shouting at them. For example, if you let them know politely: "When you tidy up your room, then I'll allow you to play with your friends."

- **Repeating warnings without following through with the consequence does not help your child.** If they cross the line and continue to do so, you show them that it will have consequences. These consequences could be in the form of taking away electronics, asking them to give more hours to studies or helping out with chores.

Disciplining your children should ideally begin from day one. It is a gradual process that does not bring about a drastic change in a day or two. It requires immense patience and hard work. But remember that once you achieve the goal you've been aspiring to attain for years, all your other worries would disappear. The joy you'll experience in seeing your little ones grow into decent, righteous, and honest individuals would be a moment of honour. Therefore, focus on disciplining them but do not punish or shout at them. By setting limits, following through them and learning from your mistakes, disciplining your children would become way easier as well as fun.

Chapter 8

The Way Forward Based on Child Development

Age group 1 – 3

Below is the way forward, a complete guideline based on how to deal with your children's behaviour and outlook from toddler to teens:

Growth and Development of Your 1-year-old-child

Twelve months between ages 1 and 2, you'll notice how your infant is gradually turning into a toddler. You'll watch your baby physically transform at this stage. The new motor skills that your 1-year-old-child begins to master would become apparent to you with each passing day. This is the time when you'll experience unique changes within your child as their personalities would start to emerge bit by bit.

Physical Development

At age 1, you will be able to see your child develop physically. Within a short period of time, chances are your child will switch from crawling to walking, and soon, they'll be climbing stairs and moving around in the house on their own.

Note:

- *Gross motor skills: It has been observed that babies take their first steps before the end of 12 months. By the time they are 15 months old, they begin walking themselves.*

- *Fine motor skills: By the time your child reaches 18 months, they are likely to eat while using a spoon, drink from a cup, and help while getting undressed.*

- *Main highlights: From age 1 to 2, you'll notice your little ones go from struggling and trying to walk to learning how to run around.*

Important Tips for Parenting

Since your 1-year-old is not aware of what objects to touch and what items to stay away from, it is advisable that you make sure to remove all the unstable objects that can be harmful to your child. This may include folding chairs/tables, breakables, tables with pointed edges, or stacked objects that can topple down. Moreover, since they've now started crawling and have begun taking small steps, it is important to baby-proof your house.

Emotional Development

At this stage, your child will try to become independent and do things on their own. They may force you to allow them to dress themselves up and may wish to test out different physical skills that they aren't already familiar with.

However, remember, they're likely to be clingy at this point and may look for your attention when feeling sleepy, drained, frightened, or lonely. When your child turns 2, you'll notice their rebellious behaviour as they keep on insisting on doing what they've been asked not to do.

Note:

- *Your child may react to unknown people or situations with uneasiness or shyness.*

- *They might imitate other people.*

- *Chances of them panicking in certain situations, particularly those they aren't familiar with.*

A Useful Parenting Tip

Separation can make one anxious. That's the reason why you must inform your child before you leave. Leaving without first informing or assuring your child that you'll be back shortly can be difficult for them to ignore.

Make sure you don't just sneak away while your children aren't looking. Informing before leaving makes matters easier.

Social Development

Although socializing at this level is not done at a higher pace, it still exists amongst children nonetheless. You will notice their desire to interact with others, particularly other kids. Their interaction with siblings and caretakers will also be noticed.

You will see that your 1-year-old would be interested in playing next to other children slightly more than playing with them. But all in all, you'll notice them being interactive with other kids their age.

Note:

- *Your child might bring a toy and place it in your hand so that you both play together.*

- *Playing basic games, including "peek-a-boo" or "where is it?"*

- *Your child is likely to show a liking for parents or specific caregivers.*

A Useful Parenting Tip

Most 1-year-olds are extremely possessive when it comes to their toys. Don't force them to share their prized possessions with other children. Rather, try giving them a few objects which are off-limits for others. This will help them have some sense of control.

Cognitive Development

Once your child turns one, you'll notice an improvement in their cognitive development with each passing day. From 12 to 24 months, your kid is likely to learn to recognize the names of different things or people, for instance, cat, dog, or bird.

They will easily understand basic games and display an enhanced ability to acknowledge as well as follow your directions.

Language and Communication

At this age, your baby will mostly depend on nonverbal communication, which mainly comprises of certain gestures or pointing towards objects of need.

However, the screams and cries of your little ones will eventually lead to distinct sounds, such as "ba," "ma," "da." Your child will slowly join these syllables and eventually be able to say proper words that are easily understandable to you.

Before your child turns two, it is likely that your child will be able to say short, simple sentences with less complicated terms. At this point, they may also point towards the items that you name.

Play

Play helps a child grow. Their curiosity to know objects, places, and people around them will enhance their skillfulness.

Hammering musical instruments or shaking them and playing with toys that include pedals, wheels, or parts that move or rotate are all well-liked at this stage. Blocks are mostly adored by kids, particularly when your child is allowed to knock down a tower that you two have built together.

1-year-old-kids are also fond of push toys. This is the time when you show and allow them to play with sturdy objects that can assist them in learning to maintain balance. This is the time that they begin to test out their motor skills.

Note:

- *Kids begin to respond to their names.*

- *They begin sticking to your short and simple orders as well as requests.*

- *They get to know what "no" means.*

An Important Parenting Tip

A useful tip for parents is to talk to their children as much as possible, even about the most random situations or objects, to help them enhance their verbal skills. If you're dressing them up, ask them about the colour of their clothes, their fabric, what they like about it.

Try using the names of everyday objects, such as spoon, toy, towel, shirt, etc. Be sure to be consistent with these terminologies and try not to come up with your own cutesy names. Labelling an item with a made-up name might confuse the child.

Remember that children, at this age, might become physically more assertive. That's because they don't realize they're hurting others or that other people can have feelings too.

You can help your kid's growing independence by giving them choices. Present them with two different toys, two different options, and let them choose the one they would like to play with. This will automatically help your child learn problem-solving skills. With time, they'll begin to improve as they work out how to operate toys or how to fix two pieces of blocks. This will eventually help to improve your child's memory skills.

When to Be Worried

Although different babies grow at a slightly different pace, you must consult your doctor if your child fails to achieve the following goals or if you observe possible delays in Development. According to The Centers for Disease Control and Prevention, you must talk to your doctor if within 18 months your kid:

1. Doesn't walk

2. Can't draw your attention to show objects

3. Forgets or loses skills they formerly had

4. Fails to imitate others

5. Doesn't know at least six words

6. Fails to grasp new words

7. Fails to notice the absence or presence of a caregiver.

Remember:

A 1-year-old-kid tries to help their parents in all the little ways that they can. For instance, some may help you while you try to change their clothes, while others may try to wash their hands or face on their own. When you feel your infant is trying to do a task to help, make sure you notice and acknowledge their efforts. A child learns what he sees, which is why it is important that you try to be the best that you can in whatever it is that you do. Make them the best versions of yourself.

Parents must remember that there will be times when your child would insist on doing the same task several times or might just scream and shout to grab your attention, much to your chagrin.

However, seeing your children learn new skills daily would be a treat to the eyes.

Growth and Development of Your 2-year-old-child

The changes that you'll notice in your two-year-olds are likely to be more prominent. These big changes will grow month after month. Kids, at this stage, are getting some freedom as they start to make sense of their environment by themselves. There's a greater chance for kids, at this stage, to show interest in trying to achieve their little goals with anyone's assistance.

2-year-olds love to display their growing skills. Whether they are running, climbing, jumping, playing, your little ones would love to show their great signs of progress between the ages 2 and 3.

At this point, you'll begin to notice that your kids are in better control of their hands, fingers, legs, which shows that they're developing the necessary motor skills. This is the time when you can expect your child to hold a book or a pencil and flip pages or draw circles.

Note:

- *Gross motor skills: When your kid's muscles become stronger, their climbing skills will develop too. 2-year-old-kids are usually capable of climbing over furniture, running, and playing with a ball by kicking it.*

- *Fine motor skills: 2-year-olds are usually capable of painting, scribbling, and piling blocks (at least four) or fix round or square pegs into their respective holes.*

- *Main highlights: Your kid will start walking more like a grownup. At this stage, they are most likely to walk next to you. Their walk is more steady, i.e., without falling down, and they are better able to navigate stairs on their own.*

A Useful Parenting Tip

Kids at this stage don't necessarily need you to plan out interesting activities for them. They are capable of making any environment turn into a play area. The only thing that you need to be careful about is their safety. Make sure the environment is child-proofed.

Emotional Development

As your child begins to grow, their tantrums can become a bit frequent too. This is when they are learning to express their emotions of frustration, agitation or crankiness, and their tantrums result from these random emotions.

Since children, at this point, do not have the verbal skills to say, *"I'm sleepy,"* or *"I want company,"* they can't voice their emotions clearly. What they can do, however, is *show* these emotions instead.

If your child sits in the middle of the floor while you're at a mall, do not be surprised. These tantrums are a part of their growing up.

Note:

- *Kids begin to show several emotions, from unhappiness to frustration.*

- *They feel great upon doing small tasks or figuring out solutions to tiny problems independently.*

- *Their mood changes frequently, which shows that your child is making an effort to take control of their desires, emotional state, and activities.*

An Important Parenting Tip

Praising your child or complimenting them for doing little tasks, such as tidying up their room, can do wonders.

This will boost your child's self-confidence and allow them to see that they are capable of achieving their goals.

Social Development

2-year-olds are mostly, if not always, "egocentric." At this stage, kids believe that they and they alone are at the centre of the universe. They are unable to grasp that people do exist outside of their world and that others can have opinions and thoughts that may differ from theirs.

That's why don't be astonished if your toddler refuses to play with other children in a customary manner. Sometimes, they might wish to play beside other kids instead of with them.

Nonetheless, even at this point, they'll appreciate interacting with others, particularly kids.

Being in the company of others provides a great chance for your kid to learn to socialize and become acquainted with social interactions.

Note:

- *Kids begin to imitate the actions and words of others and attempt to be there for others the same way you soothe them.*

- *Kids start participating in basic games.*

- *A kid at this stage might behave in a rebellious manner just to see your reaction.*

A Useful Parenting Tip

When your toddler plays with other kids, it will have a positive impact on your child. It will allow them to interact with their friends. However, you must intrude if you sense that their 'play' is getting rougher or might result in your kid or someone else's kid being harmed.

Cognitive Development

Once your child turns two, you will notice that they are coming up with creative games and joining two or more activities to make more complex and tricky structures instead of switching from one activity to another. This indicates that their mind is learning to make additional connections. They also begin to understand associations and links between different items and objects.

Language and Communication

By the time children turn two, most of them have learned to speak at least 50 words. Studies show that the language skills of boys are relatively slower than that of girls. Before kids turn three, they are able to speak short and simple sentences that are easily comprehendible.

Play

Playtime is vital for children. It is during their playtime that they get the opportunity to discover, explore and understand how things work or how people interact with others. For parents, it is essential to offer as many chances to their children as they can for fun adventures.

Once you do this, your kid will find it fascinating to carry out similar experiences time and again, for instance, stacking blocks and then knocking them over. When kids repeat actions, they begin to learn those movements. It helps boost their cognitive skills.

Note:

- *Parents must give precise, easily comprehensible instructions, such as, "Please pick up your toy and put it on the table."*

- *Children will join two or more words to create sentences.*

- *Kids begin to complete different lines in books that they are familiar with.*

A Useful Parenting Tip

Although the internet provides several interesting shows for children, it is recommended by AAP to limit 2year-olds' screen-time to only one hour per day.[40] Even that one-hour screen-time should only include high-quality programmes. Furthermore, parents are advised to remain vigilant during their kid's screen-time. Make sure they are watching content that is appropriate for kids.

Important Points

Most 2-year-olds sleep properly throughout the night (usually 11 hours). If this is not the case, make sure your infant sleeps soundly

---

[40] https://kidshealth.org/en/parents/screentime-babytodd.html#:~:text=Toddlers%2018%20months%20to%2024,than%201%20hour%20a%20day.

and has acquired the appropriate sleep associations. There are chances of them waking up again when they feel stressed or unwell.

Come up with your child's napping schedule. Your toddler might:

- Nap for short periods of time twice a day

- Nap for one relatively longer period of time

Once you make a regular napping schedule, you will realize your child is receiving a sufficient amount of sleep.

When your child learns to climb out of their cribs by themselves, it is time to transfer your child to a comfortable toddler bed. Make sure that by this time, you have already pulled down the mattress closer to the floor and detached the bumper pads. The typical age for a kid to move out of a crib varies from 18 months to three years.

When to Be Worried

Although different babies grow at a slightly different pace, you must consult your doctor if your child fails to achieve the following goals or if you observe possible delays in Development. According to The Centers for Disease Control and Prevention, you must talk to your doctor if your kid:

1. Unable to walk bit by bit

2. Fails to imitate activities and words

3. Unable to follow basic instructions

4. Forgets skills they once possessed

5. Is unable to operate with basic objects, such as spoon, cup, brush

6. Fails to say simple, two-word sentences, such as "Let's play."

Remember:

When children turn two, they aspire to explore new activities and come up with unique pastimes on their own. It is important for parents to give their children the freedom integral for them at this stage. Give them space to figure out what they like, what interests them more instead of dictating everything.

When you are carrying out a task or doing some household chore, explain to your kid what you're doing.

While keeping things simple is recommended, using a lot of baby talk might not be beneficial.

Problems Associated with Children's Behaviours and Helpful Solutions for your Toddlers (1-2-year-olds)

Disciplining toddlers can be a bit of a task. To match their energy and vigour, parents usually end up working more mainly to discipline their little ones. Disciplining kids from a young age can actually be beneficial in the long run. Teaching them good and acceptable behaviours will surely help your children drastically. One major aspect of **disciplining kids involves teaching them how to make suitable choices.** Once they learn how to do that, a huge burden will be lifted off your shoulders.

Toddlers are always active, jumping up and down, running and playing, until they finally get tired. To make sure they do not become completely exhausted, make sure to add quick little breaks. This would help calm their nerves.

Toddlers have a habit of exploring with all their senses, particularly the sense of touch. However, their budding motor skill, along with their impulsiveness, might cause them to be a little clumsy. That's the reason why it is integral to teach them how to touch objects in a manner that isn't harmful.

Kids also have a habit of insisting upon their freedom. Their independence, at this stage, is extremely precious to them. If you hear them say "No!" while asserting their independence, do not be surprised.

Disciplining toddlers can get a bit too much for some parents but remember they are your bundles of joy, and their little tantrums and tempers are temporary. To watch them grow and improve can surely be electrifying and exciting.

Toddlers have particular discipline needs because of all of these developments. They need the kind of discipline that helps nurture their individuality but still instils socially suitable behaviour.

Basic Challenges

Children can, at times, lie, but that's because they don't realize the concepts of lying or telling the truth. It might take them a little while to understand what it is to lie. Most children would reply in the negative if you ask them if they ate the cookie. This could either be due to the tone of your voice or simply your stern body language that makes them say "no."

Don't forget that toddlers do not have an extended speech and are not aware of a lot of words to voice out what they are thinking or how they feel. Rather, they usually use their bodies to let you know how they feel. This may lead to another common problem; tantrums when they are not happy or are upset. Tantrums can also take place when a kid fails to handle their sentiments or if they become a little too stimulated.

Anger is also regular. Toddlers, at this stage, do not have the skills one needs to solve a dispute in a peaceful manner. As of now, they don't know how their decisions may upset others. Remember not to be startled if they bite, hit, or toss things every now and then. One thing you can do to counter such a situation is to enforce household rules that have been set previously. Children need regular reminders and must make a habit of practising things repeatedly. Using the same language to help support your toddler to follow the rules will yield fruitful results.

Common Discipline Strategies That Help

Some of the most common yet vital discipline strategies that will help your 2-year-olds thrive are as follows:

- **Offering Physical Guidance:** When you say "Pet the cat softly" from the other end of the room, the chances are that won't be of much help. But if you *show* them how to pet a cat by placing your hand over your kid's hand and then gently petting the animal, it would do wonders. If you ever see your child being rough around cats or dogs, remind them of how you taught them to caress a cat gently. Ultimately, they'll understand to touch them more tenderly.

- **Give Children the Opportunity to Choose:** Make sure that you provide your kid with several chances through the day to make constructive choices. When they feel they are not in control of a situation, they might show tantrums. When you ask your child to choose what they want to play with or what book they want to read, you are allowing them to feel more in control.

- **Removing Children from Situations They Don't Find Amusing:** There are times when children are simply not interested in some tasks. They try to do them forcefully, which isn't good for them. If your child fails to maintain proper behaviour in the mall, it is advisable that you end your shopping trip a bit early and head home.

- **Admiring Good Behaviour:** Like adults, praise is important for toddlers too. When you admire children for their good behaviour, they are likely to repeat the same behaviour. Moreover, try to catch your child when they are doing something good. Praise them for arranging their toys, eating their snacks. This will further motivate them, knowing that you are watching.

- **Overlook Slight Misbehaviour:** Just like admiring kids for doing something great is recommended, ignoring their tantrums and cries sometimes is also beneficial. Try and look the other way, feign you are unable to hear your child cry or yell. Pretend to distract yourself with a book or newspaper. The moment your child stops whining, you tell them it's time to play or go out.

- **Knowing the Reasons Behind their Tantrums:** Getting to the depth of their tantrums may also be helpful. Observe what makes them upset. Ask yourself; Are they hungry? Are they sleepy? Do they need something? Once you understand what troubles them and satisfy their needs, they will whine comparatively less.

- **Use Timeout:** Most children are unable to handle sitting on one seat for timeout effectively. They do not have the persistence or the attention span to sit silently. But, you can use a room for a timeout. But ensure that the room is totally child-proof. Once they are in the room, close the door. For 2-year-olds, a 2minute-timeout in the room is advisable.

Note: Using a child's bedroom for timeout is not right. Your child's room is one place they feel the safest, and to associate it with something harsh, a punishment, may not work for them.

- **Averting Problems that Might Arise in the Future:** Toddlers at this age are extremely curious. They feel like touching, handling, banging on, kicking various objects present near them. For this reason, make sure you change the environment so your kid can play as well as explore safely. You can:

  - Use outlet covers

  - Put padding on corners that are sharp

  - Get rid of breakable objects.

  - Try to secure most, if not all furniture to the wall, particularly televisions

- **Plan your Toddler's Day:** Introduce a timetable to help organize your child's day. Make sure to keep their snack time and playtime consistent. Their nap and sleep time should also be steady. Your child will soon grow accustomed to the schedule, giving him a sense of order. You can help your child switch from one game or activity to another by first giving them a small warning while simultaneously making them feel involved. You can begin by telling your child that their current game is about to end, so they prepare to wrap things up. You could say something like, "Let's read one more story before it's time for you to sleep."

- **Communication:** Make sure you give your little ones concise explanations only. Since children don't have an extended attention span and soon zone out, it is better to avoid lengthy explanations of what they should or should not do. When you explain situations in fewer words, it has more impact on children.

- **Stay Relaxed:** Although disciplining your children can get on your nerves at times, it is best if you try to stay relaxed. Try to be the best role model that you can. Do things properly yourself, explain things to your kids, communicate and spend more time with them, and they'll learn the same. Do not shout at them or hit them, no matter what. If you are upset because of your kid's behaviour, take a deep breath, and give yourself some time to relax.

Raising Happy and Healthy Children

Parents of toddlers are almost always on the go. They are constantly in motion while experiencing several emotions. But as children grow, their likes, dislikes, and habits will change too. During these initial years, it is integral that you take extra care of their diet, sleep, health, security, and happiness.

Diet & Nutrition

The American Heart Association (AHA) states that the number of calories a child requires on a daily basis vary from toddler to toddler based on the child's metabolism and physical activity. According to the AHA, your little one must intake between 900 and 1,200 calories daily. Usually, 1year-olds require almost 1,000 calories every day. These calories can be split into three meals and about two snacks throughout the day.

There is a possibility that your toddler might show strange eating patterns that keep changing each day. They might intake a lot of calories at breakfast, then eat some more for lunch, and by dinner time, they don't feel hungry at all.

The next day, there are chances that they might have a completely different eating pattern. But keep in mind, all this is natural, and you don't need to be concerned.

Toddlers who do not have any food allergies should eat these food servings per day:

- 2 ounces of meat or pulses,

- 3 ounces of grains,

- 2 servings of dairy,

- 1 cup of vegetables,

- 1 cup of fruit,

- 3 tablespoons of fat or oil.

Counting calories that your toddler is taking is not as important for you as the quality of the food your kid is consuming. Check that your toddler is having a balanced diet comprising of a varied range of healthy foods.

Useful Tips on Toddler Nourishment

Toddler beverages should include water and milk. Juices are mostly high in calories as well as sugar. Children can consume snacks. Make sure to offer your toddler about two to three healthy snacks throughout the day.

Note: Don't be upset if your toddler is not willing to try new food. Tell them it's okay, then remove the food, and later try offering it one more time. Try not to associate negative emotions with food. Don't reprimand your toddler for refusing to try some new food. Offer snacks that are healthy every now and then.

Toddlers can sometimes be extremely picky when it comes to food. Give them some freedom during meals, and you'll reduce the chances of them refusing to eat food.

Usually, children switch from a high chair to a comfortable booster seat within 18 months. There is a possibility that your toddler might show less tantrums in a booster seat during meals because they may enjoy sitting with the rest of the family at the table.

Childhood Obesity and How to Control Its Prevalence

Childhood obesity is one of the most fundamental issues that is faced by the majority of the global health systems. It leads to several other issues, posing an existential threat for children worldwide. An article titled *Leeds becomes first UK city to lower childhood obesity rate* by Boseley shows how barring children from eating sweets as well as junk foods can remarkably lower the prevailing rates of childhood obesity. The study states that when Leeds adopted a similar approach, it was successfully able to lower the curve of childhood obesity.

Childhood obesity is one of the most serious problems but, sadly, less talked about. Studies show that at least 28% of children aged between two and fifteen are stout or obese in the UK.[41] This indicates the gravity of the matter of childhood obesity in the UK.

---

[41] https://www.theguardian.com/world/2019/may/01/leedsbecomes-first-uk-city-to-lower-its-childhood-obesity-rate

Other than Leeds, one other city that has successfully controlled childhood obesity is Amsterdam, Netherlands. Boseley goes on to say that childhood obesity is more rampant in underprivileged families than in the more wellto-do families (Boseley, 2019). The frequency of obesity in destitute families went from 11.5% to 10.5 % once the obesity control interventions were imposed. As for the more prosperous families, stopping children from munching on junk foods and sweets led to a drop in the dominance of childhood obesity from 6.8% to about 6.0%. On the whole, the childhood obesity ratio in the UK city of Leeds lowered from 9.4% to 8.8%.

Today, in all of the UK, only Leeds has successfully lowered the prevailing childhood obesity rate. Even its neighbours – Liverpool, Bradford, Derby, and Coventry, continue to struggle with the same issue.

Boseley believes that the HENRY (Health, Exercise, and Nutrition for the Really Young) program is responsible for reducing the frequency of childhood obesity in Leeds. The HENRY approach, which is an advanced intervention to stop child obesity and indorse a healthy start from a young age, focuses on infants and kids aged 0 – 5 as well as their families.

HENRY was presented in the year 2009. It was a part of the obesity strategy in Leeds. Boseley writes that HENRY was directed towards the most impoverished families in Leeds (Boseley, 2019). It is based on urging parents to take firm action regarding their children's diet and bedtimes. Furthermore, it encourages authoritative parenting. Through this firm parenting approach, parents make it known that they are the ones in charge. As a result of this program, parents in Leeds are not only aware but also in control of what their children

---

consume and how much time they spend in their beds, efficiently decreasing the frequent rates of childhood obesity.

An article titled *The Obesity Epidemic: Medical and Ethical Considerations* by De Vries highlights that childhood obesity can be considered to be a serious threat to the health and fitness of children in the UK. The article includes an example of the death of a three-year-old girl with a weight of 40. The cause of her death was heart failure, primarily prompted by childhood obesity.

Boseley's article also points out that childhood obesity is predominant in children of low-income parents. De Vries, too, believes the same. According to him, childhood has a facet of social class. Children who come from financially unstable backgrounds are more likely to experience obesity than those children who belong to more well to do families (De Vries, 2007).

How to Control the Prevalence of Childhood Obesity?

According to De Vries and Boseley, a more strict control regarding what children consume and how many hours they spend in bed is required. Some of the ways they propose include:

- Minimizing the intake of sweets as well as junk foods by children.

- Greater emphasis and strict control of the diet.

- Bedtimes of kids must be kept in check too.

- An effective change in the parenting techniques, having a more commanding control by parents.

- To get rid of unsuitable cultural systems that eventually lead to a growth in the dominance of childhood obesity.

In the UK, at least 28% of all children are overweight or obese. As a result, these children become more prone to contracting diseases such as high cholesterol, high blood pressure, diabetes, heart diseases at an early age, and bone problems. This is why strict parenting regarding children's diet is immensely important.

Physical Activity

The Society of Health and Physical Educators states that toddlers must get at least half an hour of organized physical activity per day along with an extra hour or more of physical activity that is unstructured. Remember that these activities should be very simple, for instance spending time in the garden with your little one or walking around the area.

Physical activity is not considered to be work for children, which makes it easier for parents to keep their kids interested. Physical activity enhances several integral concepts such as learning colours, numbers, objects, animals, and birds. It also boosts children's sense of imagination and creativity and strengthens critical thinking and problem-solving.

Note: Toddlers are usually active and always in a rush, switching from one activity to another. To keep them focused on one activity can be hard sometimes. When your child's attention span grows and their actions become more controllable, you'll come across several opportunities to try different activities.

Individual, as well as group activities, are essential for your child's development. It will allow them to become more social and learn skills that they weren't familiar with earlier. Since toddlers are curious little creatures, this is the perfect time for parents and their children to be a part of parent-child activities, such as yoga, soccer, piano playing, etc.

Inside the House

A toddler spends most part of his day within the four walls of his own house. When they are up, they would want their parents or caregiver to be with them all the time. This is the reason why it is important to make them participate in little activities that keep them occupied. Parents can ask toddlers to:

- Do little tasks, such as ask them to throw a wrapper in the dustbin.

- Help with little chores, picking up toys, and arranging books on the shelf.

- Help make their beds or tidy their rooms along with them.

Note: Communication is essential as it helps in building their language skills. Use words that describe objects or situations in your conversation, such as the colour, size, or shape of objects. When you're playing with your toddler, let them be creative and play with toys in the way they feel is right. Remember, there is no "right way" of playing with toys – their teddy bears can talk, and so can their cars.

Safety

Your toddler's safety and security should be your priority. As they are growing up, they are bound to run around, jump and go on their little adventures. They might only take a few seconds before landing themselves in risky situations.

Studies show that in the U.S., unintentional injuries are the foremost reason for death for kids under age 4.[42] Most of those injuries can be stopped if you keep an eye on some of the following basic safety rules:

- Think about **removing firearms** from the house if you have a child. If keeping a gun is vital, make sure it is unloaded. Try to lock it away in a safe place.

- Toddlers are usually known for putting everything in their mouths. Make sure the **medicines in your house are kept at a place where your kids can't reach**. Other poisonous household products should also be kept out of reach.

- Toddlers tend to take hold of whatever is nearby to steady themselves. Sadly, that may lead to grabbing the oven door that is hot or a pot handle. Try to **keep your child out of the kitchen while you're cooking**.

- **While most falls aren't problematic and are somewhat even natural, some can seriously injure children.** Stairs, sharp-edged objects, or furniture (for instance, tables, mirrors, windows) can cause severe trouble.

- It is important that **toddlers should stay in rearfacing car seats.** This should be taken care of until they turn two or until they reach the height as well as the weight that is advised by the manufacturer of the safety seat. Furthermore, **safety seats should be installed properly.** Don't make the mistake of leaving your child alone in or near the car.

---

[42] https://www.ncbi.nlm.nih.gov/books/NBK220806/#:~:text=Unintentional%20Inj uries&text=Among%20children%20aged%201%20to,and%20motor%20vehicle%2 0pedestrian%20injuries

- Only 2 inches of water are enough to drown a toddler. This is why it is important to **keep the bathroom doors shut.** Don't leave your kid alone around a bathtub or near a swimming pool or any other water body. It is important that you stay within an arm's length of your child when they're near water.

Regular Visits to the Doctor

Regular visits for toddlers usually take place with a paediatrician between 12, 15, 18, and 24 months of age.[43]

Studies show that paediatricians screen for:

- Autism at 18 months and later when the child turns 2

- Developmental issues at the age of 9, 18, and 24 months

- Obesity with a body mass index yearly which starts as the child turns 2

- Testing tuberculosis on detection of high-risk causes by 1 month, at 6 months. Then yearly, starting from 12 months

- Lead screening (blood lead level) risk valuation at 6, 9, 12, 18, and 24 months

- General health issues amongst children that include colds, ear infections, and skin problems

Note: If you have any queries regarding your child's growth, or you have any worries about their sleeping or eating patterns, or behavioural issues, get in touch with the paediatrician. Inquire about what types of food you can give your child and how.

---

[43] https://www.healthychildren.org/English/family-life/healthmanagement/Pages/Well-Child-Care-A-Check-Up-for-Success.aspx

Moreover, if any changes occur in your life, mention them. For instance, a new spouse, switching jobs, or moving to a new house could influence your child's health.

Asking your paediatrician questions regarding your child's potty-training readiness also helps. Your paediatrician will tell you ways to identify the best time to begin teaching your toddler. Many consider potty training to be a huge breakthrough for toddlers. Although it is a test for parents, several mothers and fathers actually look forward to it.

While potty training is essential, forcing it on your kids may backfire. You will know when your child is ready. One way for you to understand this is whether your child has reached the rest of the milestones that they should attain before you begin potty training.

Sleep

Most toddlers sleep throughout the night. However, some may show sleep issues, but that is nothing to be worried about. If your child has not had a good night's sleep, it can lead to tantrums and a bad temper. Remember that your child needs up to 14 hours of sleep per day. That's why it is vital that you set a routine, including plenty of naps and an early sleep time, and stick to it.

Note: Many parents feel under pressure for their child's transition from a crib to a kid's bed at this age. But keep in mind that if your child sleeps peacefully in a crib, you do not necessarily need to move them until they are older.

Younger toddlers usually take two naps each day. There is no need for you to change that unless you've observed that this pattern is changing itself. For instance, if your child is beginning to have trouble sleeping at his usual nap time and doesn't seem to be tired during the morning, it may be time for one nap a day.

Try to remove naps that are unplanned, as this will enable your child to experience longer, better, and healthier sleep. Although it may be simpler to manage that trip in the car if your child takes one short nap, it is better if you make sure they stay awake in the long run. You could even plan the tour for a time when they won't be tired or sleepy.

If your child wakes up as early as 8 a.m., a nap is bound to come around 12:00 p.m., which will last for the next 2 to 2.5 hours. When your toddler wakes up around 3 p.m., they are likely to hit the bed around 7:30 p.m. if they sleep from 7:30 p.m. to 8 or 8:30 a.m., they'll sleep for about 12.5 hours at night. When you add in the naps, that will go up to 15 hours altogether.

Don't forget that these times are approximate. Family schedules might make some alterations. But to shift the times might not always work to lessen problems. It has been observed that bedtime, as well as wake-up times, are extremely vital.

Several families tend to co-sleep with their children. Although this can have some advantages, some studies show that this sleeping pattern can be disruptive for others' sleep, particularly those of the parents.

Technology

Earlier, the American Academy of Pediatrics stated that children under the age of 2 should not be exposed to any screen time. However, this policy was later restructured in 2016, when more applications and websites started becoming more toddler-friendly.

But you, as a parent, must make sure to:

- Limit your kid's screen time as much as you can.

- Try to divert the minds of your little ones with other equally interesting activities.

- Make sure the apps that they use have quality content, including online books.

- During your child's screen time, make sure to stay with them and remain in the know of what they're watching.

- Don't leave the TV on as the background noise might affect your child's learning.

- Avoid taking your toddlers to the movies as they can be too loud for them.

Toddlers wish to move around and explore as much as they can. They are curious little creatures who are always ready for fun adventures. From experimenting with new objects to putting almost everything in their mouth, their curious minds look for answers, trying to learn all that they can in the process.

At this age, all they care about is their own needs as they don't worry themselves about the existence of others or realize the complexities of life that adults are aware of.

When you try to stop them from doing what they aren't supposed to, they'll surely be annoyed for not getting things their way. Gradually, they'll spend their time imitating those who are present around them. They'll want to try new things and foods and would wish to do the same things that you do.

You can be a confident parent only when you put in the effort to learn more about your child's development. Try to befriend other parents who have children your age. Ask questions, read books on parenting, research, and consult paediatricians if need be. But most importantly, enjoy seeing them grow.

Note: Disciplining toddlers can take its toll on parents. It isn't always easy to match your infant's energy levels. Just like it isn't easy to keep their young minds entertained all the time. But remember, these initial years are best for you to create a bond with your little champs that will bear fruitful results for the years to come.

Growth and Development of Your 3-year-old-child

When your child turns three, you'll notice that their **attention span, as well as verbal skills, grow drastically.** Because of this, they'll better be able to understand your guidelines and express their own feelings in sentences that will relatively be easier to comprehend. The switch from being a toddler to a preschooler can, however, be a little rough. At this stage, you as a parent should be ready to experience sudden unexpected tantrums, but remember that these tiny outbursts are balanced out by creativity and a whole load of joy as well.

Physical Development

At this stage, preschoolers are growing in height, weight, and motor skills too. Like everything else, the development of these talents will differ from child to child, depending on their aptitude and size. 3-year-olds are in the process of learning more about themselves, particularly their own body and the ways through which they can control it. With time, their balance will be improved, and your child will learn to carry out the tasks they weren't able to before.

Note:

- *Gross motor skills: Usually, 3-year-olds are aware of how to walk in a line. They also know how to balance, hop or run, and walk backward. Most 3year-olds know how to pedal a tricycle and jump.*

- *Fine motor skills: Preschoolers can usually wash as well as dry their hands. They can even dress themselves with a little additional help and flip pages of a book. Most 3-year-olds are able to hold a writing instrument not with their fists but with the help of their fingers.*

- *Main highlights: Some preschoolers are ready for potty training.*

A Useful Parenting Tip

Although seeing your kid running, jumping, sometimes tripping can be a bit hard for parents to handle, it is essential for the development of your child in the long run. Preschoolers must practice their motor skills in order to enhance their coordination and balance.

Emotional Development of Preschoolers

As your child starts to deal with taxing situations, their tantrums will become relatively intense. Kids at this age would insist on having a bit of freedom to carry out their tasks. And once you allow them to do so, they'll struggle with them, which will further lead to frustration.

Although not many, some preschoolers find it difficult to leave their caregivers. There are chances that your child may cry once you drop them off at preschool. They may also show sadness about going to daycare, despite enjoying being there.

Note:

- *Kids begin to comprehend feelings, both theirs as well as others'. Some of the basic sentences often used by preschoolers to express their emotions include, "I'm sad" or "I'm mad!"*

- *Although they may not always like it, 3-year-olds understand to share and take turns.*

A Useful Parenting Tip

When you use terms such as happy, sad, angry in your everyday conversations, you help your child understand the various emotions. This helps in developing your kid's emotional vocabulary and enables them to understand how they are feeling.

Social Development

When your child turns three, you'll notice a change in the way they interact with other kids. This is usually when most children start moving away from parallel play, i.e., kids playing around each other, to somewhat interactive play (kids cooperating and playing with other children). This also indicates that it is time they are helped to learn how to manage these budding relationships.

3-year-olds start understanding the concepts of friendships. They begin making friends that can sometimes be even imaginary and learn how to develop these relationships. Moreover, since they are inspired by the things and people they adore, it's natural for them to imitate their favourite animated characters from TV.

Note:

- *Kids at this age start caring for other people and their emotions. They may even try to comfort those who they see are in pain or are hurt.*

- *Preschoolers may begin to chatter if they realize some child or a sibling has "wronged" them.*

- *Display affection for those present around on their own.*

A Useful Parenting Tip

Three-year-olds start comprehending what is "theirs" and what is "yours," which is why they may struggle to share their valuables with others. Instead of telling them who will be allowed to play with what object/toy, encourage your kid to find a solution themselves. You should step in only if anyone gets hostile.

Cognitive Development

3-year-olds' cognitive development is not limited to learning the alphabet or numerals. Instead, it encompasses the whole learning process of taking in information, including asking questions and comprehending knowledge. Children are keen observers. They begin noticing the people around them and what they say. Preschoolers grasp everything they see around them. As a parent, it is your duty to help them understand how to utilize the information they have attained. As they start to focus on things for a longer period of time, they are able to learn more around them.

When children turn three, their minds, as well as creativity, begin to bloom. As their memory becomes better and they begin to comprehend more about their surroundings, you should be ready for tons and tons of questions.

There will be times when you'll be at a loss for words, unable to answer their simple yet equally mindboggling questions. Remember, do not lose your patience and try to answer them in the best possible way that you can.

Note: To know what your child understands and what they yet need to learn can be challenging for you to comprehend. But these are minor tasks that can be understood before your child turns four.

Language and Communication

3-year-olds should ideally know 300 words with additional knowledge of several other words. Along with speaking simply-structured sentences, your child's comprehension and verbal skills will be enhancing with each passing day.

Note:

- *3-year-olds like it when you read books to them. Some may even try to read books by themselves.*

- *Preschoolers are capable of identifying simple shapes as well as colours.*

- *Kids at this age know the alphabet.*

A Useful Parenting Tip

The more you interact with your child and talk to them, the better it is for their language development. This will also give them the courage to voice their opinions, and participate in speech, eventually boosting their confidence. Encourage them to ask questions, answer their queries, read books together, and speak about various events or places.

When to Be Worried

All kids grow at somewhat different paces. Sometimes, children who are a little behind will eventually get closer to their peers in the near future. Nonetheless, the Centers for Disease Control and Prevention urge connecting with your child's doctor in case your 3-year-old displays any of the following signs:

1. Dribbles or his/her speech is unclear

2. Unable to operate simple toys on his own

3. Fails to talk in simply structured sentences

4. Is unable to comprehend simple guidelines

5. Avoids engaging in pretend play

6. Lacks social skills, i.e., avoiding playing with others

7. Falls down frequently, particularly while going up or down the stairs

8. Finds it difficult to make eye contact

9. Forgets skills they once possessed

Parents must remember that these developmental characteristics are not unchangeable. Different children may develop at a relatively different pace, and that is nothing to be worried about. While some have the tendency to grow faster, others might take some time to reach there. In case you have any concerns regarding your child, it is best to talk to the child's doctor or their teacher at the preschool.

Chapter 9

Child Development Age group 4 – 7

Growth and Development of 4year-olds

Being a parent, you'll notice several changes in the outlook and behaviour of your 4-year-old. This is the time when a kid lives his life to the fullest, growing and exploring each second. So be prepared; **your child's learning skills and understanding will keep improving,** more so when they get ready to step into kindergarten.

Once you understand the main developmental signs of this age, you'll be able to know whether your child is on track or not. It will also allow you to understand your child in a better way, giving you the opportunity to see if there is any skill they need to sharpen. These developmental milestones will also help you in identifying concerns (if any) and sharing those with your child's doctor.

Physical Development

As children begin to grow, they become taller. Their gross, as well as fine motor skills, enhance increasingly. Studies show that 4-year-olds are in the process of learning ways to control their bodies and are likely to try out new things with each little success.[44]

Note:

- *Gross motor skills: 4-year-olds will gradually understand their own place. You'll notice this as they begin to bump less into others while trying to walk. Their running skills will develop noticeably.*

- *Fine motor skills: At this age, your child should possess enhanced hand-eye coordination. This will enable them to complete simple puzzles and colour inside an image.*

- *Main highlights: Most 4-year-olds are able to dress themselves. They can even brush their teeth with an adult's supervision and are typically potty-trained.*

A Useful Parenting Tip

Parents must remind their children of standard safety rules from time to time. These rules may include holding hands when outside in a crowded place, staying out of the kitchen while the parent cooks, and so on.

---

[44]https://www.healthychildren.org/English/agesstages/preschool/Pages/Developmental-Milestones-4-to-5-Year-Olds.aspx

Emotional Development

By this age, children are fascinated by the idea of having a little bit of independence and getting to do things on their own, as much as they can.

If you find your 4-year-old being cooperative one minute and then showing tantrums the next, remember that this is natural. On the whole, you'll notice them gaining better control of their feelings.

Note:

- *Children at this point become more understanding of other peoples' emotions.*

- *They start experiencing a variety of emotions, including protectiveness, eagerness, annoyance, and fear.*

- *At this age, children are obsessed with the idea of coming first and winning in games and activities.*

A Useful Parenting Tip

Saying to your child that you'll leave them behind or hit them if they don't hurry up are some of the most demotivating statements that must be avoided – even if you say it as a joke. That's because children have simple minds and might not be able to tell whether it's a joke or not.

Social Development

As your kid grows, you'll notice their tantrums become less frequent. Your child begins to learn coping mechanisms too. However, studies show that your kid's mood may get affected in case of a big sudden change. These changes may include moving to another house or a city, separation from your spouse, and the birth of another baby.[45]

Although the opinions of parents and grandparents are at the centre of your kid's attention, the views of friends and peers may also start gaining importance.

Note:

- Kids begin to create actual friendships. A "best friend" may even be made by your child at this stage.

- Starts sharing and taking turns readily with friends.

- When in need of help, a child will still turn to a trusted adult.

A Useful Parenting Tip

Don't worry if your child bends the rules to win while playing a game sometimes. Later, as they go, they are likely to change the rules to favour themselves. This can be good for their imagination.

Cognitive Development

4-year-olds get comparatively better at solving problems. They even try to look for solutions that will please everyone.

Children at this stage don't only learn the alphabet, shapes, and colours, but they also learn a lot about learning itself. They learn how to ask questions and how to sort out the basic information they acquire into understanding.

---

[45] https://link.springer.com/article/10.1007/s10578-015-0540-4

Language and Communication

As children's vocabulary improves, so does their habit of talking. They become chatty with each passing day. About 2,500-3,0004 words should be understood by 4-yearolds.[46] By the time they turn five, however, it will increase to over 5,000 words.

Play

4-year-olds' imaginations play a major role when it comes to their play. They might even create their own imaginary friends. Transitioning between reality and pretend play on and off may also occur. Their play games include playing house and dressing up, sometimes even with friends.

Note:

- *You may notice your child taking an interest in setting little goals for themselves.*

- *You'll also notice them wanting to make their own decisions by themselves. Decisions such as choosing what to wear or what snack to eat.*

- *They begin understanding the notions of numbers, i.e., the number five represents five candies or five pencils.*

Remember: If you want your child to keep learning, it is advisable that you communicate with them frequently. Let them ask questions, inquire, and quench their thirst for knowledge. Answer their questions and get them to think about different words. This can be done by asking various simple questions, including "What are you doing?" or "What do you see?"

---

[46] https://books.google.com.pk/books?id=gVdfsStbgnQC&dq=_&redir_esc=y

Moreover:

By this age, kids become aware of their sexuality. They may even ask you the differences between boys and girls or question regarding babies' birth.[47] It's vital to share with them the basic, practical information. Using correct terminology regarding your child's body parts is also important. If you see your child touching their private parts, explain to them why such behaviour is socially unacceptable. Make sure they also know that no one besides a doctor or a parent can touch them.

When to Be Worried

All kids grow at somewhat different paces. Sometimes, children who are a little behind will eventually get closer to their peers in the near future. Nonetheless, the Centers for Disease Control and Prevention urge connecting with your child's doctor in case your 4-year-old displays any of the following signs:

- Fails to jump in one place

- Cant scribble properly

- Doesn't understand or follow simple 3-part instructions

- Fails to use words like "you" and "me" fittingly

- Lack of interest in games that are interactive

- Pays no attention to other children or doesn't respond to those outside the family

- Avoids sleeping, dressing up, or using the toilet

- Fails to restate a favourite tale

---

[47] https://www.healthychildren.org/English/agesstages/preschool/Pages/Developme ntal-Milestones-4-to-5-Year-Olds.aspx

- Fails to understand simple words such as "same" and "different"

- Unclear speech

- Forgets skills they once possessed

The changes that you'll notice in the behaviour of your child between age four and five would be remarkable and noticeable. But don't fret if you observe regression sometimes. These minor setbacks are always temporary and are a part of maturing. Before you know it, these delays will fade away.

Growth and Development of 5year-olds

The growth of a 5-year-old is loaded with emotional extremes as well as conflicts. During this stage, kids are preparing to leave their preschool years and step into a new realm, becoming the "big kid."

Most 5-year-olds may be able to display greater selfcontrol than a toddler. They will not only be able to sit inside a classroom for a relatively longer period of time but will also be able to listen to the teacher's guidelines more effectively. A kid this age is still becoming aware of controlling their emotions. Although less, they will still show tantrums over petty issues, such as a lost toy.

Physical Development

The eye-hand coordination of 5-year-olds is way better than when they were toddlers. Their movement becomes more precise and coordinated as they step into their school-age years.

Children by this age lose most of their chubbiness and fat, gaining more muscle. In fact, now they look more lanky, just like most grade-schoolers. Some of the usual development goals include gaining about four to five pounds and getting two to three inches taller. It also includes achieving a 20/20 vision.

Note:

- **Gross motor skills:** A 5-year-old's capability to run, bounce, jump and skip really begins to improve. Their balance, as well as coordination, will be better.

- **Fine motor skills:** Most 5-year-olds are able to dress themselves, handling buttons as well as zippers fittingly, and learning to tie their own shows. This is mainly because their muscles have become more tuned.

- **Main highlights:** You'll notice a change during mealtime too. Children become more skilled at using forks and knives while eating. Moreover, they need relatively less help with cutting their food.

A Useful Parenting Tip

When you see your child learning new skills and becoming an expert at little things, assign them new tasks so they keep busy and challenged at the same time.

Emotional Development

5-year-olds, the "big kids," are stepping into a new sphere of better emotional control and adjustment. Most children at this age are obsessed with pleasing people, trying to be the apple of their eyes. They wish to make friends and gain positive reactions from others, particularly adults.

However, at times, you may notice their tantrums and emotional contradictions. This, however, becomes less frequent with time.

At this age, children become more aware of how they feel and what they want. They are even able to express their emotions in a manner understood by an adult. For instance, they might tell you how they do not like going to bed early.

Children are little empathetic creatures who have the tendency to care for others, especially those they see in distress. If they are upset about something themselves, they may simply state how they feel or what they're thinking.

Note:

- *Children do not become excessively upset when separated from caregivers at this point.*

- *They enjoy playing and sharing with other kids.*

- *They attend to a task directed by adults for about five minutes.*

A Useful Parenting Tip

Teaching children the socially acceptable ways of handling feelings will help them in the long run. When they understand to be in charge of their feelings, such as anger, annoyance, they will become more mature.

Some of the ways to handle feelings may include:

➢ Drawing or colouring an image

➢ Counting to themselves silently

➢ Taking deep breaths slowly

Social Development

Children at this age begin making new friends, interacting with people, and forming relationships. These may include friends, classmates, teachers, and those outside the family. Social interaction and associations will make children grow independently. The social as well as emotional milestones you notice at this age, will enable your child to move to kindergarten much easily.

This is the reason why friendships begin to be more important for 5-year-olds. They may even get close to particular friends and create small groups.

Note:

- *Wishes to please friends.*

- *They agree more with the rules and instructions.*

- *Wishes to be like other kids his/her age.*

A Useful Parenting Tip

This is the age when children form little groups, because of which some may feel ostracised. This is why it is important for parents to keep an eye on subtleties in schools, classrooms, and playgroups. Some children may also be bullied at this age. Moreover, since they do not know how to respond to that, a parent must look into it and solve the matter.

Cognitive Development

The difference between right and wrong, good and bad, becomes clear to children at this age. They will start understanding the concepts of different rules and will try their best to follow them, mainly to please adults. As a kid begins to grow, they'll be able to express their views, thoughts, and feelings on greater levels. Kids who start kindergarten will display interest in dealing with expectations regarding academics as well as behaviour at school.

Language and Communication

5-year-olds begin to state their needs as well as wants with words that can easily be understood by adults, even those who are not familiar with them. In fact, studies show that these people, who are not familiar with them, are usually better at understanding instructions that are relatively more complex.[48]

Kids' positional vocabulary also develops. They begin to understand terms such as "right next to," "under," or "on top of the."

Play

Dramatic plays are enjoyed by most children at this age. They may take their friends to another room and wish to play with them separately, away from adults. Often, they are able to resolve slight conflict themselves, without adult supervision.

Their growing physical abilities may also develop their play. The chances are that your child may enjoy riding a bike that does not have training wheels. They may also like to jump rope or play other difficult games involving balls.

---

[48] https://academic.oup.com/pch/article/17/10/561/2638880

Note:

- *Children at this point can count up to 10.*

- *They begin extending their oral language skills to read as well as write.*

- *They like to sing, dance, act and perform.*

A Useful Parenting Tip

Try exposing your 5-year-old to various experiences in order to enable them to learn different skills. This will also help them in practising the ones they already possess. To help them flourish, you can introduce new:

- crafts

- sports

- social situations

Remember: Most children at this age start losing baby teeth, and in their place appear permanent teeth in the following years. Dentists do not recommend pulling loose baby teeth. In fact, letting them fall on their own is the right way to go about it.[49]

Although most 5-year-olds know how to brush their own teeth, it is better if a parent still supervises them. They are also able to wash themselves.

---

[49] https://www.verywellfamily.com/5-year-old-developmentalmilestones-620713

When to Be Worried

All kids grow at somewhat different paces. Sometimes, children who are a little behind will eventually get closer to their peers in the near future. Nonetheless, the Centers for Disease Control and Prevention urge connecting with your child's doctor in case your 5-year-old displays any of the following signs:

- Fails to display a variety of emotions

- Shows behaviour that is extreme, including unusual fear, aggression, reluctance, or gloominess

- Is oddly reserved and quiet

- Can easily be distracted. Fails to focus on one activity for over five minutes

- Refuses to answer to people or responds only outwardly

- Fails to differentiate between reality and makebelieve

- Does not participate in various games or activities

- Doesn't know how to tell first and last name

- Faces trouble while using plurals or past tense

- Avoids talking about everyday activities or practices • Fails to draw pictures

- Brushing teeth, washing or drying hands, and getting undressed without help becomes problematic for them

- Forgets talents they once possessed

Moreover:

Kindergarten is the next step forward, not only for kids but also for parents. That's why it is understandable to have concerns regarding whether your kid is ready for starting school. In case you are concerned about a specific ability, try to solve it along with your child. But if your concern is about their lack of willingness, communicate with the child's paediatrician or a teacher for preschoolers.

Disciplining Preschoolers: Tactics and Trials

Art, as well as science, is required to discipline a preschooler. Serious alertness is also required considerably. Something that worked a few days back may not necessarily work today. Which is why tolerance and constancy can be crucial to address behavioural concerns for your 4- or 5year-old. Moreover, the chances are that you might have to do a few experiments, carry out a little trial and error sometimes to find out what strategies of disciplining work best for your child.

Usual Preschooler Behaviour

Children are obsessed with the notion of having independence and getting to do things themselves. This search for liberty can give rise to new challenges for parents regarding their behaviour and discipline requirements. Children may also show particular behaviour just to check how you'd respond.

Stepping into the new phase of life, i.e., into preschool, may affect your child. Children sometimes experience anxiety due to separation or fear because of interacting with unfamiliar faces, including children and teachers.

By this age, children may also experiment with challenging the set boundaries and restrictions. This is why they may end up showing defiance. Since their motor skill are not absolutely refined as of yet, they might struggle with carrying out a task the way they want to. This may lead to frustration and annoyance, eventually leading to disobedience, dawdling, and arguing.

Preschoolers can differentiate right from wrong. They can even follow basic rules and instructions. But since children do not understand the logic the way adults do, they can sometimes struggle to make healthy decisions.

Although preschoolers should be growing enhanced impulse control, they will still require a lot of effort in this field. You might find them saying mean things or even shouting while showing sudden outbursts. You must tell them how their behaviour can have consequences, in order to avoid it in the future.

Basic Challenges

Some of the common challenges that most parents have to deal with regarding their preschoolers include:

- **Lying:** Children lie at times. Sometimes, they do so to get themselves out of trouble, while other times, it is done simply as a result of their imaginative skills.

- **Whining:** Whining is surely one of the most common issues of preschoolers. Kids think that if you refuse to do as they ask the first time, you'll do it once they start crying and begging. But remember, you submit once, you submit forever.

- **Baby Talk:** In many households, baby talk is considered to be one of the most annoying preschool behaviours. But returning to baby talk can be a usual part of the development at this stage.

- Sometimes, it is used by pre-schoolers mainly to gain attention. Other times, they revert either because of stress or anxiety.

- **Defiance:** Most of the time, pre-schoolers are trying to help and please others. However, at times, they might feel like asserting their independence. You might hear them say "No!" to a task that you've assigned to them, mainly to see how you would respond to their disobedience.

- **Infrequent Tantrums:** Although most kids have come out of that phase where they'd show tantrums regularly, they might sometimes revert back to this behaviour. You might see them hitting, biting and, kicking, which is still a problem that needs to be addressed politely.

Effective Discipline Strategies That Work

As discussed earlier, children should be disciplined from an early age. They should be aware of the actions they are not supposed to take and the activities they shouldn't insist on participating in. Although each child is different, the following are some of the disciplining strategies that have the power of doing wonders:

- **Praising Good Behaviour:** Good behaviour that is praised is likely to be repeated by children. If you see your child trying to wear clothes himself or if you see them picking up their toys, acknowledge it, complimenting them on their good behaviour.

- **The Need for a Time-Out:** Just like good behaviour needs to be acknowledged and praised, the consequences of bad behaviour should be made clear too so that the kid avoids repeating it in the future. Time-out for the violation of important rules, such as aggression, or hitting, is necessary. You could take your child to a calm-down corner and tell them why their behaviour was not acceptable.

- **Removing Privileges:** If your child violates a minor rule, a time-out can be avoided. Instead, you could remove a privilege that is linked to their bad behaviour. For instance, if they throw a toy at their sibling, you could remove the toy and put it in timeout for 5 minutes.

- **Giving Rewards:** If you see your child struggling with an action they must learn, for example, staying in their own bed at night, try to come up with a reward system that would motivate them to achieve their goal. You can do this by creating a sticker chart and telling them that once they earn, say 3-5 stars (1 star for every night they stay in bed), they'll get a bigger reward, like getting the chance to pick a movie.

- **Preventing Future Problems:** Staying prepared for your preschooler's moods is the best way to avoid problems that can arise in the future. Most children throw a fit when hungry or tired. To avoid your child's tantrums, pack snacks and make sure they get plenty of rest so they stay fresh and invigorated. Furthermore, share with your preschoolers what they need to do throughout the day. When children are aware of what is expected of them, a sense of structure is created, allowing them to stay focused.

- **Create Clear Rules:** When you tell your child the rules that they must follow, you make it known to them what they can and cannot do. Before entering a new situation, explain to them your expectations. For instance, before going inside a museum, you tell them how to behave properly and the consequences if they don't.

- **Managing Emotions:** Many preschoolers struggle with managing their emotions. This gives rise to several other problems. Managing emotions, especially anger, is important not only for adults but even for kids. Teaching your child simple angermanagement skills will help them in the long run. For example, taking long breaths in and out, trying to count slowly, blowing bubbles, and so on.

- **Communication:** Speech that is brief, as well as effective, is way better than communication that keeps going on without reaching anywhere. Lengthy lectures are just going to make your child lose his focus. Therefore, communication should be:

  o Short, simple, and sweet

  o Talk about alternatives, how their bad behaviour could've been avoided

  o Healthy and comfortable (your child should feel at ease to share anything with you)

  o Effective and useful for your child

  o Instructive and educational (such as giving instructions)

Another important aspect that must be kept into consideration while communicating is offering limited choices. For instance, when you offer unlimited choices, saying something like, *"What would you like for lunch?"* can result in confusion and conflict. A child does not have the skills required to make appropriate choices. You can, however, offer your child two good choices to choose from. For example, *"Would you pick up your toys before or after your meal?"* Here, both the choices are favourable.

Preschooler Parenting Tips for 4, and 5-year-olds

Spending time with preschoolers can be extremely fun. This is the time when their social, physical, and emotional skills are strengthening. They are exploring the world around them and understanding new activities. This is why you must try to comprehend your kid's developmental stage first, as that will enable you to modify your parenting strategies accordingly.

Daily Life

Preschoolers are becoming more independent, trying to do everything on their own. At this stage, you can expect them to brush their teeth under supervision, button their clothes, and dress themselves. As their speech improves, they'll start speaking simple and short sentences. They may even ask a lot of questions, tell stories and rhymes, understand daily routines automatically.

Preschoolers also start interacting with kids their own age. They enjoy developing friendships and making groups, sharing toys and little secrets. Studies show that **enrolling children in preschool prepares them for the demands and decorum of school, sharpening their social as well as cognitive skills.**[50]

Diet & Nutrition

Your child's nutrition and diet should be your priority. Proper nutrition must be comprised of three meals and two healthy snacks a day.[51] Try to provide fresh fruit, vegetables, products with low-fat

---

[50] https://www.tandfonline.com/doi/full/10.1080/10409289.2013.825565

[51] https://www.healio.com/pediatrics/journals/pedann/2013-942-9/%7B21c02376-c253-429a-a8da-8e974896d9cd%7D/strategiesand-suggestions-for-a-healthy-toddler-diet

dairy and lean meats. Furthermore, limiting high sugar and high-fat foods is advisable.

The amount of calories preschoolers need may vary from child to child. It mainly depends on how active a kid is. According to The American Academy of Pediatrics, 1,200 and 2,000 calories each day are needed by preschoolers, depending on the level of their activities.[52] Telling your child what is best for them to eat and providing them with a variety may also motivate them to consume healthy foods.

Planning a diet that is low in fat, cholesterol, and saturated fat is healthy. You can also choose a diet that has a lot of fruits, vegetables, and grain products. Foods with moderate levels of sugar and salt are also recommended. Make sure you choose a diet that has enough calcium and iron as these two help in growing their bodies.

As a parent, you can also help encourage good nutrition food by:

- Setting a good example yourself

- Following a healthy eating pattern

- Providing them with healthy choices

- Allowing them to experiment

- Making mealtimes pleasant so that they feel like eating in the first place

- Limiting mealtime conversation to topics that are positive or pleasant

- Working out regularly (exercise should be a consistent part of not just yours but also your family's life)

---

[52] https://www.healthychildren.org/English/healthyliving/nutrition/Pages/Energy-In-Recommended-Food-Drink-Amountsfor-Children.aspx

- Preventing keeping desserts or snacks with highcalories

- Being vigilant with foods that your child may end up choking on

Feeding is often linked with a child's liberty as they begin to do this one task all by themselves. Although your kid may not be intaking a well-rounded diet as you would like them to, if you see your child growing normally and their energy level seems normal, there is nothing to fret over. However, if your kid is not eating well at all, you can consider giving them a daily vitamin.

Common Nutrition Mistakes

Parents must avoid the following few basic points when it comes to their children's diet:

- Do not let your child drink milk or juice in greater quantities. If they fill their stomachs with liquid, they won't be hungry for solids.

- Make sure not to force your child to eat if they are not hungry or if they don't like something in particular.

- Children usually do not eat a balanced diet every day. If their diet throughout the week is balanced, that should be enough for the child.

- Do not punish or hit your kid for not eating well

- Make sure not to comment on your child's reduced eating habits while at the table

- Avoid using food as a prize or bribe.

Physical Activity

Keeping your preschooler active should also be on your list. That's because kids who are physically fit are healthier as their muscles and bodies become stronger. Kids at this age usually love to run, jump, skip, hop, dance and climb. Their budding motor skills help them to ride a bicycle and play different sports.

According to the Society of Health and Physical Educators[53], preschoolers should receive at least **one hour of structured play, one hour of free play, and less sedentary time**.

Structured play that includes adult-led activities may comprise of playing catch, swimming, learning to ride a bike, or playing soccer ball. During free play, a child should be allowed to run around, play in the park freely. Give them the opportunity to explore. Your child's sedentary time should be limited. Make sure they do not sit still for more than an hour unless they are sleeping.

Around the House

As your child grows, they may start doing little chores around the house. This is a good time to give them instructions, allowing them to engage in useful tasks. For instance, wiping the table, picking up the toys, unloading the dishwasher, throwing used tissues or wrappers in the dustbin, and so on. Positive reinforcement is imperative for chores that your child completes. Similarly, failure to finish a task can be punished by removing a privilege temporarily.

---

[53] https://www.shapeamerica.org//

This is also a good age to make your children become more responsible. Giving them a little allowance is also an effective way of instilling a sense of responsibility within them.

Safety and Health

Ensuring that your preschooler is safe and healthy is integral for all caregivers. That's why it is essential to take certain precautionary measures to guarantee the safety of your child. This is a crucial time also because at this stage, you begin to teach your child how important it is for them to take care of their bodies and do not participate in any activity that may put their lives in danger.

Avoid talking *too much* about dangers such as kidnapping, fires, or getting lost in a mall, as it will frighten your child. However, make sure to educate them and keep them prepared in case such a situation befalls.

Common Accidents and their Prevention

Accidents are the primary reason for death for kids at this stage. If necessary precautions are taken, most of these deaths can easily be avoided. That's why it is extremely important to stay alert regarding your child's safety at all times. Some key points for your preschooler's safety include:

- Kids sometimes put small objects in their mouths and end up choking on them. Make sure you never leave tiny objects around the house that your child can have access to. Small items such as rubber, coins, pins, and parts of toys should be kept away from children.

- While teaching your child to swim is advisable, leaving them near a water body on their own is not. Even if you think your child excels at swimming, allowing them to swim without adult supervision can actually be harmful to them and, therefore, must be avoided. When on a boat, make sure they wear a safety vest.

- Focus on correctly using car seats. Preschoolers should ideally sit in a forward-facing car seat. Their seats must include long harness straps. This is before they move to a booster seat. According to Very Well Family, several convertibles as well as combination car seats "have forward-facing weight limits of 65 to 80 pounds when used with harness straps."[54]

- Don't forget to use safety equipment. In case you're using used car seats or strollers, make sure you contact their manufacturers and run a quick inquiry as to whether the equipment is safe for your child or not.

- It's integral to childproof your entire house. Some of the childproofing measures include:

  - setting your hot water heater's temperature to 120 degrees F

  - use small gates on stairs

  - cover all the electrical openings

  - put bolts on cabinets

  - household cleaners or chemicals should be kept away from your children

  - keep medicines out of reach as well

---

[54] https://www.verywellfamily.com/parenting-advice-forpreschoolers-2631976

> avoid carrying piping hot liquids or even food near or over your child

> keep your child away from stoves, heaters, burners, or other harmful appliances (especially hot straighteners).

> while cooking, make sure to use back burners. Also, turn the handles of pots inward.

> empty all water from bathtubs and buckets to avoid drowning

> keep the bathroom doors closed

> avoid leaving your child alone near any water body

> in case a room is not childproof, keep it locked

- Talking to children about their safety is essential too. Teach them pedestrian and playground safety. The basic rules of crossing streets should also be shared. Telling children not to communicate with strangers or accept anything they give, such as candy or toys, should also be prioritized. Mention how to refuse to trust a stranger if they ask them to get inside a car or tells them they're there to pick them up because you are not feeling well. Parking lot safety may include holding an adult's hand and looking out for cars.

- Make sure to keep a list of emergency numbers on your phone to be on the safe side.

When to Visit the Doctor

Your doctor will likely recommend yearly check-ups during the preschool years, i.e., if your kid is strong and healthy.[55] A few basic health problems faced by preschoolers are:

- **Constipation**: Constipation is irregular bowel movements or hard passage of stools that continue for four days or longer. It is usually caused by an intake that either lacks or is low in fiber. It can also be caused by consuming too much milk – more than 16 to 24 oz. each day. Those who do not drink enough water or wait too long to use the bathroom may also face constipation.

- **Treatment:**

  - Increase the quantity of liquids your child drinks.

  - Increase the quantity of fibre as well as bran in the diet

  - Try to decrease the sum of constipating foods, such as cow's milk, cheese, yogurt, bananas, and cooked carrots.

  - Try stool softeners if the above-mentioned steps don't work.

- **Vomiting**: In case your child begins to vomit, it is advisable to give them a little break from eating or drinking. Take this break for about an hour. After that, Pedialyte in small amounts, say 1 teaspoon, should be given every 5-10-minutes. When you see your child can easily tolerate drinking these small quantities, you can add more Pedialyte (about a tablespoon) every 5-10 minutes. Then again increase amounts as tolerated by your child and then revert back to the general formula. Make sure not to give just Pedialyte for over 12 hours.

---

[55] https://pediatrics.aappublications.org/content/131/Supplement_1/S5

Call Your Paediatrician If:

> The vomit shows blood in it

> The vomit's colour is dark green

> Your child shows signs of dehydration

- **Upper Respiratory Infections:** The upper respiratory infections are mostly caused by cold viruses. Their symptoms include a green runny nose along with a cough.

Treatment:

> Use saltwater nasal drops

> Also, use a bulb suctioner to keep the nose clear.

If the kid's condition does not improve within a week, and if their fever continues, call your doctor.

- **Diarrhea**: Loose, watery stools (bowel movements) cause diarrhea.

Call Your Paediatrician If:

> Diarrhea shows blood or pus in it

> The situation does not get better within 1-2 weeks

> You notice signs of dehydration – try preventing dehydration by giving 1-2 ounces of Pedialyte every time they have huge diarrhea stool

Annual Visits

Visiting the paediatrician annually can enable you to guarantee that your child is growing normally. A paediatrician would examine your kid's development and growth. They would review preschooler's feeding as well as sleeping patterns. Their height, weight, blood pressure levels would be measured. Furthermore, they'll be counselled on how to prevent being injured and what a proper diet is. Their vision, as well as hearing tests, will be conducted. The paediatrician may also talk about immunizations, DTaP, Varivax booster, MMR boosters, and IPV. The checkup of 4-year-olds may also contain a detailed discussion of toilet training and its progress.

Note: The toothbrush that you use to clean your kid's teeth should be soft. Take only a small amount (peasized) of fluoride toothpaste to avoid fluorosis. This should be done until they successfully learn to spit the toothpaste out.

Sleep

Preschoolers mostly require a nap during the day. Since kids this age are really active and always on the go, they become easily tired, and it is better to let them rest for a while. A one-hour nap should be enough for preschoolers. However, some might take longer naps.

Usually, 4-year-olds and 5-year-olds require sleep of 10-13 hours along with a nap of 2.5 hours. Around the age of 4, some children stop taking naps.

Note: Bedtime difficulties are common, especially for preschoolers. Remember, you are not alone in this. While some children avoid sleeping because of nightmares, others are afraid of missing out on something integral if they fall asleep. Some might just find it difficult to fall asleep.

Technology

Screen time does not always have to be harmful to your kids. You can find informative apps, introduce them to games that encourage physical activities, and sites that show various skills. Still, most of the content available online is not age-appropriate.

Pay closer attention to what your child watches on the internet. Even some advertisements can be harmful to kids. For instance, ads showing junk food or unhealthy snacks may target small kids.

On the whole, it is advisable to limit your child's screen time. Greater screen time makes children less active as they are engaged in a lot of sedentary activity. According to the AAP, preschoolers should only receive about one hour of screen time throughout the day. Moreover, preschoolers should only be allowed to watch high-quality programs.[56]

Changes You May Notice in Your Preschooler

You'll notice several obvious changes in the mannerisms and behaviours of your preschooler with each passing day. As they are growing and learning more skills, they are likely to show them off. Whether it's a new piece of information they've learnt at school or a new friend they've made, they'll like to share it with you. The alphabet that they learn and the rhymes they memorize will be repeated regularly at home.

Preschoolers experience compassion for others present around them. You may find them consoling other kids at school or daycare in case they are upset. They may also help a child who has fallen down.

---

[56] https://www.aap.org/en-us/advocacy-and-policy/aap-healthinitiatives/Pages/Media-and-Children.aspx

At this age, children like being there for others, just like they enjoy playing and exploring with their friends.

Preschoolers' imaginative skills have the tendency to take them to new places. You'll often find them pretending to be cartoon or fictional characters.

Children can find it difficult to share their stuff or take turns with others. Sometimes, because of this, they may even lash out of anger or frustration.

Note: As a parent, you'll see many physical, social, and emotional development during the preschool years. Make sure to give your child security, support, motivation, and consistency, as these will help them grow up to be happy individuals.

Growth and Development of 6year-olds

A 6-year-old's development is full of contradictions. While kids this age are glad for gaining a bit more of their precious freedom, they can sometimes be overwhelmed thinking about stepping into the big world without the continuous comfort of their caregivers.

A child may look for comfort and more attention at home as he experiences school, birthday parties, and other activities without a parent.

Physical Development

You'll notice that your toddler's chubbiness has somehow vanished and in front of you is a lanky child who seems to be growing every day. This stage of child development is known as middle childhood. During this age, a kid grows about 2 to 2.5 inches per year on average.[57]

6-years-olds generally display a variety of new physical abilities. While some show natural athleticism, others might work on achieving simple skills, for instance, catching or throwing a ball. Each kid grows at a relatively different pace. While some may be quick to adapt to new physical skills, others may require some time to master them.

On the whole, 6-year-olds are extremely energetic, burning that energy in outdoor activities. Physical activity is vital as most children at this age spend much of their time within the four walls of their classrooms. Various researches endorse that exercise and keeping fit is advantageous for cognitive function.

At this age, fine motor coordination continues to improve. Most 6-year-olds will become more skillful at writing, drawing, and colouring. Moreover, their images, as well as stories, will be much more recognizable and decipherable. Children at this stage are likely to become more capable of using different tools, including scissors.

Tying shoelaces and buttoning buttons properly wouldn't be an issue too.

Note:

- *Children often show off their growing locomotors abilities, including running, skipping, and jumping. • They display greater hand-eye coordination.*

- *They'd get better at kicking balls into the goal or throwing them at the target.*

---

[57] https://www.verywellfamily.com/6-year-old-developmentalmilestones-620703

- *Start following the basic rules of various games or sport, making the sport more meaningful.*

A Useful Parenting Tip

Playing physical games with your kid helps them grow and become stronger. Try to jump rope, kick/throw balls, run in the playground or climb over hurdles. This time is best for children to refine their coordination skills. This, in turn, will enable them to feel more assured and confident about themselves.

Emotional Development

As children grow up, they begin understanding feelings exceptionally – not just their own but even those of others. They even become aware of proper, refined concepts, i.e., not hurting other peoples' feelings by saying anything terrible about them.

By this age, kids may also show an interest in choosing their own clothes. They are likely to wash themselves and even comb their hair. It is advisable that parents support this sovereign self-care and suggest some direction.

As children start understanding the world and people around them in a better light, their friendships and other social relationships with friends and even adults grow to become more intricate, taking on more meaning.

Note:

- *Showing off skills is what kids love to do at this age.*

- *They develop better self-control abilities.*

- *They demonstrate a developed ability to continue emotional stability.*

A Useful Parenting Tip

It is better to create expected routines. These predictable routines may include nighttime fun time, activities after school, and consistent play times. These fixed activities as well as interactions will offer a sense of security kids require as they come across unfamiliar trials and events.

Social Development

6-year-olds become more skilled at directing their budding relationships with friends as well as family. They begin feeling secure and comfortable when surrounded by the people they have formed relationships with.

Sharing toys, snacks, and other valuables becomes regular for kids not only at home but also at school. However, this does not mean their minor, unpredictable fights over favourite snacks or toys won't happen. Such conflicts may arise, but in most cases, they'll be minor and fleeting. 6-year-olds will ever more achieve the social skills that will help them sort out their differences themselves, i.e., without any adult's interference.

Note:

- *Kids start paying greater attention to friendship, relationships, and teamwork.*

- *They wish to not only be accepted but also liked by peer groups.*

- *Start displaying signs of more freedom from family.*

A Useful Parenting Tip

Although your child understands other people's moods, you may need to prompt them to open up to you. You can ask questions such as, *"How do you think your classmate felt when you told them you couldn't play with them?"*

Cognitive Development

6-year-olds become more aware of what is right and wrong. Chances are they may even rat on peers who they think are doing something incorrectly or showing bad behaviour. Outbreaks, even amongst great friends, may come to the surface. But these flare-ups are mostly shortlived and usually fade away quickly, particularly with the correct guidance of parents or teachers. Most children at this age keep developing attention spans that are longer. They become more able to carry out different tasks at school as well as at home. The skill to have multifaceted thoughts really begins to grow at this stage. Their interest in their surrounding starts to grow exceptionally.

Language and Communication

Children at this stage enjoy writing stories and reading independently. Their stories are mostly either about themselves or their experiences, visits, parties, friends.

Their sight words' vocabulary starts expanding. Furthermore, they establish the ability to break down words into different sounds. Along with their vocabulary, their ability to spell more words also increases. This is the age when children start understanding the use of letter capitalization and punctuation. Enjoying reading a simple chapter and retelling the plot is an activity children take an interest in. It is likely that they may even tell you whether they liked the book or not and talk about the different characters.

Play

By this age, kids get a better understanding of what is real and what is imaginary. The things they perceive as "real" become their centre of attention. They are more likely to wish to make real food instead of pretending to cook in a made-up kitchen with toys.

Note:

- *They take part in board games or basic group activities.*

- *Kids at this age learn to tell time.*

- *They are able to copy complex shapes.*

A Useful Parenting Tip

By this age, you'll notice your child reading on their own, and you may feel it is alright if you don't sit with them while they read. This, however, is not recommended. Make sure you keep reading together. Your reading will allow them to listen and even learn new words. Furthermore, make sure you give them plenty of chances to read too.

Remember:

Children at this age wish to do everything perfectly. This may be a little difficult to achieve since their performance is not perfect yet. Moreover, many 6-year-olds see the world as black or white, right or wrong, which is why they express strong yes or no opinions about them. Being kids, they fail to see the middle ground — the grey area.

Expressing a desire for privacy while dressing or undressing is natural. Some children, however, may still enjoy having a parent around while they take a bath.

When to Be Worried

6-year-olds are either in kindergarten or first grade. For the first time, they've been told to spend extended time without their parents. Here they have to follow the rules, concentrate on schoolwork, and learn. This is the reason why at this point, a child may show signs of delay while developing. It's advisable to speak with your kid's paediatrician if you notice any of these concerns:

- Very quiet, troubled, or unhappy

- Finds it hard to separate from you

- Fails to interact with the rest

- Finds it problematic to follow a slmple 2-part instruction

- Doesn't show interest in attempting to write their own name

- Demonstrates lots of taxing behaviour

Keeping an eye on your child's development is one thing, but to compare them with other kids their age is unfair to them. Different kids will grow at a different pace. While some may be fascinated by reading and writing, others may enjoy sports more. Observe your child and see what interests them the most, make sure to always support them.

Growth and Development of 7year-olds

By this age, your child becomes extremely curious about all that he sees around him. His curiosity leads him to ask several intriguing questions. At this age, children would be little explorers, experimenters, scientists, and even researchers, inquiring about the world and trying to comprehend its ways.

7-year-olds mostly enjoy taking pride in knowing different things and even love sharing the information they collect. They are interested in showing younger children the skills they possess, and some may even brag about them a bit.

The sense of confidence of 7-year-olds increases as they become more familiar with their surroundings, particularly their school and classrooms. Their little achievements in various subjects give them a sense of pride. Children this age may even wish to share the information they've learnt at school with parents and friends.

Physical Development

Physically, children at this age become more refined. Their lanky physique will continue to grow, removing signs of their former chubby selves. Their motor skills tend to become more accurate. Because of their precise motor skills, they learn to do more combinations, including moving and dancing at the same time. They even get better at coordination as well as balance.

The more physically active a child is, the better they will be at developing these skills quickly.

A 7-year-old's growth changes are not sudden or dramatic, as they were in their previous years. Still, they do go through a growth spurt from time to time. Typically, they are likely to grow 2 to 2.5 inches yearly.

Note:

- *Children at this age learn to ride a bicycle with two wheels.*

- *They learn to make movements that can be done while standing in place. For instance, bending, turning, and circling.*

- *Demonstrate improved skillfulness at carrying out simple chores, including making their bed or cleaning the floors.*

A Useful Parenting Tip

As parents, you should do interesting physical activities together, as a family. You could play sports, attend different community events or even play outside. Kids who remain physically active are likely to get better at physical skills instead of those who spend more time sitting.

Emotional Development

Children's emotional maturity at this age is a far cry from what it was in their earlier kindergarten years. Most seven-year-olds are not only better at handling sudden changes but can also tolerate unexpected circumstances (a skill that improves drastically later, between ages 10 or 12).

Nonetheless, routines sill comfort 7-year-olds. Since at this point, a child's world opens up more and more, they begin focusing more on things and people separate from their family, they are likely to depend more on things they can count on. This includes a happy family time, a fixed bedtime routine, and consistent meals with family.

On the other hand, some 7-year-olds may also feel uncertain about themselves. Some children may even be their own worst critics. If children do not get something to look the way they want, or if they lose a game with friends or family, they may experience crushed self-respect. If your child feels the same way, make sure you divert their attention to what they learnt from the activity rather than what didn't go right.

Note:

- *Children learn to explain the causes as well as consequences of feelings, for instance, saying, "I got angry as I really wished to go outside."*

- *They handle emotions in a better way, particularly in public conditions.*

- *Self-calming strategies are now used by them. This* may include taking deep breaths in case feeling worried.

A Useful Parenting Tip

Guiding your child why or how their behaviour is bad, rather than punishing them brutally is recommended.

Try not to make them feel terrible about themselves.

Social Development

Although most children at this age enjoy making friends and playing with them, they love spending time alone too. They enjoy reading or carrying out their own activities. Studies show that this alone time can actually be significant for developing a sense of self and their relations with others.[58]

7-year-olds become more aware of the opinions and views of others. They even start caring about other peoples' thoughts. The problem of this phase of a child's development is an increased defenselessness towards peer pressure. Children will also keep developing empathy while understanding what is moral and just.

---

[58]https://www.verywellfamily.com/7-year-old-developmentalmilestones-620704

The social horizons of children at this age start expanding. In most cases, they become attached to adults other than their parents, such as an aunt or a teacher. Most children at this age begin to understand other peoples' perspectives. But minor fights and hurt feelings can still be noticed.

Note:

- *Sharing knowledge with friends and family is natural at this point.*

- *Children display the capacity to realize other peoples' actions as well as feelings.*

- *They begin treating peers with respect, particularly while playing games with them.*

Remember: This age is perfect for teaching your child what a good citizen is and how they can be good citizens too. Talking about charities or other ways of helping the environment is recommended.

Cognitive Development

The curiosity of kids at this point keeps increasing. They attempt to know all the answers to their simple as well as multifaceted questions. The more people they meet and places they visit, the more questions they ask. Their sense of adventure, along with their wish to learn, will lead them to mentor younger siblings. They'll even show off all the information they've acquired or the new names they've learnt. Their reading skills and the math gets exceptionally better, too. So does their ability to recognize words and complete simple word problems.

Most 7-year-olds become skilled at simple addition and subtraction, applying these talents to solve other more complex math problems. These may include word problems. Children will be taught place value. They will also learn to work with three-digit numbers. Most kids even start adding and subtracting mentally. Other topics they work on include fractions, learning shapes and structures around them, for example, tall buildings and homes.

Language and Communication

Your child's language also develops rapidly. Their vocabulary and the number of sight words go up to thousands. This will boost their reading skills, allowing them to step into the world of more complicated chapter books. Most kids at this point can read with more fluency with regard to speed and accuracy.[59] Moreover, they'll have more profound discussions about books. Writing complicated, clear as well as interesting stories will also be noticed.

Remember: You, as a parent, must instil a love of books in your child. This can be achieved by reading together and discussing various characters, plots, and other scenes or dialogues of the book.

Play

Seeing your child engaging in pretend play should be anticipated by you. Their enhanced learning, as well as memory skills, allow them to become more inventive and even artistic. Encouraging your child to participate in art projects can also do wonders.

Some of the great toys for kids this age include puppets, costumes, Legos, and dolls. If their toys don't have particular guidelines or restrictions, they can become more creative with them. Most children will be interested in joining playground games with their friends. They become better at sports at this stage.

---

[59] https://www.verywellfamily.com/7-year-old-developmentalmilestones-620704

Note:

- *Children can name the different characters of a book or show. Its setting, problem, and solution can also be discussed by them.*

- *They begin solving math word problems.*

- *They also use several creative strategies in an attempt to solve problems.*

A Useful Parenting Tip

Try to add in your kid's newfound math talents into normal life and while doing that, make sure it is fun. Playing around with math games with crayons while drawing objects, or in the kitchen, or on road trips can be fascinating for them. Since kids love playing on mobile phones or computers, online math games will be a smart way of making them polish their math skills.

Remember:

Although you might have to remind your children from time to time to wash their hands or brush their teeth, it is time to let them do these things on their own.

7-year-olds' fine motor coordination is quite enhanced, which is why now, they'll be better able to use dental floss. Parents should encourage their children to include flossing in their daily oral-care routine. Most children at this age have lost baby teeth and have permanent teeth now.

7-year-olds may also wish to take showers themselves instead of a bath in the evening. This can be extremely timesaving considering their busy schedules occupied with additional activities along with school. However, parents may still have to oversee every now and then to make sure the shampoo has been properly rinsed out.

When to Be Worried

While many children excel at reading and solving math problems at this age, there are a few who struggle. These struggles may have several causes, including learning disabilities, problems regarding spoken or written guidelines.

In most cases, challenges regarding academics can be stopped in the initial stages with only a little extra tutoring from a teacher, parent, or math expert. In some instances, children may require special backing or adjustments in the setting of a classroom. All in all, it is better to address these issues sooner rather than later.

Note:

- *This is a crucial time for children to improve selfconfidence. Give them some freedom. Support your child's abilities, and enable them to explore new prospects.*

- *In case you are worried about your child's growth or notice something which you believe isn't normal, talk to the doctor. Make sure to address any concerns that you have.*

Chapter 10

Child Development
Age group 8 – 11

Growth and Development of 8year-olds

For most children, third grade enhances their physical, emotional, and mental skills. At this age, the cognitive development of children improves drastically. They are able to ask questions in a better way and keep inquiring until they have acquired enough information regarding their topic of interest. 8-year-olds are growing, learning, and maturing, which is exciting for them as well as their parents.

Physical Development

Although you may not notice substantial physical changes in your child at this age, you will undoubtedly observe how refined their actions and movements have become. Their muscle control and coordination will be more developed, allowing them to carry out different chores in an upgraded way. Despite puberty being a few years away, this is the time when children start to look like "big, mature kids."

Children possessing the usual athletic capabilities may show their skills at this stage of development as their physical abilities become more accurate. Most children figure out at this stage whether they are inclined towards athleticism or not and whether they're interested in sports or not.

In any case, it is integral for parents to motivate their children to participate in physical activities. Whether your child is an athlete or not, they should still be looking forward to biking, running, swimming, and other such activities.

Note:

- *Better combination of locomotors as well as motor skills. Kids at this stage should ideally be able to run, spin, bounce, and jump.*

- *Coordination improves with each passing day.*

- *Better small muscle control keeps refining. It further makes various activities, including playing musical tools or using instruments, much simpler.*

A Useful Parenting Tip

Some children at this age might start getting affected because of their body image. Their confidence with regards to how they look may influence the way they interact with others. Make sure you focus on health instead of appearance. Try to help your kid find those activities that make them feel good about themselves, further empowering them.

Emotional Development

Most 8-year-olds display relatively cultured and multifaceted emotions as well as relations. Most of them know how to conceal their real thoughts so that they do not hurt other people's feelings. A kid may say, *"thank you for this present. I really like it,"* even when they don't just to spare someone's emotions.

8-year-olds start developing and improving their sense of self which is more refined. Their hobbies, aptitudes, relationships with friends and family members enable them to create a strong self-identity. The desire for privacy begins to form. They might even transition between selfconfidence and self-doubt.

Note:

- *The desire for more privacy begins.*

- *Although they look for caregiver's comfort and directly contact them if under stress, at other times, you may find them resisting physical contact.*

- *Know how to cope with anger, failure, and distress in a balanced way.*

A Useful Parenting Tip

Complimenting your child for coping with emotion in an acceptable manner will help them in the long run. Keep looking for opportunities to teach them by praising them for all the good emotion regulation talents they acquire and improve.

Social Development

Most children love interacting with others in social groups. As they grow older, they enjoy participating in school and start maintaining friendships that were made earlier. They may even begin to value their friends or other classmates they are close to. They may mostly be inclined towards alliances with friends belonging to the same gender.

If you notice your child refusing to go to school, make sure you get to the bottom of the issue and find out the main reason behind their refusal. It could either be due to bullying or learning difficulties. Discussions regarding how to respect others may also be focused on.

You will observe a new sense of confidence within your child and notice them expressing their views regarding different people or things in their surroundings. They may be more attentive to news events, wanting to communicate their views on the recent events.

Children may also show an interest in sleeping over at a friend's house. Some may even feel like not staying for the whole night and may end up going back home against their initial wish for a sleepover. This is mainly because children are really attached to their mothers and fathers and might not feel ready to spend the entire night away from them just yet. All this is natural, and parents shouldn't worry about it.

Studies reveal that children at this age are in the process of developing an understanding as to what can be termed as "wrong" and what can be said to be "right." Lying or other similar behaviour demanding discipline needs to be improved.[60]

---

[60] https://www.hopkinsmedicine.org/health/conditions-anddiseases/lying-and-stealing

Note:

- *A child starts to realize how another individual will feel in a certain situation because of which they will be more capable of trying to understand their viewpoint.*

- *Displays a variety of pro-social abilities, such as being kind and helpful.*

- *Wishes to follow the rules of a game strictly and be "just." At times, this can give rise to conflict within an organized group play setting.*

Remember:

Sometimes, children adopt gender stereotypes from media and begin accepting them. Boys will become soldiers while girls will be teachers is one of the most basic gender stereotypes by children. This is the reason why it is crucial that you be aware of what your child learns from media.[61] Try pointing out those characters or real-life people who prove these stereotypes to be useless.

Cognitive Development

The cognitive development of children at this age enhances greatly. They start understanding the concepts regarding money and its use – how it enables us to buy products. However, some may face problems while counting money.

The way your child thinks may also be affected by their emotions and how they feel. If they're concerned or upset about something, they may struggle to focus on the tasks at hand.

---

[61] https://www.frontiersin.org/articles/10.3389/fpsyg.2018.02435/full

Most 8-year-olds start understanding time and setting limits. If you tell them they have ten more minutes to finish their work or that the family picnic is after two days, they're likely to understand it in a better way now than they did earlier.

Language and Communication

8-year-olds' vocabularies keep developing. Research shows that children at this age learn about 3,000 new words within the year.[62] The vocabularies of those kids who read a lot expand at a faster rate.

At this age, children show their ability to play with words. They even develop verbal humour and begin to understand irony (to mean the opposite of what one says.)

Play

8-year-olds' play may vary from one kid to another. It mainly depends on the activities they've been made familiar with.

While some kids may enjoy playing outside with peers, others may take more interest in indoor activities such as drawing and painting or creating art projects. Kids this age usually love to play, dance, and perform.

Note:

- *Kids learn to pay attention to a task for about an hour or even more.*

- *They begin to see their position in the world.*

- *While doing math, they start learning to work with larger numbers. They also get better at mental math.*

---

[62] https://www.verywellfamily.com/8-year-old-developmentalmilestones-620729

A Useful Parenting Tip

Motivate your child to try and solve their challenges on their own, without any external help. This will help children develop problem-solving abilities.

In case they find themselves in the midst of a challenge, you can encourage them to think of possible ways of handling the situation. Then help them choose the most appropriate strategy.

Remember:

➢ 8-year-olds become increasingly aware of their appearance and how they look. They may start taking an interest in what they wear or how they make their hair.

➢ Kids at this age become more particular about their personal hygiene.

➢ Since their coordination and motor skill development enhance, they actively take part in personal care routines that include taking a shower and brushing teeth.

➢ You may want to make sure that they carry out their little tasks regarding cleaning and washing in a proper manner.

When to Be Worried

Although the development of one child may slightly differ from another kid's development, it is important to focus on your child's progress as closely as possible.

If you notice your child not developing physically, socially, or emotionally the way other kids around his age are, it is better to get in touch with your paediatrician. You can also talk to your child's teacher in case you notice your child struggling to interact with others or grow emotionally.

Moreover, if you see your child behind cognitively, it is recommended to talk to a mental health professional.

Don't forget that the sooner you acknowledge and address the issue, the better it was for your little ones.

Remember:

Watching your child grow up and be independent can be exciting for parents. However, there will be times when sadness would envelop you as you realize how quickly the times are changing. But, it is essential to let your child explore and learn independently as much as possible. This will give them the chance to handle situations on their own and become confident individuals.

Growth and Development of 9year-olds

At this age, children are prepared for a major shift as they find themselves at the tip of adolescence. To some extent, they are still seen as children, but on a closer look, one would observe that they're becoming more independent. They also start handling several basic responsibilities with little adult supervision.

Physical Development

9-year-olds start experiencing several physical as well as emotional changes as they begin to step into the realm of adolescence. It can be a difficult time for some children as different classmates develop at a completely different pace.

For girls, the age of puberty is usually within 8 – 12, while for boys, it is 9 – 14. Being a parent, it is your obligation to talk about these physical and emotional changes with your child. You must also talk to them about their distress (if any). Issues regarding body image may also begin to rise.

The muscle control of 9-year-olds is relatively stronger and easier. This enables them to grow their physical bounds and activities. By this age, they will enjoy their independence more and will be better at managing their personal cleanliness and grooming.

Note:

- *Girls may start showing signs of puberty a bit earlier than boys. Girls mostly exhibit signs during age 8 or 9, as for boys, the age is around 10 or 11 years old.*

- *Children may go through various physical changes, including getting taller or gaining more weight.*

- *By this time, children will be able to remain consistent in physical activity to reach an objective. For instance, while playing a sport or carrying out a physical aptness challenge.*

A Useful Parenting Tip

It is recommended to talk to your child about the changes they are going to experience during the puberty phase. This can prepare them for what is to come, making their transition easier.

Emotional Development

As children grow older, their abilities to handle conflict becomes better. Their developing individuality will allow them to pursue relationships outside of their family. This includes sleepovers at close friends' houses.

Belonging to a social group and having a place within a social structure of the school becomes the centre of their focus. This is the reason why many will become exposed to peer pressure as they want to make an impression on their friends' group.

This is the age when children learn to take on a variety of tasks and responsibilities within the house. They will wish to start taking part in decisions concerning the family.

It wouldn't be wrong to say that 9-year-olds can be epitomes of conflict and contradiction. While children mostly enjoy expanding their social groups, they will still look for comfort within the family if they ever feel uncertain. By age nine, children are still very much under the influence of their parents.

Most children at age nine profit from the liberty to exercise their developing freedom, but at times, they still look for emotional comfort and assurance from their mothers and fathers. Children may also be greatly moody. You may see them displeased one minute and then okay the next.

As kids begin to grow, they become more aware of their surroundings and the events taking place in the world that they are a part of. Incidents such as natural disasters or fires, along with personal fears such as the death of a loved one, may give rise to anxieties and distress.

Note:

- Children at this age insist on having their own way, but at the same time, they are able to listen to logic

- When and if things don't go according to their plan, their behaviour may become unreasonable or even rude. Nonetheless, they'll realize their unjust behaviour and even say sorry.

- Nine-year-olds look for friends to cope with painful emotions but are equally able to depend on their own resources

A Useful Parenting Tip

Children at this age are keen observers who want to know all that is happening around them. If they ask you anything about the events going on in the neighbourhood or the community at large, answer their questions honestly in a language that is appropriate for them. While at it, focus on the positive aspects too and how people are willing to help those in need, particularly the victims of some natural disaster.

Social Development

As friendships begin to take more importance, social skills become integral. At this age, your child should ideally be able to:

- ➢ Realize that friendships can have various levels.

- ➢ Understand how peer pressure has the power of negatively disturbing their emotional and mental health.

A nine-year-old's social world is starting to open up in a manner that was so far not even imagined. Some kids get their own mobile phones and become a part of social media. This gives them the opportunity to explore the internet and do the things that were otherwise unreachable for them, such as online bullying or content that is inappropriate.

It goes without saying that most children at this age have one best friend. In case their best friend is away, they may feel lonely. For a child's development, it is always good if they have a close friend.

Note:

- *Kids at this point learn to communicate their needs as well as wants in ways that are socially acceptable.*

- *They learn to work helpfully towards common goals.*

- *They regularly accept the views and thoughts of other people.*

A Useful Parenting Tip

This is the perfect age to familiarize your kid with the environment. With their improving sense of social awareness, it is advisable to urge them to participate in activities regarding their community's well-being. In this way, they'll contribute greatly to society.

Cognitive Development

From reading books attentively to playing sports, you will notice how they carry out the activities that interest them with great focus and attentiveness. The attention span of a nine-year-old is relatively longer. However, they still shift their interests quite quickly.

Children at age nine usually work cooperatively in groups at school. They work well in a collective project. Working on a topic or doing a task till they absolutely master it is also noticed.

At this point, children begin to face challenges related to academics at school. Those kids who are good at studies excel, but those who lag behind may become frustrated with the classroom's decorum.

In the fourth class, math becomes more complex. They start solving multiplication as well as division problems along with learning geometry and fractions. Making graphs and charts with the help of data and solving word problems while using logical thinking also becomes necessary. By the end of this class, kids will be capable of adding, subtracting fractions. They'll also be aware of different angles, how to measure them, and how to collect, arrange and share figures in reports as well as presentations.

Language and Communication

People, even strangers, easily understand the language spoken by your child at this age. They should ideally be using proper diction and make no grammatical errors while speaking.

Children at age nine are able to read as well as write skillfully. Most of them would also be able to give their opinions using complicated and refined vocabulary as well as the content.

Nine-year-old children are able to write and read skillfully and will be able to express themselves using complex and sophisticated vocabulary and ideas.

By this time, your 9-year-old kid would be able to read books of different genres, including fiction, non-fiction, historical fiction, poems, and even biographies.

Kids at this age are also expected to write different kinds of writings such as essays, answers, fiction, and reports.

Nine-year-olds learn how to research by using different books in the library and by using the internet to write about various topics.

Play

It has been observed that children, at this age, usually prefer to play with peers of the same gender as themselves.[63] At this age, their play may have less pretend-play and more sports-related games or board activities.

Note:

- *Although their attention span increases, their interests may keep changing.*

- *They begin to learn how the world is not divided into black and white, right or wrong. A few situations, events, and even emotions can be grey too, and for this, one needs to be aware of the middle ground.*

- *They show an interest in collecting stuff and acquiring hobbies.*

A Useful Parenting Tip

Introducing children to research tools, including age-appropriate websites and informative magazines, can help children in the long run. Taking your child to a library or a museum so that they learn about art, history and culture is also recommended.

Remember:

Children, like adults, look for some kind of organization in their routine. You might see your child keeping track of their daily activities or having a basic to-do list.

---

[63] https://www.verywellfamily.com/9-year-old-developmentalmilestones-620731

Most kids at the age of nine also enjoy being part of youth groups and school clubs. Organized activities within these groups can allow children to have a sense of structure, and their will to achieve a common goal improves.

When to Be Worried

Although one child's development may slightly differ from another kid's development, it is important to focus on your child's progress as closely as possible.

If you notice your child not developing physically, socially, or emotionally the way other kids around his age are, it is better to get in touch with your paediatrician.

You can also talk to your child's teacher in case you notice your child struggling to interact with others or grow emotionally. Moreover, if you see your child behind cognitively, it is recommended to talk to a mental health professional.

Remember:

Nine-year-olds crave more responsibility than they can handle. It is integral to assign them tasks and give them the opportunity to carry out simple chores themselves.

Make sure to keep an eye on what your kid does while using the internet or who they spend their time with. Keeping an eye on their development must also be your priority. In case of any concerns, get in touch with your child's doctor.

Behavioural Difficulties and Useful Solutions for Your 8 and 9-year-olds

It is fun to be around 8 and 9-year-olds. But, at times, it can be a challenge too. Their refined talents will make it necessary for you to acquire some important sophisticated strategies in order to discipline them. The way you discipline your child today will reflect in their personalities when they grow up. Your disciplining strategies will turn out to be great lessons for them.

Usual Behaviour of a School-Age Kid

Your child can no longer be considered a baby, nor would he be included amongst the big kids. Age 8 and 9 is the period of transition that will be evident through their behaviour.

On the whole, school-age children have a longer attention span. They'll also show patience in case faced with a challenge or minor setback. They'll be able to display longer concentration and focusing on multiple activities.

Their cognitive, as well as physical abilities will be better, allowing them to carry out routine tasks more easily.

This means they'll get less frustrated or show tantrums and will be better at controlling themselves and their emotions. This is the time when kids learn to create a balance between school, social, and home life.

Most school-age children wish for some independence, which is why assigning them household chores or other simple tasks will help them stay focused and capable of carrying out their tasks on their own.

Challenging Behaviour

- Disobedience

- Lying

- Rivalry and brawling against sibling

- Dilly-dallying

- Whining

Basic Challenges

Some of the common challenges that most parents have to deal with regarding their 8 and 9-year-olds include:

- **Defiance:** As children become more independent and verbal, their behaviour of talking back or being defiant can become more challenging too. In school age kids, defiant behaviour is more common. So don't be worried if your child checks your reactions by refusing to see to almost all the tasks you assign to them. Mostly, disobedience is a stage that comes for a little while throughout childhood and then goes for good.

- **Lying:** School-age kids can sometimes lie as well. Some of them adopt this behaviour in an attempt to show themselves in a positive light, i.e., by boasting about something that never really happened. Others lie to try to get themselves out of trouble. In case left unaddressed, lying can surely become a bad habit.

- **Sibling Rivalry:** Children usually adore their younger or older brothers or sisters. However, there will be times when they would treat them as rivals, ready to fight and teach them a lesson. Remember, this is a natural phase of childhood bound to occur.

- **Dawdling:** Another annoying behaviour is dawdling. Sometimes kids take ten minutes to do one simple task, or even longer, which can be extremely frustrating for you as a parent. Maintaining calm is the only way to tackle this challenge.

- **Whining:** Crying or throwing a tantrum can also become vexing. Most parents get frustrated because of their kids' whining.

- **Over-confidence vs. Self-doubt:** Kids at 8 and 9 may swing between sessions of obvious overconfidence and uncertainty, doubting their own abilities. Some may compare themselves to those present around them and might feel they aren't as talented as others are. That's why it is necessary to show your child that they can improve their skills too only with practice and determination.

Discipline Strategies That Work

As discussed earlier, children should be disciplined from an early age. They should be aware of the actions they are not supposed to take and the activities they shouldn't insist on participating in. Although each child is different, the following are some of the disciplining strategies that have the power of doing wonders:

- **Praising Good Behaviour:** Good behaviour that is praised is likely to be repeated by children. When you praise your kid's efforts genuinely, it boosts their self-confidence and encourages them to do the same thing again. *"Great work for folding your clothes!"* or *"Great job preparing for your exam!"* are some of the statements that encourage good behaviour.

- **Placing Your Kid in Time-Out:** Time-out is best even for school-age kids. It can be a good way of cooling off your child's mood or when they refuse to do as you ask.

- **Using Words Cleverly:** A slight modification in the way you speak or the words you choose can change a consequence into an incentive or a valuable prize. Instead of saying, *"You cannot play with your friends right now because your clothes are dirty,"* you could say something like, *"You can play with your friends as soon as you change your clothes."* Then, your kid will understand he can get a reward by making appropriate choices.

- **Providing Rational Consequences:** In case your child does something he isn't supposed to, for instance, refusing to stop using mobile, then use consequences that affect them directly, such as taking away the privilege of meeting friends for the next 24 hours.

- **Natural Consequences:** Letting your child face a consequence naturally is also going to help them in the long run.

- **Creating a Simple Economy System:** Introducing a system where your child earns tokens or snacks for their good behaviour will encourage them to continue this conduct.

- **Preventing Future Problems:** As your child gets older, their school work becomes more challenging, as well as time-consuming. In case they don't understand the work, they may show signs of frustration and annoyance. Children, at this age, try their best not to be known as someone who doesn't understand math. You can help your child manage and handle school work on their own in some of the following ways:

➢ Enable your child to adopt good habits which will be useful for them, especially at school. Build a separate area for homework.

➢ Assign a fixed time for homework.

➢ Keep an eye on your child's learning progress.

Slight concerns can be attended to during afterschool time, either with a teacher or a tutor. Major concerns may lead to some mental health issues, including ADHD or dyslexia.

According to Very well family: "Research shows an authoritative approach to parenting leads to the most successful outcomes in children. Establish high expectations for your child but give plenty of support and warmth."[64]

- **Creating Clear Rules:** When you tell your child the rules that they must follow, you make it known to them what they can and cannot do. Also, tell them politely the consequences that they will face for breaking the rules. These attempts will allow you to become a more respected parent, which is important for making your child grow up to be a mature and accountable adult.

- **Paying Attention:** Kids depend on parents for comfort and safety. One basic way of providing them with assurance and a sense of protection is by giving enough attention. Take out a few minutes each day only for your children. You should give them complete attention as it will nurture the bond you two share.

---

[64] https://www.verywellfamily.com/discipline-strategies-forschool-age-kids-620099

Communication and Speech

Speech that is brief, as well as effective, is way better than communication that keeps going on without reaching anywhere. Lengthy lectures are just going to make your child lose his focus. Therefore, communication should be:

- ➢ Short, simple, and sweet

- ➢ About alternatives, how their bad behaviour could've been avoided

- ➢ About the house rules

- ➢ Healthy and comfortable (your child should

- ➢ feel at ease to share anything with you)

- ➢ Effective and useful for your child

- ➢ Instructive and educational (such as giving instructions)

While conversing with your child, make sure you remain patient and give them the chance to speak too. Through dialogue, you can also resolve various issues, both personal and academic-related. It gives you a chance to understand your child in a better way. Even your kids will find it okay to share their secrets with you, further strengthening the parent-child bond.

Raising Happy and Healthy Children

School-age children are full of energy. Their natures are pure, and they establish some distinct pursuits and skills. In trying to understand your kid's needs, you are, in turn, helping them stay active, healthy, and happy. These tactics can also enable you to inculcate lifetime healthy practices in your child.

Daily Life

Children at age 8 and 9 tend to carry out most of their personal hygiene routines on their own. They are likely to be able to bathe with minimum adult supervision. Children at this age are usually aware of how to brush their teeth. However, they might need a little push or encouragement to do these tasks. In the case of flossing, children may require a little help from adults.

While most school-age kids are quite obedient when it comes to personal hygiene, some may require a little additional support.

Diet & Nutrition

Grade-schoolers are extremely fussy about food in general. Your child who once loved having carrots may now start hating that vegetable. Research shows that these changes in eating habits have less to do with the food itself and more to do with trying to adopt other children's eating patterns.

Studies show that at age 9, boys require about 1,600 and 2,600 calories while girls require about 1,400 and 2,200 calories. This ratio may vary from child to child, depending on their activity level.

To make sure that your child is fit and healthy, here are some ways you can adopt:

- **Stocking houses with healthy foods,** including fruits, fresh vegetables, milk, yoghurt, and cheese, can make it easier for your child to choose healthy food to eat.

- If your child intakes a lot of water, milk, or juice before a meal, chances are their tiny tummies will have no room for solid food. That's why try to **limit fluids before a meal.**

- **Try making mealtimes pleasant** so that they feel like eating in the first place. Also, limiting mealtime conversation to topics that are positive or pleasant also works.

- Make sure you **do not punish your children for not eating.** Food should be enjoyed, and associating it with something negative will just backfire.

- Children usually do not eat a balanced diet every day. If their diet throughout the week is balanced, that should be enough for the child. **Make sure not to force your child to eat if they are not hungry** or if they don't like something in particular.

- Set a good example yourself by **following a healthy eating pattern.**

- **Avoid giving them desserts, sweets, cakes, or snacks with high-calories.**

If you feel your child is not eating well, you can think of giving them a daily vitamin. However, this isn't something that most children need.

Physical Activity

Children require about two times as much physical movement and activity every day as needed by adults. According to the Centers for Disease Control and Prevention, school-age kids get about an hour or even more of physical activity every day. This activity must comprise of aerobic activity, such as playing football, running in the playground, or riding a bicycle. Activities for strengthening muscles are also essential. Playing on the monkey bars or hiking little hills or trees are some activities that are suitable for strengthening their muscles.

Bone-building activities that include running, bouncing, skipping rope, tennis, and basketball, or playing hop-scotch are also important for kids this age. Although gym class, recess, and sports activities are recommended, they alone are not enough. Try to make physical activity an important part of your family life. For instance, going on a walk after dinner, hiking together, exploring new places, and going swimming. Playing with your family and having friendly tournaments/matches is also advisable.

Children learn what they see. If they observe you taking care of your physique and diet, they are sure to follow you in your footsteps.

Inside the House

Most school-age children are excited about taking on some kind of responsibility of their own. Although most kids at this point make their own bed and try to pick up and put away their stuff, they can welcome other chores that are relatively more "adult-like." For instance, being the selected dishwasher emptier or the one in charge of throwing away trash.

Giving children a variety of chores to choose from will also give them a sense of control. Make sure you don't pay them for carrying out these tasks. Doing household chores is a way of contributing to family teamwork. It strengthens the bond between family members and, therefore, shouldn't involve any money. What you can do is appreciate their efforts in helping the family and encourage them to maintain this behaviour.

One great way of teaching children how to value and use money is by giving them an allowance. This can be a weekly allowance. When children begin to manage small amounts of money, they begin to value the importance of saving.

Children at this age also love spending their time with their families. They enjoy playing board games with their parents as well as siblings or watching a movie together. This is the best time to introduce them to new activities and sports so that they get the opportunity to explore new games and learn different rules.

Safety and Health

Teach your children aged 8 and 9 the ways through which they can keep themselves safes, secure and healthy. Although it is important to remain watchful of them, it is good to allow them to make healthy decisions on their own.

When to Visit the Doctor

Healthy children are expected to visit their paediatricians annually for a regular checkup. During these visits, a doctor will examine your kid's growth and development. A doctor is likely to review their diet as well as sleep timetables. They'll measure the kid's height, weight, and blood pressure. Their school performance will be reviewed along with a vision test.

Some of the basic health issues in 8 and 9-yearolds include nosebleeds, constipation, vomiting, diarrhea, earaches, upper respiratory infections, and skin issues such as rashes.

Mental Health

Caring for your child's mental health should also be on top of your list. Mental health problems may begin during the school-age years. Children can become sad or nervous, or they may display symptoms of ADHD.

In case you have concerns regarding the mental or physical health of your child, make sure to get in touch with your child's doctor.

Sleep

The bedtime for children varies from child to child. While some kids can go up staying till 9 pm, others may sleep around 7:30 – 8 pm. In any case, sleep is essential for your child to keep them fresh and active. School-age children should ideally get about 9 to 12 hours of sleep every night.[65]

You would know your child is not getting enough sleep if they:

- ➢ have trouble getting up in the morning

- ➢ face trouble while staying awake throughout the day

- ➢ seem excessively emotional

Creating a bedtime routine for your children gives them a sense of structure. A couple of hours before your child sleeps, make sure to shut off electronics. Urge her to read different books or participate in quiet activities before sleeping.

Safety

Grade school is the best time to enable children to understand to watch out for their own protection.

- **Being street smart:** Teach your child how to crossroads and how to be mindful of the traffic. Tell them what to do if a stranger comes to them or tries to interact. Ensure they know they aren't supposed to walk off with strangers or sit in anyone's car, even if they are told you have sent them.

---

[65] https://www.verywellfamily.com/parenting-advice-forschool-age-kids-620716

- **Teach your child how to deal with an emergency.** They should be aware of how to dial 911 and what to say in case of an emergency.

Accidents are the most common risks your child can face at this stage. The following few strategies can lessen the death or injury risks of your child.

- **Don't get rid of the booster seat even if your little one begs you to do so.** This must be done only when your child is big for his age. The American Academy of Pediatrics (AAP) states that car accidents are the major cause of death amongst children.[66] If your child is not 4 feet, 9 Inches tall, make sure you keep him in a booster seat.

- **Carry out safe play.** Safe playing means providing your child with the necessary equipment required for his activity. For example, if your child is skating, you make sure they are wearing the proper kit with a helmet that fits. Similarly, they must wear knee pads, and mouth guard when playing sports.

Technology

School-age children are usually interested in using the internet. By this time, some of their friends even have mobile phones or other electronic gadgets.

Technology has its pros and cons for children. Make sure you are watchful of what your child watches on the internet. Some of the dangers of using the internet without adult supervision include:

---

[66] https://pediatrics.aappublications.org/content/127/4/e1050

- Presence of online predators

- Video games with mature content

- Junk food advertisements

In the year 2016, the AAP revised the screen time recommendations regarding kids stated by them earlier. While earlier, they endorsed no more than 2 hours each day for school-age children, they now suggest that parents think through the positive as well as negative influences of electronics on kids. Parents are now recommended to use common sense while setting screen-time limits.

Although high-quality programs that are educational can be useful for kids, too much screen time can be damaging. They alert parents not to allow screen time to affect adequate sleep and physical activity.

The computer games that your child wants to play or the movies they want to watch should first be approved by you.

Also, try to find out what your child will have access to at a friend's home. Using parental controls is also important.

Try to establish healthy restrictions on screen time.

Make sure you DON'T:

- Let your kid have a TV inside the bedroom

- Let him play limitless video games

- Allow them too much sedentary activity

Instead:

- Encourage them to spend most of their time playing outside

- Interacting with peers

- Exploring new and fun activities

8 and 9-year-old's World

As children grow older, their school work starts becoming more challenging. During this time, while some kids thrive, others struggle.

In many households, homework is often a big strain. At ages 8 and 9, several students run away from studying, especially while preparing for a spelling test or solving math problems.

Children during this stage are interested in sports and participate in activities even after school. Many also spend their time on their digital gadgets.

Remember: Keep your child mentally as well as physically active as much as possible.

Friends start becoming the centre of attention during this age. You must encourage your child to make friends, meet new peers and socialize. Support them if they want to play with other kids in the playground or want to attend their friend's birthday party.

Bullying can become problematic during these years. It's imperative to speak to your child regarding kindheartedness and respect so that they don't become a bully. It is also vital that you have a word with them regarding how they should react if someone bullies them.

Growth and Development of 10year-olds

By the time children become 10 years old, most of them will begin considering themselves as almost teenagers. However, not all kids think alike. While some children will act more mature and "adult-like," there are some who still remain child-like. Their immaturity would be visible both physically as well as emotionally.

10-year-olds are in the midst of transition. It is a phase of change that can put forward challenges as well as pleasures as children begin to accept the coming of adolescence.

Physical Development

By the time children reach fifth grade, they will notice significant growth spurts. Girls grow at a relatively faster pace than boys. They may find themselves towering above boys of the same age.[67]

On the other hand, most boys at age 10 only begin to show signs of approaching puberty, while others need to wait even for the signs till they turn 11, 12, or even 13. This difference in growth can give rise to distress in several children, either due to growing too fast or not growing fast enough.

Note:

- *10-year-olds show enhanced alertness, promptness, coordination, as well as balance.*

- *They start to show several signs of puberty, including:*

---

[67] http://www.vintagehouse7612.com/prism-tv-tojw/drawingfor-10-year-old-boy-e8b51c

> ➢ Oily skin

> ➢ More sweating

> ➢ Growth of hair in the genital area and also under the arms

- They also see an increase in small muscle coordination.

A Useful Parenting Tip

Don't let the changes in your child make you believe they don't need to go to bed early. Make sure your 10-yearolds are getting ample sleep – between 9 and 10 hours, every night.

Emotional Development

This is the age when children begin to understand who they are and what's their place in the world. Many are getting ready for starting middle or junior high school. They are also preparing to find their way towards new social settings.

Girls usually mature physically at a faster pace and step into puberty before boys do. For them, the move into adolescence can generate a horde of emotions, including; eagerness, doubt, anxiety, and even awkwardness.

By age 10, you'll notice your child having more control over feelings and may see her being skilled enough to handle conflict and negotiate resolutions with peers. Simultaneously, you may notice some instability in her emotions.

One major factor behind the mood swings is the pressure and strain that a usual 10-year-old may be under as she tries her best to handle the physical changes as well as other minute alterations in her life. 10-year-old children may be struggling to carry on with ever-more hard school work, trying to fit in and interact with friends, and handling the physical changes of developing.

Note:

- *10-year-olds have high regard for older youth and even try to imitate them.*

- *They start to question authority and who's in power.*

- *They are more accepting of those beliefs supported and endorsed by parents or family.*

A Useful Parenting Tip

Ensure you teach your child how to handle unpleasant situations or emotions, such as anger, annoyance, dissatisfaction, guilt, nervousness, unhappiness, and boredom.

Social Development

10-year-old girls interact with groups and socialize with circles being an insider as well as an outsider or sometimes being both almost every day. This is also the age when most girls often become possessive of their close friends and may even become jealous of each other.

In contrast, boys of this age have a more straightforward take on friendships. That's because their relationships are usually formed based on similar interests rather than personal feelings.

10-year-olds, both girls and boys, are good at sensing the emotions and feelings of others. They are even aware of reading facial as well as the body language of an individual. At age ten, recognition and appreciation by the fellow group is a crucial step that appears to have a strong influence on the following level of growth.

Poor peer acceptance at this age may give rise to possible behavioural as well as emotional difficulties in adolescence.

Most children at this age are attached to their immediate and extended family. Although, at times, they may quarrel over petty issues with their siblings.

The pressure of peers can play a huge role in most children's social relationships at this age. Children try to fit in too. They'll do this by wearing the right attire, listening to the music popular among peers, or enjoying and abhorring the same things as their friends.

Note:

- *Children at this age often create private codes as well as passwords with their buddies.*

- *They start identifying with people of the same gender as themselves.*

- *They wish to work in groups and start enjoying collective activities.*

A Useful Parenting Tip

Let your child have some sort of privacy with close friends. Having private chats or sharing secret stuff is socially acceptable at this stage. In fact, it can be constructive for your child's vigorous growth.

Cognitive Development

Parents may observe that as their children turn 10, they begin acting, reasoning, and even sounding almost like adults. 10-year-olds are on the tip of adolescence. They acquire appropriate language skills and thinking ability to collect information and articulate effective views and thoughts. It wouldn't be wrong to say that most

10-year-olds can be an enjoyable company at meals or at social gettogethers, who are able to voice their thoughts on presentday events, different books, art, and other related subjects.

For several children, the development stage around 10 years old is filled with knowledge and quick cognitive growth. Learning increases greatly in fifth grade as kids get ready for the middle-school years. In fifth and sixth grades, children start to handle more difficult content in math, as well as reading.

The math for fifth graders include:

> fractions

> multiplication as well as division

> complex geometry concepts

> symmetry of shapes

> using formulas for calculating the area and volume of geometric shapes

They may even begin early algebra. 10-year-olds start practising more mental math abilities. They will be progressively more able to practice logic and mental thinking to crack oral math questions.

As for other subjects, such as history and geography, children will increase their research capabilities while using additional resources, including books from the library or different informative websites found online. Fifth graders are mostly eager to learn. They are delighted not just in collecting their research but are even fascinated by constructing their opinions and having others praise their hard work.

You will notice your 10-year-old moving towards more independence in dealing with school work as well as homework. At this age, they are likely to require less regulation from adults.

Language and Communication

Children's reading skills improve significantly by this age as they start reading and even enjoying lengthier stories and chapters. Concepts such as metaphors, similes, and other literary devices are understood by them. They begin to understand stories and might even comment on their plots and characters. Their capability of thinking rationally becomes more noticeable. They are able to write convincing essays and debate viewpoints and thoughts with more selfconfidence and structure.

Play

Most 10-year-olds enjoy running, riding a bicycle, skating, and playing sports. They like team sports and also single activities.

By this age, children have their favourite sports clubs and players. They'll also be aware of the details of their favourite shows and programs on TV. Their awareness of famous singers and celebrities also increases. Most 10-yearolds enjoy using electronics. Taking pictures with phone cameras and playing video games online is common.

Note:

- *They start learning to use better judgment.*

- *Most children begin exhibiting an interest in pop culture or different sports clubs.*

- *Their attention span increases, allowing them to spend longer periods of time thriving on their favourite activities.*

A Useful Parenting Tip

Make sure you set your kid for educational accomplishment by fostering good study and reading habits.

Assign a fixed time and a selected area for homework. Make rules, for example, no TV or mobile phones during homework time. This will enable your child to become successful.

Remember:

Children at age 10 may also begin to focus more on physical appearance and the way they look or how they dress. They would like to conform with kids their age more than they used to.

Body image concerns can also grow at this stage in a few children— especially girls. You, as a parent, must be a role model to your children when it comes to issues regarding body image. Try not to make any comments against your own body and focus on supporting eating habits that are healthy. You'll notice a great desire for privacy in children at this age. As they are becoming more aware of their bodies, they'll like to change clothes or bathe in privacy. They'll also start focusing on what others wear or how their friends carry themselves.

When to Be Worried

If you see your child getting upset or being in a bad mood temporarily, then that's not an issue. However, if you notice them being aggressive almost all the time, so much so that their relationships are being affected, then it is time that you consult a doctor. Talking to your kid's teacher or doctor in case of behavioural changes such as trouble while eating or sleeping or refusing to go to school is also recommended.

Different children mature physically at different degrees. It's vital to talk regularly about your child's changing body and if they have any concerns. Ensure to focus on the importance of health rather than appearance.

Remember:

If you are concerned that your kid is not growing as they should, remind yourself that this is the time of change for your 10-year-old. There isn't a fixed place as to where your child should be at this age. Although some children will find it amusing playing with dolls or reading their younger siblings' books, others will be more interested in makeup or sports. All this is fine and perfectly natural.

In case you are still worried that your child Is falling behind, talk to your paediatrician. Your child's doctor will be best qualified to evaluate your kid's growth.

Growth and Development of 11year-olds

Before you know it, your child enters his/her tween years. With this change, several prospects, as well as challenges, arise for parents. Spending time with your 11year-old can be fun since they're beginning to comprehend the world they live in and communicate like tiny adults.

But the power and the fuss of a teen-to-be— particularly for girls—can be somewhat exasperating and demanding for a parent to control. This could either be due to the confusion arising from complex social dynamics at school and the emerging bodily changes.

Physical Development

You can expect noticeable physical changes in your child at this point. Girls, by this time, have already experienced puberty, while for boys, the changes are now bound to occur, i.e., around age 11-12.

Physical Changes in Girls at Age 11-12	Physical Changes in Boys at Age 11-12
• enlarged body fat	• larger muscles
• the start of breast enlargement	• oilier skin and hair
• first menstrual period	• vocal changes
• growth of pubic hair	• the starting of underarm
• widening hips	• growth of facial and pubic hair
• oilier hair and skin	• testicle and penis growth
• growth of underarm hair	• darkening scrotum

You may notice some physical awkwardness as tweens begin to grow and become comfortable in their new bodies.

Note:

- *Tweens begin to show visible signs of puberty.*

- *They also display better-quality handwriting and a developed capability of using various tools.*

- *Keeping in mind their growth spurt and the pains and cramps that follow, it is important that they sleep and eat more and healthily.*

A Useful Parenting Tip

Since your child's sweat glands are starting to get activated, you might smell unanticipated odours. This is the reason why keeping them aware of the significance of bathing and using deodorants is recommended.

Emotional Development

Prepare yourself for a crazy ride with the moods of your 11-year-old. As your child runs into puberty, anticipate irritability and mood swings.

Although most 11-year-olds are still accepting of family beliefs and identify adults as authoritative individuals, this is also when they start to question that power. Some might get introduced to detrimental habits, including smoking or drinking for the first time.

Note:

- *Their ability to make better decisions develops.*

- *They start to question authoritative individuals.*

- *Most begin to refrain from physical fondness from parents.*

A Useful Parenting Tip

Despite 11-year-olds' desire to socialize and spend time with friends, they have still not resisted the notion of "family time." This is the reason why they participate in family events, including going to church or dining out with grandparents.

Social Development

Although this isn't the first time your child is talking to his friends or interacting with them, this is the time when friendship becomes essential for them. The notion of a "group identity" becomes active, and close groups can appear. Peer pressure begins to affect your child, making them do the things they wouldn't have done otherwise.

Note:

- *The begin to create strong as well as meaningful friendships.*

- *Children at this point start taking more interest in*

- *friends rather than in family.*

- *They explore their own identities through clothing, activities, and friends.*

A Useful Parenting Tip

Because of their friends' influence, children might start testing your restrictions and might even try to bend the rules. Use this for your own good. Make it clear that getting good grades and avoiding drugs and cigarettes is compulsory. As for choosing what to wear or how to style their hair, give them some freedom.

Cognitive Development

Earlier, it was difficult for children to think about the consequences of their decisions in the long run, but now, they are becoming more aware of it. They also begin to understand the complexities of situations and emotions. Not everything can be divided into black or white; there are grey areas too.

Language and Communication

The speech issues that children faced earlier are, by this time, mostly resolved. Some children do struggle with the "r" sound. For that, you can register for therapy regarding speech to fix problems.

Play

At this age, children begin moving past their earlier playdates habits. They are now more interested in staying at friends' homes or going out to the movies. They continue to participate in sports.

Note:

- *They start to realize that thoughts are personal.*

- *They begin experiencing a better sense of accountability.*

- *Children show an improved attention span but can also display rapid changes of likes/dislikes.*

Remember:

Most 11-year-olds start going through brain changes. This will allow them to transition into becoming more selfgoverning. However, their frontal cortex is still developing, and their need for approval can give rise to increased risktaking conduct. You might notice your child making poor decisions at times. Don't ignore that completely. Use them as examples and teach how better decisions could have been made. Motivate them to think before they act.

When to Be Worried

All kids grow at somewhat different paces. Sometimes, children who are a little behind will eventually get closer to their peers. Don't worry if your child is not displaying typical tween behaviour. As for puberty, if it doesn't occur by the age of 14, then it is time to consult a doctor. You can also consult a doctor if you feel your tween may fall into some injurious pattern of behaviour.

An Advice

Don't forget that no two children will act, think, live, or feel in the same manner. All children are different and grow at different paces. Some children, who lack social or interactive skills and haven't matured emotionally yet, may struggle with isolation, loneliness, or separation.

It's imperative to help your child hone their talents when (and if) you notice shortfalls. Moreover, if you're worried about possible growth delays, get in touch with your child's paediatrician. It's essential to tackle any issue now before it gets too late.

Chapter 11

Child Development Age group 12 – 15

Growth and Development of 12year-olds

As the tween years begin, your child starts to grow taller with each passing day and transforms into a full-grown teenager. Luckily, the social, physical, and emotional changes that your child encounters at this stage happen gradually, giving you enough time to prepare for what lies ahead.

Generally, kids at this age may go from behaving like a kid you are familiar with to being a sensible, mature individual. This is the time for you to know what to expect from your child in terms of their physical, emotional, cognitive, and social growth.

Physical Development

This age is precisely in the middle of the phase when young girls start puberty. This age is also at the starting of the usual age at which a boy begins experiencing the process.[68]

In young girls, you will observe the following physical changes:

- ➢ breast development
- ➢ hair growth
- ➢ menstruation

In boys, the following changes will take place:

- ➢ the penis and testicles get bigger

- ➢ hair growth in the pubic area

- ➢ hair growth in underarms

- ➢ facial hair growth

- ➢ the voice deepens

- ➢ muscle growth

Note:

- Children at this age start to show signs of puberty. While girls go through menstruation, boys experience muscle growth.

- They become more and more trained in sports.

- They experience a development spurt.

---

[68] https://www.healthychildren.org/English/agesstages/teen/Pages/Stages-of-Adolescence.aspx

A Useful Parenting Tip

Ignoring your tween's budding sexuality is not the right thing to do. Although it might be a little hard for you, talking about your child's growing sexuality and the changes they may experience from that point onwards will help in preparing them for what lies ahead. In case you're not sure how to bring up this topic, talk to your child's doctor.

Emotional Development

Your tween's emotions shouldn't be taken lightly. Chances are, you will come across your child's wild emotional changes within this and the following year. Although they love their parents, they might not want to interact with them a great deal. They feel triumphant and then feel as if they have failed at everything. There will be instants of cheerfulness, episodes of sadness, which will only repeat from time to time.

At this age, individuals begin to discover their leadership qualities. They even start to recognize the notion of being generous to the community they are a part of. Boost these talents by encouraging them to take part in supervisory processes in the home first and by favouring participation in community or school happenings.

Note:

- *They begin to display a stubborn streak.*

- *They try to take their freedom from their parents; nonetheless, they often want adult support.*

- *Questioning family values and evolving personal morals are also a few changes that can be noticed.*

A Useful Parenting Tip

By maintaining house rules and keeping your child safe, create a balance between freedom and management. Talk regularly about the things your tween would like to do on their own and constantly make settlements when it feels suitable.

Social Development

At this age, your tween's friends are more significant than ever. However, people of the opposite gender are gaining importance as well. Your child believes it is essential to belong. This often means gaining liberty from parents as well as other members of the family. However, this gives rise to the risk of peer pressure.

Note:

- *You may notice your child displaying concerns regarding being adored and accepted.*

- *They may show interest in events, including those of the opposite gender.*

- *They start to acknowledge other people's perspectives.*

A Useful Parenting Tip

Make sure you let your child know that they can always come up to you to talk regarding all their concerns and queries. Your tween may experience a certain situation they are not prepared for or are unaware as to how to deal with, together with the struggles of peer pressure and growing up. Although your child is maturing up, they would still want to know they have their parents' support.

Cognitive Development

Although your tween's brain has ceased to grow in size, it is still not done developing. The following tasks become easier for your child:

- ➢ Problem-solving

- ➢ Abstract thinking

- ➢ Logic and judgment

Nonetheless, their organizational skills, as well as impulse control, are still immature.

Language and Communication

12-year-olds have strong control of language, and their communication skills continue to improve. Now, they will be better able to understand proverbs, idioms, and expressions. They'll also be able to comprehend sarcasm, the tone of your voice, and whether to interpret everything literally or not.

Play

Children at this age engage in:

- ➢ Organized sports

- ➢ Activities with friends

- ➢ Video games

Make sure you are aware of how many hours your child spends in front of the screen. Also, try to encourage them to participate in active sports. Discuss how it will benefit them.

Note:

- *Tweens begin to comprehend the consequences of their actions.*

- *They begin applying reason to circumstances and problems.*

- *The concepts such as justice and equality are understood by them.*

A Useful Parenting Tip

Staying in touch with your child's teachers (but not too much) and remaining active in your child's academic life is recommended. Make sure you don't wait till the end of their academic session. Becoming aware of your child's academic progress only when they come home with the report card is not enough. If your child is facing difficulty while studying, try to resolve it without getting upset or infuriated.

Remember:

Tweens begin to discover the standards of their social group. If your tween announces they want to take on a new way of living or perhaps explore a new religion, probably that of their friend's, don't be surprised.

Discovering morality is an ordinary phase of the growth process. Although it is essential that you explain your morals and the beliefs and rules of your household, do not worry if your child says they disagree with your beliefs.

When to Be Worried

Physical and emotional changes do not always occur at the same time. If you notice your child is emotionally not ready for the activities that other children of his/her age are, do not worry.

Stay mindful of your tween's emotional state of mind, and always be aware of any lingering mental health issues, including depression, that can occur at this stage. Although a little moodiness at this point is understandable, if you notice severe concerns regarding your tween's mental or physical well-being, get in touch with their doctor. You must also contact a doctor if you notice your child lagging in academic life. This includes their failure to keep up in class.

Important Advice

Ensure that your child acquires the talents he/she is going to need to flourish during their teenage years. In case they do not possess suitable social skills, you'll see them struggle as they step into high school. Keep looking for areas where your child might require help in improving their abilities. Provide additional backing by educating, supervising, and practising together. In case your encouragement doesn't have an influence, reflect on looking for professional help.

Disciplining and Handling Challenges with Tweens

As children tread on the path of becoming tweens, they've outgrown some of the disciplining tactics that were effective earlier, i.e., when they were younger. Moreover, the conducts that need to discipline are more likely to shift as well when children grow. It's vital to address problems regarding behaviour with active discipline stratagems that will enable your tween to acquire the talents they're going to require to succeed during the teen years.

Usual Behaviour

Your child, who once used to baby talk and showed tiny, short-lived tantrums, may now begin to talk back and show signs of sulking. This is a part of their natural growth progress. 12-year-olds struggle with various issues. These include hormonal and physical changes, peer pressure, and academic workload.

Some other usual habits that tweens display include:

- Spending greater time with friends, instead of the family.

- Becoming increasingly self-conscious. A child may feel a sense of insecurity seeing their peers developing faster. Some may feel embarrassed for growing earlier than their friends.

- Managing academic work. While some students may thrive in academics, others may struggle.

- It's common for 12-year-olds to struggle with a push and pull association with self-esteem. You might hear them say, *"I am the best,"* one minute, only to say, *"Everyone dislikes me"* the next minute.

- One main reason behind this uncertainty is the budding interest in how others observe them. You'll notice your tweens worry about how their peers view them. They may also worry about what other students think about them.

Basic Challenges

Some of the basic challenges you'll notice in your tweens include trying to act cool, attempting to fit in, and showing themselves as fully grown individuals. For this reason, many may even start using foul language, along with cursing, only to impress others, particularly their peers, and act all grown-up.

They may also become annoyed over apparently small things. A quarrel with a friend, bad test grade, or coming home to a not-so-favourite cooked meal may trigger their anger. This frustration may lead to shouting, grumbling, or banging doors.

At this age, you'll notice your tween displaying an attitude that suggests they know everything. Although their problem-solving abilities begin improving, they start believing that they can do all the tasks on their own now.

So don't be shocked if your kid keeps repeating, *"I know! I know,"* every time you remind them to finish their school work or brush before going to bed at night.

Your 12-year-olds may start looking for gaps in your rules too. If you tell them, *"No mobile after dinner,"* they might end up delaying dinner to increase their screen time.

Effective Discipline Tactics That Work

It's imperative to ensure your discipline approaches are in accordance with your child's requirements. In case your child breaks any pre-established rule or misbehaves, make sure you use discipline strategies. This will allow them to make healthier choices in the future. Some of the most useful discipline strategies for children at this age include:

- **Taking away privileges**. House rules are established for a reason. In case those rules are not followed, then punishment in the form of taking away privileges becomes mandatory. If you see your child misbehaving, remove an important privilege. Taking away electronics for the next few hours or refusing to allow them to go see their friends over the weekend always work. Taking away these privileges temporarily asserts the fact that you are still in power. It also makes it clear that privileges need to be earned.

- **Rewarding and appreciating good behaviour**. A basic reward system can be essential in helping your tween stay on the right track. Giving them an allowance for carrying out their chores or allowing them to invite a friend over for movies only if they finish their homework on time can also do wonders. You can also build a token economy system. This will help them run through new behaviours.

- **Creating a behaviour contract.** A contract based on behaviour summarizes what tweens must do to earn as well as keep additional privileges. For instance, if they want a cellphone or want to go out, watch a movie with a friend, explain how they could display that they're ready for these changes through their behaviours. Write down the behaviours you'd need to see from them, such as getting their chores done on time and putting away their other electronics without arguing.

- **Participate in problem-solving**. Instead of telling your tween what to do, try and engage with them while they solve problems. Highlight an issue they are facing currently, and give them possible scenarios that will help them solve those problems.

- **Natural consequences**. Letting your child face a consequence naturally is also going to help them in the long run. If they forget to take their sports gear to school, let it be. This is how they're going to learn and be responsible.

Avoiding Problems in Future

A few basic strategies can go a long way in stopping behaviour problems before they even begin. Following are some of the ways that help you can inspire good behaviour from your child.

- **Don't put labels on your child**. Putting labels on your tweens such as "the studious one" or "my athletic child" is not recommended. We all know negative labels are harmful to children but did you know that even the positive ones can be destructive and misleading for children. As children begin to grow, their interests may shift too. A kid who was crazy about arts and crafts might not be interested in the same hobby anymore. These labels might stop them from doing what they actually like.

- **Explain what you expect from your tweens beforehand**. Several issues can be avoided if you tell your children how you expect them to behave. Before dropping them at a friend's house or taking them to a library, make sure you explain how they are supposed to behave. Also, make clear what you expect them to do in case they encounter any problem.

- **Tell them the primary reasons behind your rules**. When kids are told the reason why a certain rule is made, they are more likely to obey it. Tell them the reasons why they need to eat healthy food or how it is going to benefit them. This will enable them to understand why they need to make good choices, even when you aren't around.

- **Observe your tween's everyday activities**. It is true that your tween will want a lot of independence but, at this age, they do not have the appropriate skills needed to make decisions regarding life's challenges. This is the reason why it is essential to observe their day-to-day activities. You, as a parent, must know who your kid's friends are and who do they generally hang out with. You must also be aware of what they do online.

- **Giving your tweens some liberty**. Make sure not to turn into a parent whose sole purpose is to pry into the lives of their kids. Giving your children a wee bit of freedom and allowing them to make small decisions on their own, without your interference, is good for their confidence. This will also help them hone their problem-solving skills.

- **Teaching anger management skills**. You will notice that several issues regarding your tween's behaviour arise due to anger or frustration. This is the reason why you must effectively teach your child what to do or how to react when angry due to a sudden change of plan or for losing a soccer match.

- **Show them that privileges need to be earned**. Your tween's privileges include activities such as watching TV, using a tablet, or visiting a friend. Allowing your child these privileges only when they behave maturely is advised.

- **Being the role model**. What you do and how you act are essential in your child's upbringing. They live with you and surely learn from you a great deal. This learning is not limited to a few hours per day. Rather, it is an ongoing process. This is the reason why it is important to make sure that you yourself are setting a good example. Adopt ways and mannerisms that you'd want to see in your children. Remember, they'll learn what they see.

Communication Guidelines

It isn't easy to communicate with a tween. You may notice them talking a lot sometimes while at other times, they'll hardly say a few words. Following are some effective strategies that will help you build a special bond between yourself and your child:

- **Remind your children of household rules without distressing**. It is important to make clear the rules that your child must follow. However, don't go overboard while explaining them. Moreover, constantly talking about these rules may also irritate them. It's also vital to always address matters such as these with gentleness and respect.

- **Listening to your child's view**. Listening to an individual speak and taking into consideration what they say is a way of showing that their voice matters.

- It also shows that people around them are willing to listen. When you begin to value their opinions, they become more confident to speak. Their critical thinking skills are enhanced too.

- **Asking open-ended questions for discussions**. Asking questions regarding different fictional characters of books or movies, discussing various topics, talking about your child's friends and their associations will allow you to know your child in a better way. Talk to them about the decisions they make, the choices they opt for, and the reason behind them to understand your child's views that might be different from yours.

- **Talking about gaining more liberty**. You can talk about how your children can get more freedom. That is, if they continue to do their tasks without anyone reminding them to do so, you'll be able to trust them more and will be more likely to give them independence.

- **Listening to what your tween has to say about the set rules.** Allow children to speak about all their concerns (if any). Talk to them about the rules. Try to find out if they are comfortable with them. Allow them to answer honestly, without any worry.

Tween Parenting Tips for 12Year-Olds

This is the time of transition. Tweens are not young enough to be considered little kids, neither are they old enough to be called adults or teenagers. This is the reason why one tween may vary from the other in terms of their maturity level.

For these reasons, it is the best time to teach children the skills which they are going to need to thrive in life.

Everyday Life

Most tweens are usually independent. They are not only aware of taking care of their hygiene on their own but can also carry out their chores with few reminders. Most children at this age complete their homework too. However, some children may need additional support. If you notice that your child is not as independent as other kids his/her age are, it is important that you help them be more responsible. The moment they gain enough confidence to take charge of their life, they'll begin to grow into healthy individuals.

Food and Nutrition

The overall health of your child depends on their nutrition. Appropriate nutrition must include eating three meals each day along with two nutritious snacks.

Make sure you restrict high sugar as well as high-fat foods. Persuade your tween to eat as many fruits, vegetables, lean meats, and dairy products with low fat as possible. A diet that is healthy is vital to enable your child to grow physically to their maximum potential.

It's natural for 12-year-olds to go through variations as far as their appetite is concerned. In most cases, growth spurts can eventually lead to an escalation in appetite. The top nutrition advice in order to keep your child fit includes motivating them to:

- Eat a whole lot of different foods

- Balance the food they consume with regular physical activity

- Eat enough grain products, fruits, and vegetables

- Choosing foods that are low in fat, saturated fat, as well as cholesterol is advisable

- Sugar and salt intake must be moderate

- Enough calcium and iron must be consumed to satisfy their developing body's needs

Store the kitchen with meals, desserts, and snacks that are low in calories and fat. Make sure your child only drinks low-fat milk. Moreover, try your best to keep highcalorie chips, drinks, and other snacks out of the house as much as you can.

Put in the extra effort of making mealtimes fun where the whole family sits and eats together. Arguing about issues regarding academics or behaviour during mealtimes is not advisable. Make sure to keep the conversation as pleasant as you can.

If your tween doesn't want to eat anything, let it go. Don't force them to eat. Offer meals; if your child is hungry, he/she will eat on their own. You don't have to cook a separate dish for your tween if he doesn't want to eat what you're providing.

Never use food as a means to bribe your tween. If your child is a picky eater, don't make a fuss about it. You'll be making matters worse by focusing too much on it.

For moderately active 12-year-old boys, the advised calories are 2,200 calories per day. As for girls the same age, the recommended calories are 2,000 calories each day. The term moderately active applies to those tweens who take part in at least 1 hour of physical activity five days per week. Those who are less active should ideally intake lesser calories. At the same time, those who are more active may require more calories.

Physical Activity

One hour of physical activity per day is recommended for tweens. Because most of the tweens do not have recess anymore, it becomes essential to ensure you are focusing on physical fitness at home.

Some of the basic physical activities include:

- Aerobic activities that constitute of riding a bike, playing sports, and jogging. These activities are mostly enjoyed by tweens.

- Activities that strengthen muscles. This may include strengthening exercises and lifting weights.

- Bone-building activities comprise of running, skipping rope, and playing basketball.

- Playing catch, kicking a ball, going through an obstacle course are some other physical activities that help in keeping your child active.

- Going on a walk in the morning, arranging a friendly match with family members or friends, or going for bike rides during weekends are also good ways of keeping your tween physically fit and active.

Incorporate healthy living into your lifestyle and make it an important part of your family. If your tween grows up to see his/her parents being mindful of what they eat and whether or not they exercise will automatically affect them too. Be a good role model and adopt a healthy lifestyle culture so that your tween grows up to be the same.

You may also notice body image issues rising during the tween years. This is why it is imperative to emphasize on exercising to stay fit and build strong bones instead of losing weight or looking better.

Inside the House

Spending time with friends and socializing amongst peer groups is what tweens enjoy the most. Although they still take an interest in family matters and events, chances are they'll prefer to hang out with friends (in case they call and suggest meeting up) than be a part of a family gathering.

Still, this, in no way, means that you avoid your special family weekend nights. It goes without saying that your tween will love spending time with you. Playing board games with them, taking part in physical activities together, or going to new places will contribute to making the parentchild bond strengthen.

At times, you may notice your tween becoming disrespectful, and you may realize they need disciplining. You'll notice them trying to assert their independence or show how they are aware of everything, implying they do not need anyone's help. The best way to deal with a situation such as this is to give them appropriate options to choose from. For instance, *"Do you want to finish your homework before or after mealtime?"* Here, both the options are favourable.

Tweens should ideally possess the talents to do most of the household chores. In case you allow your child to do the cleaning that requires household chemicals or if you allow them to cook, ensure that you are mindful of covering the safety precautions. The basic and suitable chores may comprise mopping floors, cleaning windows and bathrooms, vacuuming, and emptying dishwashers. Making a chore chart is also a smart way of reminding your child of the chores they are expected to carry out.

Offering incentives or little treats when they behave responsibly is also advised.

Fitness, Safety, and Security

By this time, your child may be able to stay alone at home for short time periods. But before considering your child to stay at home by themselves, make sure you are aware of the local or state laws.

But not all children may feel comfortable without an adult at home. This is the reason why you must make sure that your tween is ready for the experience or not.

Tweens are old enough to understand basic first aid. So teach them this important lesson. Prepare them to handle basic injuries such as a cut on hand or foot. Teach them how to use different things present in your first aid kit. The local hospital in your locality may also offer short courses to prepare tweens as well as teens as to how to use first aid or CPR. Try and take a class with your child so that your tween may get prepared or knows what to do in case of an emergency.

Safety

Accidents are the most common risk your child can face at this stage. The following few strategies can lessen the death or injury risks of your tween.

- **Keeping your tween in a booster seat if you deem it necessary**. Older school-age children should ideally sit in a belt-positioning booster seat as soon as they reach the height and weight harness strap limits of their car seat that is facing forward. According to the American Academy of Pediatrics (AAP), car accidents are the major cause of death amongst children. If your child is not 4 feet, 9 inches tall, and between age 8 and 12, make sure they do not use an adult seatbelt.[69]

- **Do not let your tween sit in a pickup truck**. A pickup truck's cargo area is not secure for tweens who are younger than 13. Do not let them ride these trucks, even if they are enclosed. That's because, in an accident, kids in the back of a pickup truck are hardly protected from serious injury or death.

- **How to ride a bicycle and what measures to take**? Don't allow your child to ride a bicycle without wearing a helmet. Teaching safety rules with regards to traffic, footpaths, and intersections is also advised.

- **Apply food safety**. Teach children to eat fruits and vegetables that are washed properly and cleaned. Teach them not to eat

---

[69]http://thewhitterinstitute.com/tween-parenting-tips-for-10-11-and-12-year-olds/

meat or poultry that is undercooked or drink milk that is unpasteurized.

- **Persist on safety equipment.** Teaching your tween to wear the suitable safety equipment such as helmets, pads, mouth guards required for the sport they are participating in is essential.

- **Set up smoke and carbon monoxide detectors**. Make sure you have a preplanned escape plan ready. In case of a fire in your home, make sure to use flame-retardant sleepwear. Teaching your tween about fire safety, such as not to play with matches or lighters, is also integral.

- **Locking away firearms (if any)**. Think about removing firearms from the house if you have a tween. If keeping a gun is vital, make sure it is unloaded. Try to lock it away in a safe place. Moreover, talk to your child about gun safety.

- **How to deal with an emergency.** They should be aware of how to dial 911 and what to say in case of an emergency.

It's also significant to talk to your tween about the various social issues regarding alcohol, sex, and drugs. Although you may think your child would never be a part of such adult activity, the chances are that some of their peers are already.

It is vital for tweens to understand how to handle peer pressure and identify dangers when they come across them.

When to Visit the Doctor

Healthy tweens are expected to visit their paediatricians annually for a regular checkup. During these visits, a doctor will examine your kid's growth and development. A doctor is likely to review their diet as well as sleep timetables. They'll measure the kid's height, weight, and blood pressure. Their school performance will be reviewed along with a vision test. The doctor will also counsel them on how to prevent injury. Counselling regarding a proper diet and dental health can also be carried out.

Doctors may also check for immunizations: Tdap (tetanus booster), HPV vaccine (boys and girls), and Meningococcal vaccine (Menactra or Menveo).

Tweens may have to see a doctor in case of any issues related to puberty. Some tweens may face acne once puberty hits them.

Note: Some of the basic health issues that tweens face at this age include respiratory infections as well as constipation. Some tweens may also experience gynecomastia – enlargement of breast tissue in boys. Although the breast lump is visible to the individual, its presence is normal and mostly disappears within the following few months. Other issues involve injuries due to sports or physical activities, including broken bones, sprains, or bruises.

Sleep

The American Academy of Pediatrics endorses that tweens get about 9 to 12 hours of sleep every night. However, it is possible that some tweens may sleep less than the recommended time.[70] At this age, homework, friends, family, physical activities, and electronics usually take much of the time of your tweens. If they take up the time of your tween's sleeping hours, sleep deprivation is bound to take its toll.

---

[70]http://thewhitterinstitute.com/tween-parenting-tips-for-10-11-and-12-year-olds/

To make sure your tween is getting enough time to sleep, keep an eye on how much sleep they are actually getting. Once you figure that out, you can adjust their schedule.

Winding down before going to bed is also important for your tween. To wind down, your child can read, listen to his/her favourite music or take a hot, relaxing shower before hitting the bed.

If your child has trouble waking up in the morning or if they have difficulty staying awake throughout the day, it may suggest that they're not sleeping enough.

Using Technology

Although most tweens adore using electronics, it does not mean they should be allowed to do so without adult supervision. Most children at this age are aware of using social media and the internet as they have their own smartphones.

We cannot deny the fact that we can have access to several informative, useful and educational websites through the internet. But while the internet has its pros, it also has its cons. And particularly for tweens, it can impact negatively. From online predators and cyberbullies to online harassers, the dark online world can be unsafe for young minds.

Tweens who use the internet without an adult's supervision are likely to encounter adult content online.

Sexting can also be a problem during these years. While some tweens may ask someone to show them unsuitable photographs of someone else, others may be the ones sending them.

This is the reason it is recommended to create clear rules which will defend your tween's confidentiality. Make sure they know they aren't supposed to share their home address or location with anyone.

They shouldn't share the social security number or the numbers or names of their family members.

If you let your child use social media, pick a nickname different from their actual name. Make sure you go through the social media site and see the possible risks and uses before you let your tween join.

Teach your child how they're supposed to respond in case they receive an inappropriate message or see an offensive post or picture. Urge them to be open about it to you.

Ensure that your tween uses their electronics in the presence of other family members. Try to keep an eye on their phone's screen every now and then and see what they're up to. Using parental controls to make sure your tween can only have access to kid-friendly content is also important.

The World of Your Tween

For tweens, middle school can be a little difficult. Although they really want to fit in, sometimes they aren't sure as to how to do that. The academic challenges of middle school increase too. Even those tweens who haven't had any difficulties regarding academics earlier may begin to struggle with studies now.

Additional activities can enable your child to make new friends, become confident, and acquire interests. Motivate your tween's interests. Don't be astonished if they move from one interest to another often. Remember, this is the age when tweens are trying to explore their personalities. Be tolerant as your child decides through different possibilities and motivate them to seek out fresh experiences.

During these years, bullying can be a huge issue too. However, they may not disclose to you that they've been bullied mainly due to embarrassment. This is the reason why you must talk about bullying to your child and allow them to be open to you. Avoid asking direct questions such as *"Have you been bullied at school?"* instead, ask questions such as *"Is bullying common at your school?"* You may notice them talking about bullying more generally at first.

It is also important that you keep an eye on whether your child bullies others or not. Although you, as a parent, would never think your child would ever do anything like that, the truth could be different.

"…almost half of all tweens admit they have bullied another child at one time or another,"[71]

– The Whitter's Institute.

As tweens begin to grow, they become more aware of their surroundings and the events taking place in the world that they are a part of. Incidents such as natural disasters or fires, along with personal fears such as the death of a loved one, may give rise to anxieties and distress.

You do not necessarily want your tweens to sit and watch the news with you. However, you can talk to them about these topics. You can also talk about ways through which they can be responsible citizens.

Effective Tips

Since most children at this age begin experiencing puberty, some tweens may feel scared or even confused. This is the reason why it is

---

[71] http://thewhitterinstitute.com/tween-parenting-tips-for-1011-and-12-year-olds/

important to have a dialogue with your child. Make them feel comfortable to talk to you openly about their concerns (if any).

In case you do not know the answer to a particular question, feel free to inform them that you need to do a little bit of research first. Talking to your tween about their puberty and sexuality will allow them to ask questions more comfortably.

Some tweens may begin displaying interest in romantic relationships. Some may even start looking forward to dating as well. Try to hold as many conversations about strong relationships as you can. Talking about sexual activity at this point can also be thought of.

Growth and Development of 13year-olds

You will notice a whole lot of changes when your child moves from being a kid aged 12 to an adolescent aged 13. As kids start to see themselves as teenagers and the physical changes they experience, they undergo a mental shift. Early adolescence can be an exciting time for 13-yearolds.

Most 13-year-olds become sensitive while experiencing bodily changes. They also begin to notice the changes in their friends. Some may even begin to worry that they aren't growing the way their peers are. They may even have concerns as to why they haven't hit a growth spurt till now.

It can be a little difficult to handle your teens' concerns as most of their issues aren't really practical. But for them, they are crucial. Comfort your teen that everyone matures at slightly different rates. Tell them it's natural for some teens to grow quicker than others.

Physical Development

Most 13-year-olds are handling the emotional as well as physical changes that come with puberty. If your teen feels uncertain, sensitive, or moody, don't be surprised. Most teens at this age undergo these mood swings and can even be self-conscious sometimes. For them, it becomes more vital to fit in with their friends.

Boys who grow physically the earliest are mostly more confident. However, girls who mature the earliest tend to be more unsure and even insecure about their bodies. They not only grow taller but also gain weight. It is during middle adolescence when girls fully develop physically. While in the case of boys, they fully develop physically by late adolescence.

Their quickly changing physical look can result in self-conscious thoughts. It is common for teens to struggle with issues regarding being overweight or acne. Other body image issues, including eating disorders, may also come to the forefront during these years.

Note:

- *Teens at this point undergo quick physical changes.*

- *These changes can vary from one teen to another. This, however, can make young people anxious.*

- *They tend to display a wide range of patterns regarding growth between genders.*

A Useful Parenting Tip

Talking about body image with your teen and how they feel about their undergoing bodily changes is essential.

Emotional Development

Because 13-year-olds are undergoing hormonal shifts, they can experience mood swings. Moreover, peer pressure and school stress issues add to their moods, going from good to bad and then the other way around in minutes.

Young teens are beginning on the path to becoming free young adults who have a say regarding their likes, choices, bodies, and so on. You'll notice them needing a space for private conversations with friends.

13-year-olds usually feel as if the world rotates around them. Some might believe others are staring at them or may think everyone else's behaviour is in some way due to them.

Most teens at this age face great variations in their self-esteem. For them to feel good about themselves one day and feel worthless the next day is quite common.

Although teens claim they want to do everything on their own, you may find them seeking adult affirmation.

Note:

- *Teens are anxious about physical growth and how they look.*

- *They see themselves at the centre of everything.*

- *Although they attempt to get liberty, they still want an adult's approval.*

A Useful Parenting Tip

Although mood swings are normal, it is vital to stay aware of your teen's mental health problems (if any). These issues may include anxiety, depression, or other common health issues for this age group.

Social Development

Desiring more freedom from parents eventually makes 13-year-olds depend more on friendships. They open their hearts to their peers more and wish to spend less time with family and more time with friends.

Because teens want to have a sense of belonging, peer pressure can be a problem at this age. As teens grow up and their interests shift, so will their peer groups.

Unruly behaviour is sometimes normal for the teens of this age group. Teens may also cultivate changed personas or experience various phases. Some teens try to surprise their parents and dress differently.

Dating as well as romantic relationships mostly become central during the early teen years. It's standard for them to cultivate sexual interests as well.

Note:

- *They search for trust as well as approval from their friends.*

- *They may reject resolutions proposed by parents.*

A Useful Parenting Tip

It is better to talk to your teen directly regarding topics such as smoking, drinking, sex, and drugs. To believe whatever you say about these topics, acknowledge how teens can be tempted by these activities, and then tell them the consequences.

Cognitive Development

Although 13-year-olds are good at problem-solving, they may face difficulty while thinking about the future. They may also notice their behaviour and think about its consequences before they act. This is because of the fact that various parts of the brain develop at different rates.

Most 13-year-olds tend to believe they are safe from everything dangerous as If they are immune to it. This is the reason why they are more interested in taking risks.

They may also consider themselves to be unique, thinking no one can understand them. As they grow, they start looking at the world with a different mindset and how others see them.

Language & Communication

Generally, 13-year-olds converse similarly to adults. They understand non-concrete language, including figurative language as well as metaphors and examples. As they begin to comprehend abstract concepts, they can become concerned with moral issues. With time, they'll understand how breaking rules is not always wrong and that there can be exceptions too.

Play

13-year-olds' play includes camping out in the yard, playing board games, and staying over at a friend's house for a slumber party. Most teens at this age love to socialize and stay active with their peers.

This is actually good for your teen. It allows them to manage stress and acquire a sense of belonging, giving them reasons to stay confident and active.

Note:

- *Teens begin improving talents in the use of logic.*

- *They start finding honesty and fairness to be significant issues.*

A Useful Parenting Tip

Talking to your child about the ways through which they can solve a single problem is good for them. Motivate them to brainstorm different solutions before making a firm decision. This will give a boost to your teen's judgment.

Remember:

Most teens at this age have their own accounts on social media and are quite active on these platforms. It gives them a chance to stay connected with their friends and talk to them openly. But, for some teens, electronic communication can be intimidating. It can be a means of stress. They may feel forced to be a part of online conversations to be approved by their friends. By looking at their friends' pictures and posts online, some may even feel as if their friends are having way more fun than they are.

When to Be Worried

Different children tend to grow at a slightly different rate, and that is natural. However, if you come across any of the following issues, it is important to seek professional help:

- Your teen's refusal to shower or keep him/herself hygienic.

- If you see them struggling with their studies. Learning disabilities or ADHD usually become apparent in the teen years.

Talking to your child's teachers or paediatrician if you have concerns is recommended.

Remember:

When (and if) your teen makes mistakes, try looking at it as a chance to help them improve their abilities. In case you see them struggling with the same issue repeatedly, seek out professional help.

Growth and Development of 14year-olds

This age can be extremely crucial. Some teens become more responsible and start walking towards the right path. Others may falter, rebel, and even become a part of the wrong crowd. It's an imperative time to make sure you're giving your teen enough direction and encouraging them to learn the skills they need for a thriving future.

Physical Development

By age 14, most children have experienced puberty.

Physical changes in girls include:

> ➢ Pubic and underarm hair

> ➢ Menstruation

> ➢ Breast development

Physical changes in boys include:

> ➢ Pubic and underarm hair

> ➢ Enlargement of the testicles and penis

> ➢ Some may experience nocturnal emissions

While these bodily changes can be a reason for pride for some, they can be a source of concern for others. Some teens may feel embarrassed due to their visible physical changes, while others may be proud because of them.

It has been observed that boys who experience puberty later tend to feel bad about themselves. They may even face body image problems when comparing themselves to their friends. It is common for girls to come across body image issues too. They can become concerned about their weight or how they look.

Note:

- *Teens can grow some inches in a number of months, followed by a time period of exceptionally slow growth.*

- *Since bodily changes with regards to one's appearance take place at different rates, it can be a source of great concern for some teens.*

- *They begin to display a varied range of sexual maturity amongst genders.*

A Useful Parenting Tip

You may find your 14-year-old being hungry most of the time. This is why it is essential to stock your house with healthy foods and snacks. Talking about health, instead of weight, should be focused on.

Emotional Development

Most 14-year-olds behave as if they know everything and give off the vibes 'know-it-alls.' So, do not worry if you see your teen arguing about everything you say or if they tell you how you don't know what you're talking about.

Most teens at this age face great variations in their self-esteem. For them to feel good about themselves one day and feel worthless the next day is quite common.

Mood swings can still occur at this stage. However, their intensity lessens. At this age, teens become more eventempered as they grow.

They have mostly established the talents they require to handle uncomfortable emotions in suitable ways. They may depend greatly on their own approaches, like maintaining a journal or listening to music. They may even look for their friends' support.

It's typical for 14-year-olds to feel ashamed of their parents. They may not like being seen with their parents, especially being dropped off by them or going to an event with them.

Note:

- *They naturally become more easy-going.*

- *They start recognizing their own strong points and also their weaknesses.*

- *Can feel embarrassed due to parents.*

A Useful Parenting Tip

You may notice your child complaining about how the rules that you insist on are too strict or that you're expecting a lot from them. Make sure they know they have power over their privileges. Assign tasks and expect them to do their school work on time, without a reminder.

Social Development

It's natural for 14-year-olds to stop telling their parents their little secrets. In fact, now they turn to their close friends and begin confiding in them.

Teens at this age wish to be admired and accepted by peers older than them. Individuality is not important for them, but being a part of the group is.

In case your teen doesn't feel like he/she fit in, they may become anxious. It could affect their self-esteem, and they may end up seeking support from the bad crowd if they don't find a suitable place to fit in.

Most 14-year-olds cultivate an interest in developing romantic relationships. They may start having crushes on people near them or on popular celebrities.

Note:

- *14-year-olds have a great interest in romantic relations.*

- *They feel restless to be accepted.*

- *They have a big social circle comprising of friends belonging to both genders.*

A Useful Parenting Tip

Take an interest in your teen's hobbies. Ask questions that will tell you what's happening in your teen's life. Show them your care about them and their activities.

Cognitive Development

Issues related to justice, equality, and fairness become important. They are also prepared for experiences that are long-term or interests that are less temporary.

They often wish to discover the world that exists beyond their own society. They start taking an interest in finding out all that is present beyond their school and state.

Language & Communication

14-year-olds can communicate less sometimes. However, this is a natural part of development as your teen starts solving problems and handling emotions by themselves.

You may find your teen preferring to stay in electronic connection with peers. Messaging, as well as social media, become really significant during this age.

Most teens tend to make their inclinations known.

They usually have favourite books, movies, and activities.

Play

Play usually includes video games and watching different sporting events with acquaintances. Most of their activities include their friends.

Note:

- *14-year-olds start focusing on the future.*

- *They begin setting goals for themselves.*

- *Some may even challenge the expectations and resolutions proposed by adults.*

A Useful Parenting Tip

Make sure you respect your teen's thoughts and views even if you disagree with their opinions. Take more interest in finding out the cause of their ideas or particular beliefs. Oftentimes, teens just wish for others to listen to their point of view.

Remember:

Although many teens at this age desire to earn money, they usually do not acquire formal employment. You might help your 14-year-old in finding unusual jobs that enable them to earn some money. These jobs could include looking after a neighbour's pet or mowing lawns.

By this age, most teens should know how to perform the basic chores that are done by you around the house. Consider paying your teen for doing the jobs you may pay someone else to carry out, such as washing the car or mowing the lawn.

When to Be Worried

It is natural for different individuals to grow at somewhat different paces. There can be 14-year-olds who look and behave more like adults. At the same time, there will be teens who might still be a lot child-like. Generally, you don't need to fret about it as they eventually mature.

That said, if you are tensed about your teen's childishness or irresponsibility, it's vital to connect with your child's physician. A doctor can guide you whether or not your child needs a specialist. You need to keep an eye on whether or not your teen suffers from eating disorders as they can develop during these years. Make sure you observe how and what your teen eats. If you see them skipping meals, or purging diets, feel free to seek professional help.

Remember:

- Make sure your teen possesses all the talents they require to become an adult.

- Get focused on educating them on life talents and giving them chances to practice those abilities independently.

Growth and Development of 15year-olds

The years from 15 to 18 can be involved in enabling your teen to develop and hone the talents they need to become responsible adults.

Teens, at this age, are most likely to believe they are capable of controlling the world now. You may find them insisting on the fact that they know everything. With this, you may also notice frequent rebelliousness.

It is essential to understand your teen's growth in order to discipline them successfully during mid-adolescence.

Physical Development

By age 15, most girls reach their full height. Many of them feel uncertain when it comes to their appearance, particularly their weight. Studies reveal that nearly half of all high school girls diet in an attempt to lose weight.[72]

15-year-old boys may keep on growing for the following year or two. Mostly, during this age, the voices of boys become deeper. They may even start to grow facial hair. 15-year-old boys increase muscle speedily at this age.

Note:

- *The voice of boys grows deeper.*

- *Teen boys start growing facial hair.*

- *By this time, girls reach their maximum height.*

A Useful Parenting Tip

Acquaint yourself with the symptoms of different disorders, including eating ailments and other mental health issues. It is important to find professional help in case you notice your child is facing eating disorders, body image problems, or mental maladies.

Emotional Development

By the time teens turn 15, they start thinking out various possibilities. For instance, what would it be like to travel alone?

Some may start imagining themselves at different colleges or getting their own little apartment.

15-year-olds may also get tensed about their scores, romantic relationships, and other teenage matters. They may even be very much concerned with what they look like.

---

[72] https://www.verywellfamily.com/15-year-olddevelopmental-milestones-2609027

By the time teens turn 15, they argue less with their parents, and their conflicts with them begin to fade. However, they show more individuality and freedom from their parents while simultaneously showing great respect for the rules when privileges and freedoms are dependent on their behaviour.

Many teens are handling a fair amount of pressure at this point. Their stress may be due to academics or romantic relationships and maybe even due to their first sexual encounters.

Note:

- *Their disputes with parents become less frequent.*

- *They display increased freedom from parents.*

- *They also show great skills regarding emotional regulation.*

A Useful Parenting Tip

Making your teen's privileges reliant on their capability to be responsible enables them to be more mature. Ensure they know they can earn independence only by showing that they can handle more freedom.

Social Development

Friends are at the centre for most 15-year-olds. Make sure you are aware of who they are spending their time with because most children tend to adopt their peers' behaviour patterns and try out different activities that interest their friends.

Most teens aged 15 are greatly interested in romantic relationships. Although some may want to stay in touch with their love interest over text or online, others may want to spend time with them.

Most 15-year-olds are not only aware of their sexuality but may also display a growing interest in sexual activity. You would also notice your child's preference to stay alone in their room.

Note:

- 15-year-olds' interest in romantic relationships bloom.

- As they mature, they become more caring towards others and are more able to develop intimate relationships.

A Useful Parenting Tip

Keep an eye on who your teen is hanging out with.

Cognitive Development

Teens at this age can be argumentative, for which there is nothing to be worried about. To assert their independence and show how they know it all, they may go against what you have to say.

A lot of teens begin to think about their future. Many even decide what field they would major in at college and what career they want for themselves.

Language & Communication

Despite being with friends at school the whole day, they can still talk to their friends on the phone the entire evening. However, when it comes to talking to their parents, they have little to share.

They are also interested in staying active online, communicating via texting, and may even write blogs to voice their thoughts and feelings.

One factor because of which their language, as well as vocabulary develops, is reading. They also learn to talk like an adult and hold proper conversations. They can even tell more engaging stories and know how to use more cultured communication skills.

Play

Teens at this age are interested in particular activities. In most cases, they're interested in watching movies, playing video games, surfing the internet, or listening to music. They may also be great fans of sports and follow different athletes.

Although some 15-year-olds like being on their own, others prefer spending time with friends.

Note:

- *They start thinking more about their future.*

- *They also display more defined work habits.*

- *They will better be able to explain their choices/decisions.*

A Useful Parenting Tip

Take a greater interest in your teen's life and the activities they enjoy. Learn more about their world, what games they enjoy and what sports they like to participate in. Find out who their favourite celebrities are, what kind of movies they like, and so on.

Remember:

For most teens, this is the time when they begin to take driver's education. Attaining a learner's license can be a huge deal. With this, the responsibility multiplies too.

However, you as a parent must be sure that your teen is ready for this kind of responsibility. Make sure you don't rush them into believing they are prepared for it. It's not necessary that all 15-year-olds are ready to drive.

When to Be Worried

Make sure you are well aware of your child's behavioural patterns. Get professional help if you notice the following changes:

- Difficulty in sleeping
- Refusal to attend school
- Changes in appetite
- Loss of interest in activities
- If they seem sad or dejected
- If they tell you they've been thinking about suicide

You can also connect with a doctor in case you are worried about your child's development.

Important Advice

This can be a big year for teens. You will notice several changes during their 15th and 16th birthdays. Although at times you might feel they are not ready to go out in the world, remember, you just have two more years to prepare them for life after their high school ends.

Take time to teach them all that will aid them well in their adult life.

The Self-regulation and Emotional Development of Adolescents

Adolescence indicates to the transitional stage of development from childhood to maturity. It starts with the beginning of puberty and ends with successfully gaining freedom from parents (Steinberg & Morris, 2001). However, a paradox can be seen at this age. Human adolescence sees an upsurge in mortality as well as immoral behaviour relative to their childhood (Steinberg & Morris, 2001). This can be a little difficult to accept, keeping in mind that adolescents are becoming stronger at this age, firmer with greater disease tolerance and honed cognitive skills. Then how can there be a rise in morality?

It must be remembered that the higher mortality rate in adolescents is not because of various diseases but because of other harmful incidents such as accidents, suicide, or homicide that are mostly fatal. This is generally a result of adolescents' lack of self-control which compels them to put themselves at risk. In other words, it is because of the lack of the ability to methodically control unsuitable feelings, wishes, and actions (Steinberg & Morris, 2001). I believe that self-regulation differs from one adolescent to another. Moreover, we can explain and even predict behaviour that is inappropriate or reckless just by focusing on the concept of emotional development in adolescents.

The adolescence period can be a unique stage of development characterized by a radical change within the manners as well as feelings of people. However, as abovementioned, adolescence is the peak time of physical health. They are mostly healthier, stronger, more immune to various diseases and have sharp mental capacity. Yet, this age can be a period of behaviour that is risky with heightened emotionality. Because of their desire to seem confident, they can end up putting themselves in risky situations or engage in dangerous endeavours. Due to these reasons, the chances of them dying during this age increase drastically.

In 2017, 56% of the deaths of 10-24-year-olds were because of external causes.[73] These external causes included intentional self-harm, using toxic substances, assault, drowning, and accidental poisoning. It goes without saying that a substantial proportion of this ratio can be prevented if more emphasis is laid on a healthy diet, self-control, and extensive public health involvement.

We can explain this trend of engaging in risky behaviours within the frameworks of restraint and emotional growth. Lately, several types of research have been conducted especially with regards to neurobiology, where most research has highlighted that adolescents face issues regarding self-control. They don't have any prefrontal cortex. In Bell & McBride's words, it's a car with just gasoline, no brakes or steering wheel, whatsoever (Bell & McBride, 2010). These statements can have both hostile as well as positive consequences because adolescents are used to justifying their restricted ability of forming decent life choices and their weakened responsibility for corrupt and wrong deeds.

Many studies regarding the behavioural changes in individuals of this age, carried out in recent years, show that adolescent behaviour is unexpected, deviant, or illogical. This can be understandable, keeping in mind the fact that this stage is often characterized by heightened occurrences of criminal activities as well as psychiatric disorders (Spear & Varlinskaya, 2010). Their main overgeneralizations are made on the descriptions behind the augmented prevalence of

---

[73] http://www.youngpeopleshealth.org.uk/wp-content/uploads/2019/09/AYPH_KDYP2019_Chapter2.pdf

dangerous behavioural and untimely deaths within the adolescence phase:

Overgeneralization 1: Adolescents are Incapable of Forming Ideal Decisions

As an adolescent begins to gain more liberty and is expected to rely less on the family as he/she grows up, it places new demands on the individual.

By definition, adolescence places new demands on the individual as he or she transitions from dependency on the family system to relative independence. Rises in trying for innovation, forming relationships with peers, and rebelling against parents or caregivers are some of the characteristics found not only in humans but also in other species during this growing stage. It is believed that these behaviours have evolved to gratify adaptive functions, for instance, effective mating and acquiring resources for survival (Spear & Varlinskaya, 2010).

A higher sense of understanding towards socially appropriate signs (for example, monetary acquisition, peers) would seem to be the best device for overcoming these types of developmental issues. However, when the impact of these socially conscious cues comes at the price of long-standing objectives and the adolescent's overall well-being, such a device can appear to be less than perfect (Spear & Varlinskaya, 2010). In the framework of emotional signals, self-regulation –here, the suppression of influential actions – shows an exceptional cognitive pattern than when it is absent or when there is no sensitive info present (mainly in males), many teenagers act as well as adults, and even better (Tottenham et al., 2011). When decisions are made in the heat of the moment, suggesting when various emotional cues are present, the performance of adolescents weakens considerably.

In particular, adolescents have a difficult time overpowering responses to appetitive social cues rather than those that are neutral (Tottenham et al., 2011). This decline in the ability to make the correct decisions is neither observed in children nor in adults (Spear & Varlinskaya, 2010).

Overgeneralization 2: All Adolescents Undergo Similar Heights of Pressure

It is important to understand that not all adolescents struggle with these changes, as Stanley Hall proposed in his theory of adolescence (Arnett, 1999). It wouldn't be wrong to say that adolescence can be somewhere between Hall's storm-and-stress adolescence concept and Mead's cultural theory of the same age group (Côté, 1992). Basically, our behaviours are a result of genetics as well as environmental influences that sway the brain's ability to react to different environmental hassles. While some of these environmental demands are consistently accepted, others can be new to a person. Biological restraints and previous knowledge decide how well we respond to the environmental demands that are changing (Côté, 1992). Consequently, even being adults, our skills to respond to new tasks and suitably control our actions can differ. A vital assurance of self-regulation is the skill of a person to refuse the attraction of an immediate gain in return for better rewards.

The impulse-control capabilities of adolescents are strictly tested in emotional situations in contrast with children or adults. Extravagant responses when it comes to incentive-related circuitry are also noticed. These are relatively difficult to control due to the absence of top-down regulation because of prefrontal connection absences in adolescents.

Specific differences in the clash between regulation and motivational structures may add to increased or reduced self-control during this period. To define adolescents as "all gasoline, no brakes, and no steering wheel" is to underestimate this critical phase of growth (Casey & Caudle, 2013). Certainly, if adolescents' aim is for adolescents to attain liberty from their caregivers or parents, then providing them with opportunities to tackle new responsibilities is a serious matter (Casey & Caudle, 2013). This period's developmental objectives will be tough to attain unless resources and communications are delivered to help develop the adolescent's brain.

Overgeneralization 3: Adolescents Lack a Prefrontal Cortex

Several proofs from the studies of animals and human imaging of the structural, neurochemical, functional, and brain changes during development have given rise to the growth of the uneven model of brain development, a hypothetical account of adolescence (Somerville & Casey, 2010). This theory states that subcortical regions and reward-related prefrontal control do not interact during development in the same manner. Particularly, emotional and motivational sub-cortical links evolve before the prefrontal control connections. Because of this developmental difference, the regions of motivational subcortical depend on more than the prefrontal regions throughout the course of development (Somerville & Casey, 2010).

In contrast with adulthood, when this developmental circuitry is entirely developed and during infancy when it is still budding, this growth disparity leads to a relatively greater dependency on the motivational subcortical regions than the prefrontal regions during adolescence. With experience and age, the link between these regions builds up, offering a medium for top-down adjustment of subcortically controlled emotional behaviour that increases the capacity of self-regulation (Rubino et al., 2015). Numerous brain imaging analyses have attempted to confirm this model and carry out a test for any exceptional brain activity patterns in adolescents involved in typical risky behaviour in the sense of recompenses. These findings call into question that adolescent self-regulation is a result of the less developed prefrontal cortex, contributing to less active behavioural regulatory control (Rubino et al., 2015).

In social sciences, identity growth is one of the main notions. Several psychologists, as well as sociologists, have tried to explore the association between the development of identity and the rise in psychological ups and downs in the adolescence phase of progress. Researchers believe that adolescents aged 12, 13, and 14 are considered to be the most exposed to hostile psychological variations. Brown believes that the following four major psychological tasks are considered to be the most important to accomplish by adolescents (Brown et al., 1986):

- to be easily noticeable or stand out (work at autonomy and cultivate an identity),

- to measure up (look for mechanisms to attain as well as improve competency),

- to gel in (acquire acceptance from friends and find affiliations that are comfortable),

- to take hold (make promises to particular opinions, objectives, and actions).

Furthermore, Brown defined two characteristics in which these major activities are connected to teenagers' threats. First of all, different risk behaviours may either enable or hinder the effective accomplishment of these tasks. Next, to cope with the failure to do well in these tasks, adolescents may end up engaging in behaviours that are risky (Brown et al., 1986).

In adolescents, the link between risk-taking and the development of identity is apparent. This has been understood as an individual psychological mechanism by some sociologists as well as psychologists and a social process mechanism by others. Adolescents' risk-taking is seen as a mechanism to distance oneself from the views of other people, particularly parents. Erik Erikson originally proposed this view. Erikson believed that the reason why adolescents engage in risky behaviour is to develop a sense of who they are and the behaviour they would like to be known for (Montgomery, 2020). Suppose the process of identity formation is not completed. In that case, individuals will likely tend to engage in risky behaviour, including drug exploitation, reckless sexual behaviours, and suicide ideation.

Researchers have also identified other aspects of identity development. These consist of sexual orientation, gender and also, ethnicity. Adolescents must evaluate these potential identities' parameters, examine them, and think through whether and how to incorporate them into their sense of individuality (Kroger, 2014). The immigrant youth may find this process particularly hard. That's because they must, at times, interpret the culture of both their families as well as their nation or ethnic group, and also of the society into which they've now settled. Many studies on immigrant youth reveal that they either stick to the culture of their home, following traditional norms, or reject that choice in place of the immigrant country's identity (Kroger, 2014).

Autonomy development is greatly connected to identity development. In most cases, this is thought of as essentially an interpersonal or psychological procedure. Brown believes that a few psychologists have suggested that individuals develop healthy autonomy through a universal mechanism (1986). Those individuals who develop a greater sense of agency (for instance, taking responsibility for their behaviours) while also keeping in mind functional relationships with adults cultivate healthy autonomous and relational self. This implies that such adolescents are less likely to take part in risky behaviour (Montgomery, 2020). If this procedure is not accomplished, the affected adolescents will likely adopt risky behaviour, that can lead to adverse life outcomes. Besides, teenagers spend considerably more time with peers than with younger children, meaning they notably influence them more.

Adolescents' desire for friendship and support at this point makes them more vulnerable to peer pressure, encouraging the quick creation of new relations. Researchers have also found a direct link between age and the frankness to peer control (e.g., Brown et al., 1986), with the height of openness to different antisocial influences being fixed at around 9th grade.

The highlights mentioned above show the significance of nurturing social maturity, one of the most critical tasks during adolescence. The skill of effectively taking part in social relationships is crucial for both identity growth and attaining approval from favoured peer groups (Montgomery, 2020). Impulse control, as well as emotion management, are two abilities that are especially significant for refining social competence. It has been observed that those individual teenagers who efficaciously control their sudden whims have a rather different set of social relationships than those adolescents who do not, implying that their chances of engaging in different kinds of aggressive behaviours are less (Montgomery,

2020). Thus, even more adults would avoid teens who are impulsive, leaving them to be swayed by peer groups made up of hostile teens. Stability shown by peer groups in this category is rather less than others.

The Attachment Theory

It is true that a child needs the mother most. The attachment theory focuses on the mother-child relationship at length. The consistency of this relationship as well as the care and nurturing the mother provides and how that support builds a special, stable bond, are some of the key points of this theory. According to the attachment theory, this bond plays a crucial role in upholding a healthy attitude towards future relationships and responding to challenging life situations. Secure attachment is closely connected to useful adjustment to emotive experiences. On the other hand, methods of insecure people for dealing with negative feelings and situations fall into a range of efforts to enhance or mitigate attachment needs. These strategies have exposed a person to danger and increased venerability to the risk and self-destructive behaviours (Blesky, 2002). Individuals displaying insecure attachments look for self-regulation in other areas that may include drinking, smoking, or doing drugs. Therefore, emotion-based coping mechanisms may be used to affect the force of drug abuse, smoking regularity, and alcohol intake.

Studies have shown that in the case of people who have secure attachments, they are more likely to look for social backing when they need to confront emotional stress (Barrett, 2020). This probably explains why this group of adolescents is characterized by a heightened skill to confront emotional strains. Thus, they are likely to keep away from adopting antisocial behaviours such as too much alcohol drinking to manage negative emotions. This contrasts with the behaviours displayed by individuals who show insecure attachments (Barrett, 2020). This group of individuals smokes or drinks alcohol greatly and maladjustive mechanisms of releasing pressure. Those individuals who demonstrate avoidant attachment tend to reject the significance of attachment figures. As a result, they tend to avoid them when they come across emotional stress. Furthermore, ambivalent youths have also been found to have high respect for attachment figures. Still, they don't deem it necessary to construct functional relationships with them. This results in development issues regarding selfregulation and problematic emotional growth (Barrett, 2020).

Insecure attachments pave the way for adolescents to participate in risky behaviours that include drug substance abuse, suicide ideation, or smoking by generating psychological conflicts. Therefore, adopting these behaviours can be seen as an ill-advised mechanism of selfmedication for emotional stress problems. They can also be thought of as mechanisms of dealing with the loss of selfregulation as well as emotional instability (Barrett, 2020). Perhaps the lack of trust among parents/caregivers and adolescents, parents' inattention of the emotional needs of adolescents, the failure of parents to show reasonable feelings towards adolescents, or to express empathy to adolescents who undergo traumatic events, all contribute to the growth of adverse behaviours in adolescents (Barrett, 2020). We learn from the storm and stress model that secure attachment in adolescence is mainly associated with greater self-esteem, tougher ego identity, honed social fitness, and effective psychological adjustment (Barrett, 2020). It is also imperative to note that the nature of attachment in adolescents greatly influences the kinds of relationships formed throughout this developmental stage. Sroufe et al. states that teenagers, who display secure attachments, are more likely to forge effective romantic relationships and better self-regulation (2010).

This is a period of change for adolescents when they are more susceptible to various undesirable behaviour, including drug abuse, risky sexual activity, and behavioural adjustment issues. Early engagement in such risky behaviour and transition issues are incredibly distressing because they are connected with various adverse effects in later life stages, such as adult alcoholism and early pregnancy (Wellens, 2020). Factors within a child and within the child's environment have been linked with the increase of these risky behaviours.

Latest studies point out that dysfunctional emotional regulation styles and behaviours that are emotionally induced in adolescence can be a noteworthy indicator of risky behaviour. Adolescents who are unaware of how to deal with their feelings are more likely to take part in risky actions to handle their negative emotions. The stress vulnerability model shows that individuals who do not possess good strategies for handling their emotions may adopt harmful substances to lessen their negative emotions (Wellens, 2020). Emotion avoidant approaches are also connected with greater levels of drug abuse. Related studies have linked risky sexual activity with the clamping down of negative feelings, backing up the model. This lack of abilities may result in concerns regarding regulating emotions, being cognizant of one's feelings, and efficiently communicating emotion.

In studies of risk behaviour, emotion regulation has hardly been studied as a separate indicator of affect regulation but instead in conjunction with impulse control, behavioural, or cognitive regulation (Wellens, 2020). For example, some studies have displayed that the absence of or low self-regulation during early adolescence is categorized by a tendency of the affected adolescents to take on many sexual partners in the course of the later stages of adolescence (Raffaelli & Crockett, 2003). Moreover, the absence of behavioural ego control in childhood and adolescence has been predictive of an increased rate of hard drugs and marijuana during the later stages of adolescence (Wellens, 2020). However, greater emotional restraint in adolescence is associated with lower rates of hard drugs during early adolescence. All these results back the statement that emotion regulation has a substantial impact on adolescents' tendency to participate in risky behaviours.

Conclusion

It goes without saying that the adolescence period is a difficult developmental stage in human beings. That's mainly because it is related to many behavioural as well as psychological changes. The cause of these behaviour and psychological changes has never been completely comprehended. While some researchers believe that it is caused by biological effects, others suggest that it is a result of environmental effects. A few studies have proposed that adolescents' lack of prefrontal cortex is responsible for youths' adverse behaviour. This opinion has been questioned by the advocates of theories believing that several factors are responsible for adolescents' adverse behavioural as well as psychological changes. All in all, one thing is clear from all these theories on adolescent behaviours; many adolescents do not possess self-regulation, making them susceptible to engage in risky behaviours.

Furthermore, adolescents who show low emotional competency, insecure attachments, and an absence of proper identity are more likely to take part in ruthless habits, including drinking alcohol excessively, smoking, irresponsible sex behaviour, and the use of strong drugs. For example, Erikson claims that adolescents involve in risky behaviour to develop a sense of who they are and the behaviours they want to be known for. However, to say that adolescents are "all gasoline, no brakes, and no steering wheel" is an overgeneralization of the psychological, behavioural issues that face adolescents, as there are several causes that contribute to this phenomenon. Besides, some adolescents can achieve normal development in spite of the developmental challenges that face a part of adolescents.

Chapter 12

Child Development Age group 16 – 18 & Onwards

Growth and Development of 16year-olds

Sixteen-year-olds know how to bring both happiness and vexation to their parents or caregivers. For example, parents may have several reasons to take pride in the accomplishments of their daughter or son and bloat with happiness while seeing their children thrive. Still, even during that time, they are bound to come across multiple challenges too. These challenges can be regarding risky behaviours, sudden impoliteness, all of which parents have to deal with.

It goes without saying that you'll love spending time with your teen, going to different matches together, tagging along while they get a driver's license. It all trickles down to how you balance the relationship with your teen.

Physical Development

At age 16, the physical differences between girls and boys are most obvious. Although girls are beginning to somewhat slow down in their physical development, boys seem to be just starting.

In case you have a son, you should expect physical changes to continue in them. This includes fast growth in their height and also the growing of facial hair. During this phase, you may find your teen (both boys and girls) eating and sleeping more in order to carry on with that development.

Note:

- *16-year-olds need more sleep. That's also because the time at which they generally fall asleep alters given their biological wiring for staying up as well as waking up later.*

- *They keep growing and physically mature. The boys grow facial hair.*

- *Boys start paying more attention to how they look and whether or not they gel in with others, particularly girls.*

A Useful Parenting Tip

Talking about outlooks, dangers, and prospects directly without avoiding tough topics such as alcohol intake, sex, or drugs is helpful. Make sure they know how you'd want them to react if, for instance, there is drinking at the party they're at.

Emotional Development

Adulthood is not far from teens of this age, and they are quite very well aware of that. At this point, they'll begin making decisions. Sometimes, the decisions that they make might not be the correct ones. In case their decisions worry you, have a word with them. Keep an eye on the changes in their behaviour, mainly if you feel your teen looks sad or unhappy. Connect with a professional if need be.

Note:

- *16-year-olds develop worries concerning their physical development.*

- *They not only show considerable independence, but they also engage in less fight with parents.*

- *Teens at this age go through episodes of unhappiness.*

A Useful Parenting Tip

Although you might hear your 16-year-old say they don't need you, they can't be further from the truth. Make sure you continue to build up your connection with your teen by taking an interest in their everyday life and by admiring them for their little endeavours. Allow your child to fail sometimes but ensure they have the abilities they require to deal with the distress that turns up with disappointment.

Social Development

Sixteen-year-olds are embedded in a social domain that is dominant with friends and romantic relationships. Spending less time with families and more time with friends seems important. They may even wish to spend more "me time" alone, preferably in their rooms.

Every so often, teens have intense sexual desires and may even become sexually active. During this time, they'll start understanding more about their sexual preferences and who they're attracted to.

Note:

- *In search of intimacy, 16-year-olds step into profound relationships, both platonic or romantic.*

- *They display signs of self-confidence.*

- *They also start to show increased resistance to peer pressure.*

- *They get to know their sexual orientation.*

A Useful Parenting Tip

Talking about topics that are usually not talked about openly, such as sex, sexual orientation, and consent, often helps teenagers understand different aspects of relationships. If you keep ignoring these issues, your teens are only going to get more curious and might end up doing something they shouldn't.

Cognitive Development

Children, who once used to think about themselves only, now begin to pay more attention to the world they are a part of. During the mid-teen years, teens become mindful of the entire world and their role in it. 16-year-olds also begin abstract thinking, the things that could be. Their reasoning, as well as problem-solving skills, improve considerably.

Language and Communication

For the most part, teens can talk the way adults do. They can understand abstract as well as concrete thoughts, grammatical and punctuation rules, particularly at school. They also learn to read and write difficult sentences, often profound in meaning.

Play

It wouldn't be wrong to say that teenagers are usually overscheduled. This isn't always great for their growth. Teens need some free time to explore their likes and dislikes, for instance, arts, reading, and sports. They need to figure out for themselves as to what interests them and what doesn't.

Teens, at this point, may even try to relax themselves by simply watching tv, or playing an online game.

Note:

- *You may notice 16-year-olds changing language and behaviours depending on where they are, for instance, whether they're at school, home, or with friends.*

- *They display well-defined work ways.*

- *They may clarify the logic behind their views or decisions.*

A Useful Parenting Tip

There isn't a standard path that is "ideal" for teenagers, but you may feel your teen needs help in exploring the different options they've got. They must understand the pros and cons of a decision they are planning to make and how that decision is going to affect their future. Make sure you help your child plan for life after school/college.

Remember:

Usually, teens start driving at the age of 16. However, driving duties means greater risk. You must make sure that your teen is ready to deal with the responsibility of driving before you teach them to drive or before you allow them to take the car out by themselves. As stated earlier, accidents are one of the top reasons for death for teens. Make sure your teen is sure of how to stay safe on the road.

When to Be Worried

At this phase, two aspects are worth getting concerned about. One, if your teen is lagging behind academically, and second if you notice any signs of mental health issues. For the first aspect, make sure you help and support them, making them believe they have what it takes to succeed. Try to help them organize their schedules and provide them with useful tips that will enable them to focus on their studies. As for the second aspect, reach out to a mental health doctor instantly, before the issues grow bigger.

Important Advice

Some 16-year-olds need to be reminded sometimes to finish their homework and carry out their everyday chores. Others may be struggling to get out of bed and get dressed for school on time. In case your teen needs a lot of help, remember they only have a few more years before they are done with their school. This is why doing everything for your teen on your own may not be a wise move. Allow them to learn the important life talents while you still watch them.

Growth and Development of 17year-olds

While most 17-year-olds are excited about their future outside the four walls of their school, others are scared about stepping into the grown-ups' world. Even some parents may think that nurturing a 17-year-old may be a bit frightening.

For example, you may fret over whether you've prepared them for the adult responsibilities or not. To make sure that you've raised them well, think about their growth and help them accordingly to ensure they are ready to enter the real world and handle challenges on their own.

Physical Development

By this age, most girls and boys are completely developed physically. They are done with their puberty and hence have reached their full height. That said, boys may still continue to grow muscles. They may also grow more facial as well as underarm hair. You may notice that their voices continue to deepen too.

Issues regarding body image are quite basic at this stage. Some teens may not entirely be pleased with the way they look now. Acne issues are also common.

Note:

- *Most 17-year-olds have reached their maximum height.*

- *They are done with their puberty phase.*

- *Boys may continue to grow muscles.*

A Useful Parenting Tip

Make sure you have a dialogue with your child about the significance of good health rather than appearance. The focus should be kept on eating healthy, nutritious food instead of dieting or eating mindlessly.

Emotional Development

Each 17-year-old develops emotionally at a different pace. While some are looking forward to entering the adult world, become increasingly responsible, and have all the freedom, others may be afraid of letting go of their previous, carefree habits. They may become petrified of the truths of awaiting adulthood. This is the reason why some of them may even seem lost, confused, and worried while thinking about the future. Struggling to show signs of responsibility when it comes to their homework, chores, and everyday responsibilities is also common. 17-year-olds may feel fearful about entering into the adult world.

On the whole, a 17-year-old teen's tempers are relaxed and composed than they were earlier. That's mainly because of less hormonal shifts and a heightened sense of control. However, teens will still struggle with their sentiments when, and if, they face a difficult problem. Whether the issue is regarding a broken, weeping heart or a rejection letter, remember that most 17-year-olds are handling adult-sized issues for the first time and are still in the midst of understanding how to deal with them.

Similarly, most children at this age are goal-oriented.

They're starting to picture the type of life they want to form outside of their high school. That's why make sure you are giving them enough space to find out who they are, where they see themselves, and what they want to do in life.

Note:

- *At this age, teens begin to display more freedom from parents.*

- *Their capacity to develop more intimate relationships grow deeper.*

- *Much to their parents' relief, they take less risks at this age.*

A Useful Parenting Tip

Letting your teen drive a car, stay home for one night by themselves and get a job are some of the ways that will enable them to become an adult. It's also essential to stop and guide them in case they're making bad decisions.

Social Development

Most teens at this age are capable of forming strong, meaningful relationships. They cultivate loving friendships and are less likely to move from one group to another. They also learn that it's vital to be dependable and steady. Every time they make promises to their peers, they would wish to fulfil their commitments.

You may find your teen spending most of their free time with friends. When they are home, they may like to stay in their room alone, all by themselves. The relationship you share with your teen may experience several changes during this phase. While some grow apart from their parents after getting enough freedom, others may get closer to them as their rebellious nature begins to fade.

Note:

- *17-year-olds begin to look for intimacy.*

- *They wish for adult guidance roles.*

- *They are able to make as well as keep their commitments.*

A Useful Parenting Tip

Establishing clear-cut rules regarding dating is advisable. Try to talk about healthy relationships, dating, what safe sex is, and the importance of consent.

Cognitive Development

By this age, most teenagers have proper administrative skills. Therefore, they can effectively deal with extracurricular events and activities, part-time jobs, and school homework. However, even though most 17-year-olds think of themselves as adults, their brain powers still are not yet completely matured.

In other words, while they may have the talents to control their desires, they may still act irresponsibly sometimes.

Most teens at this age also start to think about their future. They start to form more solid plans for college and their life after school. Because of their increased fluid intelligence, 17-year-olds have an enhanced aptitude to deal with new difficulties and circumstances.

Language and Communication

The communication of most 17-year-olds is as good as that of adults. But, they may not ask for an explanation or speak up when they come across a word they aren't familiar with or perhaps the meaning of a term or expression.

During these years, slang is also common among teenagers. That may have more meaning than formal language during this age.

In the meantime, some 17-year-olds might still struggle to comprehend double negatives. Moreover, although they have enhanced attention spans, it's common for them to lose track of detailed, difficult questions.

Play

For a 17-year-old, the play might include going to a movie with a friend or perhaps taking part in a hobby. Most 17-year-olds participate in similar free-time activities as adults. It is also possible that many of them have ripened hobbies and pastimes that give them a chance to relax.

Note:

- *17-year-olds can hold a conversation like an adult.*

- *They might use slang words occasionally.*

- *Their ability to deal with new issues and different circumstances become better.*

A Useful Parenting Tip

Motivate your 17-year-old to read as much as possible. Reading will enable them to build their vocabulary, allowing them to improve their writing skills.

Remember:

17-year-olds might be going through various emotions and situations for the first time. For instance, getting a driver's license, acquiring a new hobby, or perhaps getting into a relationship. Some may be applying for and getting part-time jobs, while others may be trying out some riskier behaviours such as sex, drugs, or alcohol.

Therefore, be prepared and observe your teen cope with these adult-like issues.

When to Be Worried

As a parent, if you are worried thinking about sending off your child out in the real world in a few years, then that's understandable but remember, you are not alone. In most cases, there is a lot of development between the ages 17 and 18.

During this one year, teens get ready to step into college or the working world. However, if you notice the following characteristics in your child, it is better to get in touch with your child's doctor.

- If your teen seems to be particularly inadequate for the challenges of adulthood.

- You must also be worried if you observe some major changes in their mood or behaviour.

- Declining grades, variations in sleeping habits, a change in weight or appetite are a few signs implying a mental health issue or some other hidden issue that needs to be addressed.

Important Advice

When your 17-year-old graduates, you may begin to think about whether or not you have raised them well. You start thinking if you have done everything to make them ready for life outside of the comfort of your home. But, it's vital to remind yourself that it's never too late for teenagers to adopt new talents like handling money, keeping themselves safe, or cooking for themselves.

Look for areas in their life where they might still need a bit of training or guidance. As a parent, help them overcome their fears and teach them all that you think is essential for them. In case you struggle with something, connect with your paediatrician or a professional.

Growth and Development of 18year-olds

By this age, teens are somewhat scared and at the same time excited about the future. They have to make several decisions right after their graduation. It goes without saying that 18-year-olds think a lot about what lies ahead of them or the kind of life they want for themselves once they've been given the opportunity to do so.

Those teens who possess multiple life talents are mostly looking forward to moving out of their homes and starting a new chapter of their life. However, those going through self-doubt may retreat a little as they think about entering into the unknown.

Physical Development

18-year-old boys and girls are physically mature. By this age, puberty is over, and they've mostly reached their maximum height.

Although boys may still grow more facial hair, and their voices may also alter to some extent, on the whole, they're fully living in grown-up bodies.

By this time, most teens grow accustomed to the physical bodily changes they experienced earlier and may even begin to accept those changes.

Note:

- *18-year-olds are less preoccupied with bodily changes.*

- *By this age, their growth has lessened or, in most cases, ended entirely.*

- *They have attained sexual maturity.*

A Useful Parenting Tip

Make sure you tell your child that their brain hasn't developed entirely as of yet. And in case they consume alcohol, their brain development could get affected.

Emotional Development

18-year-olds are starting to find out where they will fit into the world of adults. This is a time for substantial changes filled with substantial amounts of freedom and pleasure, sometimes together with episodes of longing and uneasiness.

Several 18-year-olds seek advice from adults, particularly their parents, again and are quite comfortable with that. They understand that they want some direction and assistance to sail across the adult world. 18-year-olds are more welcoming to advise than they were earlier, i.e., during their younger teen years. By this age, teens are better able to control their emotions. In fact, most teens are aware of dealing with different emotions properly.

However, the fear of the future and failure can still be big issues. While some teens will start to settle these problems effectively, others will struggle with them.

Note:

- *18-year-olds become more comfortable pursuing adult advice.*

- *They start to accept adult duties.*

- *They can manage feelings in a socially suitable way.*

A Useful Parenting Tip

Regulate your teen's feelings. Many teenagers will think they are the only ones who are going through these changes. Make them believe they are not alone in being fearful about the uncertainty that lies ahead. Remind your teenager that they don't have to figure out every aspect of their future at this point. Things will begin to take shape as they progress.

Social Development

Most teens have had close relationships. By this age, they are better aware of their sexuality.

Social groups that once had an immense influence on teens now seem to be somewhere in the background as teens begin to assess their thoughts without blindly accepting the same ideas as others. Many teens are seen taking a strong stance on different social issues.

18-year-olds have a developing skill to make autonomous decisions and also, to cooperate where necessary. This helps them exceptionally as they are establishing new friendships as well as close relationships.

Although most teens are not yet thinking of settling down, many may start thinking of the kind of life partner they'd want.

Note:

- *Teens can assess their own thoughts and views rather than just following the crowd blindly.*

- *For teens this age, close relationships become vital.*

- *They start accepting adult duties.*

Cognitive Development

18-year-olds begin to think a lot like adults despite the fact that their brains are still developing.

They can think abstractly and are mostly, if not always, future-oriented. At this age, they begin to think about their future, plan, and understand what they want in life. This is the reason why they show a lot of concern for what lies in the future. Sometimes, they may feel speechless when people inquire about what they're up to or what their future plans are.

Many teens are philosophical and ideological as well. However, they have a better capability of using insight.

Language and Communication

Teens at this age communicate differently with friends than they do with family members or school teachers. You may notice them using slang or social media acronyms while with friends. Those teenagers who have a habit of reading more are likely to have an extensive vocabulary. By this age, teens can communicate very well, just like adults.

Play

Spending time with friends or talking to them is important for teens at this age. They mostly have similar pastimes and interests as adults around them.

A Useful Parenting Tip

It's usual for parents to be a little sad, seeing their child turn into an adult. But make sure not to let the sadness you might feel burden your teen. Let them know that although this is going to be a huge change for you, you are happy that they are heading into the adult world nonetheless.

Remember:

18-year-olds may sometimes be troubled with morality. They may be evaluating their morals and the kind of life they want to live as they grow older.

Teens may also think about their spiritual beliefs. Teens at this age sometimes begin to question the beliefs they have held important their entire lives so far. While some may continue with the same beliefs, others may start practising or exploring a new religion.

When to Be Worried

If you find your teen concerned with body image or academic issues and experience a change in appetite or behaviour, chances are they could be experiencing a mental health problem. Substance abuse problems are also quite common during this age.

If you're worried about your teen's growth, urge them to talk to their doctor. Support them if you see them arranging an appointment. Try to accompany them to the appointment and speak about any worries that you have.

Remember:

Although your teen is 18 now, remember he/she is still your child, and your parenting is not over yet. This is the time when you become more of a mentor and guide for them.

You'll see them grow into responsible adults soon.

Behavioural Problems and Effective Solutions for Teenagers

Your parenting style changes exceptionally when your kid enters his teen years. You'll notice yourself being more like a guide, a mentor instead of an enforcer. This does not mean that you don't intervene in case of danger. What it does mean is that by this time, you should allow your kid to make some decisions on their own. Let them make their own choices.

Usual Teen Behaviour

Adolescence can be a riotous time for teenagers as they begin to experience physical, emotional, and social change. Some of the typical behaviour patterns include:

- It's **usual for teens to seem responsible sometimes while still continuing with their child-like behaviours** in other areas.

- During this phase, **friends and intimate relationships become ever more important.** It goes without saying that they'll love to spend as much of their time with friends as possible. This eventually means less time for the family.

- **Teenagers' desire for more privacy continues to grow.** You'll find them interested in keeping their conversations private (especially on social media).

- **Teens love spending time in their rooms,** alone, preferably with the door closed.

Teen behaviour tends to be upsetting for parents at times. But remember, all of these changes are natural. This is just a phase of life that your child will grow out of within a few years. That said, make sure you are on the lookout for any mental health issues, drug abuse, or alcohol intake.

According to Verywell Family:

"Depression, anxiety, eating disorders, and substance abuse issues may emerge during the teenage years[74]."

---

[74] https://www.verywellfamily.com/discipline-strategies-forteens-1094840

Basic Challenges

You still have a few years ahead of you to make sure your teen is ready for the real adult world. For most parents, this can be tricky. The key is to balance the freedom they can have and the guidance you provide. Neither shouldn't be too much or too little at this point.

Teens, as stated earlier, wish for absolute freedom. Often you'll see them asking to go to a party or staying up late with friends.

There will be times when you'll be told you don't know anything about what it's like to be a teenager. But try to stay patient, this is temporary, and things will ultimately rule out in your favour.

Teens may stress their freedom by insisting on doing things when they want to. For instance, when you tell them to help with dishes, chances are they'll complain or perhaps tell you that they'll do the task later.

Being short-tempered, becoming distressed over relationship issues, friend troubles, and school-related problems is common. Some teens also lie only to get themselves out of trouble.

Discipline Strategies That Work

A time-out will no longer work on your kid, but it doesn't mean you can't instil effective outcomes. However, make sure the consequences will teach life lessons that will be helpful for your teen in the long run. Some of the most effective consequences for teenagers can be:

- **Removing Electronics.** Teens are very particular about their gadgets that include laptops, tablets, smartphones. Putting a restriction on your teen's electronic privileges can be an efficient consequence that they'll remember. But make sure it's time-limited. Twenty-four hours without a phone should be enough for your teen.

- **Taking Away Time with Peers.** If your teen is misbehaving due to friends or perhaps under peer pressure, take away their time to see their friends for a while. Grounding them for a couple of days or cancelling their weekend plans also works.

- **Tighten Up the Rules.** In case your teen breaks a rule, they may be displaying they are not yet ready to handle the freedom you are giving them. You can tighten the rules by reducing the time they spend on their electronics or by giving an earlier curfew.

- **Giving Extra Responsibilities.** Taking away some of your teen's privileges until they carry out extra errands or complete certain tasks is also advisable. The moment they begin to show they are responsible, you can return them their privileges.

- **Performing Acts of Compensation.** If your teen has hurt someone, it is time to make amends. Teach them the importance of being apologetic for their rude behaviour or for hurting others.

- **Facing Natural Consequences.** In certain cases, natural consequences turn out to be great teachers. However, make sure the natural consequence will teach your teen a life lesson that is important for them. If it is, back off and allow your teen to face the consequences for the choices they've made.

- **Offering Reasonable Consequences.** If you see your teen breaking something, make them pay to fix the object. In case they are reckless with the car, take it away for a day or two. Make consequences that are directly connected to your teen's poor choices.

Avoiding Problems in the Future

If you behave like an overprotective parent, your teen will never be able to make healthy choices on their own. Similarly, if you're too lenient, they will not adopt the skills they must have to become responsible adults. The top tactics for averting behaviour problems in teens include:

- **Averting Power Struggles.** If your teen says they'll do a certain task later, fight back the temptation to dispute. Rather, set a fixed limit and follow through with an aftereffect. Make sure not to get sucked into an intense power struggle.

- **Making Your Expectations Well-known.** Before allowing your teen to go to the movies, make sure they know how you'd want them to react in case they encounter a problem or what time you expect them to be back home.

- **Earning Privileges.** In case your teen wants an expensive sports kit or a later curfew time, make sure they earn their privileges.

- **A Good Role Model.** You, as a parent, are your child's biggest teacher and model. Your child is likely to learn the ways and values you follow, so make sure they are fit for them.

- **Spending Time Together.** Spending quality time with teens and nurturing the bond you share with them eventually builds an unbreakable bond. Take an interest in their lives, communicate and value the things they hold dear. Go on trips, shop together, watch movies to form a connection.

- **Being Responsible.** Your teen will listen to you and follow your instructions as long as your expectations are reasonable.

Communication Guidelines

There will be times when you'll notice your teen talking to their friends on the phone for hours, but the moment you try to talk to them about anything, they'd have little or nothing to say. This is natural, and talking to your teen can be a bit difficult at times. But make sure you keep trying. Some effective tips are:

- **Communicate Repeatedly.** We all know that healthy communication is the key to a fruitful relationship. It's essential to talk about everything that is worth talking about. Your chat can be about peer pressure, your teen's ambitions, their friends, or even their interests. Once they understand they can talk to you, they'll come up to you for guidance and advice.

- **Communicating During an Activity.** Sometimes, it can be difficult for teens to open up if you especially ask them to sit with you and talk. But if they are busy doing an activity with you, they are likely to talk more, more like a reflex.

- **Problem-solving Together.** Instead of telling your teen how to do things, ask them to watch you solve them. When they accompany you and brainstorm ideas with you, they will learn quickly. Motivate your teen to choose a possible solution.

- **Don't Insist Your Teen Talk to You Only.** There will be times when your teen may be hesitant in talking to you about a particular topic. In that case, make them know other healthy adults they could turn to. For instance, an aunt, grandmother, teacher, coach, and so on.

- **Get to Know Your Teen's World.** Your teen may talk more openly over social media, on comments, or through online messages. That's why you should be willing to enter your teen's world.

Talking to them in whatever way they seem most relaxed opening up in should be practised.

Tips for Parenting Teens

During the teen years, it becomes essential for parents to make sure their children are going to be prepared for life beyond school. You'll observe your teen being independent in many ways. However, you'll also notice certain areas where you'll feel your child still needs to improve.

In case you observe your child struggling in a particular area, teach the skills necessary for them to handle whatever the situation is. Moreover, give them several opportunities where they can be responsible and act independently. If you focus on healthy ways now, you can prepare your teen to take care of themselves in the future.

Everyday Life

Although teens may insist on knowing everything, there will be times when their fresh skills need improving. It goes without saying that teen years are filled with new opportunities. Landing a part-time job or getting a driver's license are some of the ways that will allow your teen to practise being in charge of his/her own actions.

For now, it's vital to teach your teens how they are to take care of themselves or how they should perform daily activities that will make them ready for the future.

Diet and Health

According to the USDA guidelines, your teen must get all the important vitamins and minerals through a wellrounded diet. There are greater chances of adolescents falling short of the daily advised portions of calcium, zinc, iron, and vitamins, particularly vitamin D.

It's better to attain nutrients from food instead of dietary supplements unless one's blood tests or a paediatrician's assessment disclose a particular deficiency.

Calories required by moderately active boys are:

- 13-year-olds require 2,200 calories

- 14-year-olds require 2,400 calories

- 15-year olds require 2,600 calories

- 16, 17, and 18-year-olds require 2,800 calories

Moderately active girls ageing between 13 and 18 need 2,000 calories each day.

Those teens who are energetic more than an hour each day may require more calories. Similarly, those teens who aren't much active may require fewer calories to sustain a healthy body mass index.

You must have noticed that teens like making their own choices when it comes to food. They might find it better to grab a burger while with friends. That's why you must instil in them the need to eat healthily and make appropriate choices.

The focus should ideally be on health rather than weight. Discuss the significance of charging his body as well as the brain. Stocking the kitchen with healthy eatables is also a good way of promoting healthy living at home. Make sure you reserve sweet, sugary eatables for special occasions only.

Keep an eye on your teen's dieting or body image concerns, particularly in girls. Girls in their teens are often aiming to lose weight, because of which, many of them limit their food intake. Some even start to eat only a few kinds of food. Disorders related to eating often arise during these years.

Physical Activity

Physical activity is a must for children. The physical activity of teens should at least be for 60 minutes each day. It should ideally include:

- Aerobic exercise must be the main practice of activity.

- Muscle-building movements are also vital for good health. These may include:

  ➢ Strength training,

  ➢ Bone-building exercises, for instance, jumping

Other physical activities can be:

- Going for a walk every day

- A bike ride

- Swimming

- Kayaking

- Go hiking twice a month

- A relaxing evening walk after dinner

In case you feel your teen is not interested in being a part of a sports team, don't impose it on them. Instead, look for other fun activities that you're sure your teen would love. Making physical activity a family activity can also be fun.

Make sure you restrict your teen's screen time. Motivate them to take part in outdoor activities and be active. Discuss the significance of having a healthy body and mind.

Inside the House

The teenager phase is a crucial time for youngsters to understand how to make decisions by themselves and be granted more duty. It is better to understand that if your teen is able to handle more responsibility right now, in the future, they'll struggle less, particularly during their shift to adulthood.

Some of the responsibilities teenagers learn at this age include:

- Carrying out different tasks proficiently and properly at not just home but also at school and work.

- Taking care of their personal hygiene as well as belongings.

- Being compassionate for people around them.

- To be publicly responsible with regards to their everyday lives.

- Manage their feelings and socialize suitably with different people.

- Realize that sexual activity has the tendency to lead to consequences.

- Must be aware of handling peer pressure conditions, for instance, situations that include doing drugs, drinking, or smoking.

- Grown-up privileges such as driving or having an account in a bank.

- Holding a job and working properly with those who are a part of the team.

- The skill to earn as well as spend money sensibly.

It is essential that your teen knows how to perform important tasks such as cooking and doing laundry. Try to rotate some household chores and give them the chance to learn as much as possible. This will help them maintain the house in the future.

Giving privileges to teens according to their responsibility level is also recommended. Moreover, spending quality time with teens works magic in strengthening the bond. Having a movie night on weekends can be a great way of staying connected. Eating meals together is another way to do the same.

Health & Safety

It's essential for your teen to understand how to take care of himself, particularly his health. Risky behaviour is the leading danger that teens face. So teach your teen regarding the dangers they come across and remove privileges if you see your teen making bad choices.

Visiting the Doctor

Teens can keep seeing their doctors until they turn 21. Wellness checks carried out annually are advised for teenagers.

Some of the common causes that make teens visit their paediatricians between their annual visits include:

- Sports injuries
- Asthma

- Acne
- Skin issues
- Respiratory infections

It's significant to give teens a chance to have a word with the paediatrician in private. Some may have queries with regards to sex, STDs, sexuality, drugs, alcohol, or other delicate issues that they might not be comfortable speaking about in front of you.

A paediatrician should ideally check a teen's body mass index. They should offer to counsel about physical activity, food, and nutrition. They should also discuss what sexually transmitted infections are. Screening for mental health issues, including depression, should be carried out by paediatricians.

Those teens who are sexually active may be regularly tested for sexually transmitted diseases. These include Chlamydia and gonorrhoea, despite not having any symptoms.

According to The American College of Obstetricians and Gynecologists, **girls should visit a gynaecologist from age 13 to 15.**[75]

The Centers for Disease Control and Prevention suggests that when teens turn 16, they should have their second dose of the Meningococcal vaccine[76].

Safety

The biggest issue regarding safety that teens face is their risky behaviour. Teens are known for being impulsive sometimes, and unfortunately, at times, it only takes one wrong decision to end up being in the hospital bed.

---

[75] https://www.acog.org/womens-health/faqs/your-firstgynecologic-visit?utm_source=redirect&utm_medium=web&utm_campaign=otn
[76] https://www.cdc.gov/vaccines/vpd/mening/public/adolescent -vaccine.html

As stated earlier, motor vehicle accidents are the foremost reason for death for teenagers in the U.S. Those teens aged between 16 to 19 are at a greater risk of death or damage while in a car accident than any other age group.

Before you allow your teen to get behind the wheel, it's essential to recognize the chief dangers that result in teen motor vehicle crashes. Some of the leading factors of these accidents include driver inexperience, distracted driving, and speed.

Creating clear rules for your teens from the start and letting them know what you expect of them is important. Speak to them about consequences for irresponsible behaviour, including speeding or getting into the car with a friend or peer who is drunk.

Violence is the third biggest risk to a teen's health.[77] The 2017 survey of the Centers for Disease Control and Prevention (CDC) reveals that 19% of teens have been bullied throughout the previous year. **The ratio of students carrying a knife or a gun was 16%.**[78]

Therefore, it is essential to talk to teens about how they can keep themselves safe. How to handle a violent situation should also be discussed.

The third major cause of death amongst teens is suicide. Although several issues can lead to a teen commit suicide, the leading factors are depression, loneliness, anxiety, and family troubles. Make sure you keep an eye on your teen's mental health. In case you suspect your teen might be suffering from a mental health issue, look for professional help. You can begin by communicating your concerns to their paediatrician.

---

[77] https://www.verywellfamily.com/parenting-advice-for-teens-2609022#citation-4

[78] https://www.cdc.gov/healthyyouth/data/yrbs/pdf/2017/ss6708.pdf

Sleep

According to the AAP, teens should receive about 8 to 10 hours of sleep every night. You can do several things to make sure your teen gets enough sleep. Some of them include:

- Speak to them about their nightly routine. Tell them how to unwind before they go to bed. Reading at night or taking a bath are some methods to relax.

- Make sure your teens turn off all electronic devices early. Smartphones, TVs, and laptops should be turned off at least 30 minutes prior to bedtime.

- Naps after school can hinder night-time sleep and, therefore, must be discouraged.

- Your teen's sleep routine should be kept consistent. Staying up too late on holidays or sleeping in on weekends can disturb the biological clock of your teen.

Technology

With each passing day, technology seems to be getting more and more important for teens. Technology today has changed the way they live their lives, socialize and talk. This is the reason why you, too, must be aware of the latest trending apps that your teens are using. You should also know what devices they are using and to what extent. It is less likely that your teen will listen to your warnings if you yourself are not aware of the dangers of the online world.

Cyberbullies, as well as sexual predators, cause several risks. But there are other online dangers your teen may face too. Someone may try to steal their identity. Teens may also be invited to take part in activities that are fraudulent.

On the whole, you must be aware of how they interact with others online and whether or not they're making healthy choices. Make sure they realize the significance of handling their reputation online.

The World of Your Teen

It's natural for teens to think they are at the centre of the world sometimes. Some might even believe in the existence of an "imaginary audience" that is obsessed with them. Teens might feel this audience follows all their moves and even judges them for their actions. This thought arises from the bigger concept of adolescent egocentrism, according to which teens think the world revolves around them. Because of this belief, they think everyone is keeping an eye on how they look or what activities they take part in. This is a typical stage of social development in teenagers.

Along with becoming more involved in social relationships, teenagers will also become more mindful of social matters. They may even participate in helping a charity. As teens grow, they'll start thinking more about the values they hold dear. They may begin to explore other lifestyles or religions and question their own faith.

It's natural for all teens to feel as if they are not understood by others. At times, their confidence may also wear out. For those teens who are often the victims of bullying and are disliked, adolescence can be a rough time for them in particular.

Think of getting professional help if you notice your teen struggling to fit in socially. Isolation could result in mental health problems. Moreover, be mindful of the stress level of your teen. Issues regarding academics, society, sports, or the uncertainty of the future can be crushing at times. It is important to ensure that your teen is not overscheduled. Remember, downtime is essential.

Important Advice

Each teenager will have different habits, hobbies, and likes. While some may be interested in sports, others might love to read or write. Whatever it is that interests your teen, support them and their efforts to be a unique individual. You, as a parent, should be proud of the person your child is growing up to be. Remember, soon they'll go out into the adult world, and their days of depending on you are becoming lesser. So cherish all these moments. You must healthily deal with your feelings and do not let your emotions hold back your child.

To end with, remember that your teen doesn't have to agree with everything that *you* say or believe in. They can have their own outlook towards the world, so allow them to be their own person.

Chapter 13

From Childhood Risks to Problematic Adulthood

A great number of studies and research highlight that there is a need to invest in addressing susceptibilities in the early years of children. There is a considerable indication that an individual's health status when he grows up is greatly affected by their socioeconomic status. A person's habits and way of living is highly influenced by several factors including,

- Schooling

- Earnings and occupation

- Where they live

- Presence or absence of a disability

The Connection between Risk Factors of Childhood and Adult Outcomes

Many studies have found a connection between early childhood and teenage problems and fitness and emotional concerns in adulthood (Hayward & Homer 2017). These challenges can only be discovered by analysing identity, emotional, and attachment problems in childhood. Moreover, behavioural theories, cognitive-developmental theories, and psychodynamic theories can explain the predictive factors that can lead to problematic adulthood. This chapter will discuss the theories as well as processes that describe the relationship between childhood dangers and adult outcomes.

We know through BBC News that brain scans have the tendency to predict a child's future. The report goes on to say that childhood factors such as low IQ, weak selfcontrol, and parental disregard are greatly related to adult outcomes, including obesity and smoking (Nursing Times 2016). According to the report, these outcomes are "socially costly."

The research focused on the lives of 1,037 people, analysing their lives from the early stages to midlife in New Zealand. The socioeconomic status of a child, their intelligence quotient (IQ), along with susceptibility to the mistreatment or disregard of parents, and level of self-control were all taken into consideration. The researchers wished to find out if these factors could foretell adulthood results like criminal thoughts, smoking, obesity, all of which are pricey to the economy regarding healthcare and social services (Nursing Times 2016). After proper research, the researchers revealed a clear relationship between the abovementioned four factors and the poor outcomes in adulthood. The researchers mentioned their study did not intend to single out some kids or to "blame the victims." Rather, they wished to use this information to classify children who would profit from early childhood programs, such as parental training and pre-school tutoring (Nursing Times 2016). They stated that spending money on such interventions is better than spending money later on harmful things in the long run.

Finding trustworthy interventions that solve these diverse problems, such as social inequality, is quite challenging. The above-mentioned study was a Dunedin Longitudinal Study, which is a potential cohort study that tracked down the lives of 1,037 children. In the study, the possible dangers faced in childhood that could foresee poor adult outcomes were looked at. It was conjectured that a small part of the population is responsible for putting a noteworthy economic burden on economies. This could be foretold reasonably and accurately from childhood. Prospective cohort studies may enable researchers to find out if exposure and outcomes are linked in any way. For example, here, it is between the exposure of childhood and possibly destructive adult outcomes (Nursing Times 2016). However, the nature of the research makes it difficult to prove the effect and cause relationship. Part of it is because there is a possibility of the impact of several other causes.

On the whole, the study revealed a clear connection between unusual adult outcomes and risk factors in the early years of children. These factors also include being raised in a socially disadvantaged neighbourhood, child abuse, low IQ, and showing signs of weak self-control. These four factors elevated the threat of unfavourable outcomes by 18 to 31%, along with the presence of a greater number of these factors forecasting a higher danger (Nursing Times 2016).

These four childhood risk factors were connected to various other monetary pressures. The crime was the next appropriate predictor, with other risk factors in the early years being poorer predictors of results, such as obesity and accident claims. The researchers concluded that the study produced two results. First, the study recognized a group of the population, having great costs in the social as well as health sector (Nursing Times 2016). Secondly, the report offers the highest effect sizes to date, assessing the link between unsafe childhood and unfitting adult outcomes in the population.

Looking at the findings in the stimulus material, we can say that there is an association between childhood occurrences and damaging behavioural and health results in adulthood. Particularly, those children who are raised in challenging environments are more likely to struggle from disorders that include depression, anxiety, hypertension, obesity, and other harmful conditions (Nursing Times 2016). This is the reason why proper strategies should be introduced to classify children who are underprivileged or are facing traumatic events in the early years of their lives to relieve possible illnesses during adulthood.

Concepts, Theories, and Concerns

Focusing on the Psychodynamic Viewpoint

The psychodynamic perspective is centred on Sigmund Freud's psychoanalysis. It is necessary to highlight that according to Freud, human behaviour, which includes violence and crime tendency, is the outcome of "unconscious" forces in an individual's mind (Ryan 2019). Freud believes that experiences in childhood have a huge influence on adult and teenage behaviour. According to Sigmund Freud, conflicts that occur at different developmental phases, for example, can have a bearing on the capability of a person to become a normal working adult (Bartol 2002). He believes that hostile behaviour is a major human instinct that is suppressed or bottled up in normally functioning people, particularly those individuals who were not subjected to childhood dangers. However, if the aggressive behaviour is left unregulated or is suppressed to a great extent, it may be shown unconsciously, resulting in impulsive actions of violence. This is exactly what Sigmund Freud meant by "displaced violence."

It is integral to remember that Freud himself did not comment on anything regarding crime or abuse. A renowned psychoanalyst named August Aichorn is closely linked with the analysis of crime (Tambling 2019). Unlike several of his colleagues, Aichorn was not of the view that being displayed to extreme social circumstances unavoidably led to crime or abuse. He believed that many people, although exposed to high levels of trauma, never partake in severe criminal goings-on. According to Aichorn, stress and tension only began criminality in individuals who experienced a mental state issue called latent delinquency. Aichorn was of the viewpoint that latent delinquency grows because of poor or unsatisfactory childhood socialization and shows a wish for instant gratification (impulsiveness), a lack of compassion for those around, and an absence of remorse. These features are generally taken to the adult phase. Moreover, such people expose atypical qualities such as leaning towards violence, strain, despair, and fretfulness, giving rise to other issues, for example, hypertension.

Psychoanalysts typically see violent people as "ID dominated." They are viewed as individuals who cannot control their pleasure-seeking manners (Toch 1979). People prone to violence also have destabilised or delicate "egos." This is usually because of problems such as childhood abuse or desertion, making them unable to cope with demanding circumstances in present-day society. It is also believed that youth with fragile egos display immaturity and irresponsibility. They are easily affected by deviant acquaintances into carrying out misconduct and abuse.

Superegos can cause "psychosis," that is, the failure to be compassionate towards victims of crime in their simplest form. The most thoughtful critique directed at the psychoanalytic viewpoint is that it is created on data obtained from the subjective insights of engagements with only a lesser number of participants. In another way, this assumption has not yet been scientifically confirmed. Nevertheless, important psychodynamic notions are applied in the elaboration of criminological theory. For instance, some theories of abuse stress upon the principle of one's family and early childhood experiences. Additionally, numerous criminological, as well as sociological theories highlight that violent offenders do not have sympathy for others and are generally reckless.

Behavioural Theories

Through behaviour theory, we understand that all human behaviour is developed through contact and connection with the social world. Behaviourists believe that people do not come into this world with a violent disposition. In fact, it is due to their everyday encounters that they begin to think or act in a violent manner (Bandura 1977). According to believers of behaviourist tradition, this may include seeing family members or associates being admired for aggressive leanings or even observing violence glorification in the media. For example, family life studies show that violent adolescents of children frequently copy their parents' aggressive demeanour. Studies reveal that people who inhabit societies regarded as violent usually obtain their neighbours' hostile behaviour.

Behavioural theorists believe that the following four major causes contribute to the happening of violent behaviour:

1. Arousal is intensified by a worrying stimulus or incident, including an attack, a danger, or challenge.

2. Destructive skills or practices learned as a result of noticing others.

3. A confidence that violence will be publically rewarded by, for instance, decreasing frustration, improving self-respect, offering material goods, or receiving the admiration of others.

4. A system that permits aggression in some social settings.

In the initial empirical experiments, the abovementioned four notions were considered to be favourable (Bartol 2002). Consequently, behavioural theory inspired the development of social learning theories. These include the differential association theory, subcultural theory, neutralization theory, and so on. Damaging behaviour from early periods that is not properly handled had developed to become undone in later life. It is true that our system has false praises from the early stages. Children in the early stages are not to be told *NO* or *Naughty!* The sad truth is that when violent individuals turn 18 years, false praises on their behaviour which have so far damaged their character can now all be addressed. This is done by using the correct ways which could have helped them to know good and acceptable in the society. As a result, they are sent to juvenile or prison for the correction of behaviour, which, unfortunately, causes more damage than good.

Personality and Violence

In psychology, personality has been defined as steady behaviour patterns, outlooks, or actions that differentiate one person from another. Several early criminologists reasoned that a number of personality styles have a greater likelihood of involving in unlawful behaviour. For example, haughtiness, self-assertiveness, extroversion, distrust, and narcissism were some personality qualities associated with violence by Glueck and Glueck. Egoism, aggression, unkindness, lack of understanding, and jealousy are all connected to violent behaviour in contemporary years (Bandura & Hall 2018). Criminals, too, have been found to be missing motivation and persistence. They have been seen to struggle with handling their temper and are more likely to hold unconventional views than the general public.

The two famous methods of evaluating the personality behaviours of young people include the Multidimensional Personality Questionnaire (MPQ) and the Multiphasic Personality Inventory (MMPI). These scales constantly disclose a statistically substantial link between specific personality characteristics and a greater likelihood of participating in criminal behaviour (Bandura & Hall 2018). Teenagers who are inclined to hostility are more likely to be subjected to strong negative moods in response to annoying incidences. While facing hostile social situations, they often feel dejected, irritable, and anxious. According to psychological testing, young people who are prone to crime are normally paranoid, impulsive, aggressive, and hostile.

Psychopath and Violence

Extremely aggressive people typically have a severe personality flaw known as sociopathy, psychopathy, or antisocial personality disorder. Psychopaths are usually impulsive. They have low morality levels and every so often invade other people's rights. Psychopaths are not capable of justifying their acts, making them seem sane and acceptable all of the time. Edens, along with his co-workers (2007), summarized data on adolescent recidivism with regards to psychopathology in the latest meta-analysis. From 1990 to 2005, the authors looked for and examined unpublished as well as published research. While researching, they studied American and Canadian samples and one sample from Sweden.

The conclusions of their comprehensive study reveal that the identification of psychopathy in early childhood is a useful predictor of adulthood violence (Edens et al., 2007). Also, the findings show that psychopathy is greatly connected with violence as well as general recidivism but not strongly associated with sexual recidivism. Astonishingly, psychopathy is an inferior sign of violent recidivism, especially in populations that are racially diverse, as per the findings. Some of the adolescents have acquired the personality of wearing clothes like a goon. Their personality just indicates who they are. They might not be criminals, but their looks and personalities give them up. This has been the most important issue that has led to many unlawful convictions for children in black communities.

Parents must be able to advise and address these issues. Being a parent, you should instruct your teenagers to avoid bad crowds. You must be aware of the kind of people your child hangs out or plays with and who their parents are. Participate in a chat about how things are going in your teenager's life. Ask them the things they do when they are with their friends. Make sure you check their bedrooms and bags frequently, at least once a week, if not more. This can identify if your child is hiding any harmful substances or weaponries that can be dangerous to others or themselves. This also makes them understand how they are being monitored by you.

Intelligence and Violence

Another vital aspect of the investigation in psychology is the possible link between crime and intelligence. Back in the early 20th century, criminologists every so often argued that intelligence is connected with criminal behaviour. Specifically, they claimed that individuals with a low intelligence were more likely associated with people with greater ratios of intelligence to participate in a crime. This hypothesis was further confirmed by research that mainly compared the intelligence quotient of teenagers with the IQ obtained from a rather general population (Nyarko et al., 2020). The notion that low IQ results in delinquency and crime have led to disastrous outcomes a lot. For example, back in the 1920s, people who were suspected to be having low IQ or other unwanted psychological qualities were allowed to be sterilized as a result of the enactment of the "negative eugenics" bill passed by the governments of Alberta and British Columbia (Nyarko et al., 2020). It is imperative to note that only the disapproval by the Catholic church compelled the annulment of the sterilization rule in other states like Ontario and Quebec. In approximation, 5,000 citizens in Canada could have been qualified for sterilization according to these rules, which continued until the 1970s. These rules were suspended in 1999. As for the governments of Alberta and British Columbia, they settled to a payment of more than $82 million to the victims.

Cognitive Theory and Violence

Cognitive theorists review the ways in which people understand and learn to resolve their problems within their social surroundings. The most narrowly linked division of cognitive science with the analysis of violence and crime is the cerebral and mental growth outlook. Piaget was one of the earliest psychologists who stated that the intellectual aptitudes of people develop in a balanced and systematic manner (1932). He observed that youngsters respond to their social setting in a simple manner during the first progressive phase known as the sensor-motor stage. They do this by concentrating their interest on exciting objects and refining their motor skills. Children who have developed into adults are able to attain abstract and complex thinking by the time they arrive at the final developmental stage.

Criminal behaviour by using the notion of moral development was studied by Kohlberg (1969). He declared that **each individual goes through six levels of moral growth.** People only follow the rule at first as they are scared of vengeance. People go along with the law by the sixth stage because it is an expected duty. Also because they have positive viewpoints about the universal standards of justice, fairness, and respect for others. Kohlberg believes that aggressive youth have considerably poorer moral growth than those who are nonviolent, even when modifying for socioeconomic causes (Kohlberg et al., 1973).

According to studies carried out after Kohlberg's innovative efforts, people who live their lives in accordance with the law only to get away from retribution (i.e., because of self-interest) have a greater probability of committing cruel acts than those who recognize and value the rights of others. In contrast, greater levels of moral thinking are connected to acts of altruism, nonviolence, and generosity. To conclude, the data confirms that people who display low moral reasoning are most likely to commit acts of crimes and abuse if they know they can get away with it. Crimes have been committed by young people who have never been caught due to how they have planned and mastered the whole idea. Most cases involve in knife crimes have never been caught. The victims' parents are still seeking justice for the death of their loved ones.

Attachment Theory

The emotional connection built by an infant with their primary caregiver is called attachment. The value of this relationship experienced initially, in accordance with the attachment theory, founded by psychiatrist John Bowlby and psychologist Mary Ainsworth, generally describes how favourably a person interacts with others and replies to affection in their life (Crittenden et al., 2017). The behaviour shown in a bond, specifically when the relationship is endangered, explains attachment manners or forms. When confronted with relationship challenges, the individual with a firm attachment approach is likely to freely state their point of view. But at the same time, they'll be showing a willingness to look for help. On the other hand, those who have insecure or unbalanced attachment mannerisms mostly become anxious or dependent in most of their cherished relationships. They end up acting manipulatively or rashly when they feel weak. Sometimes, they just avoid relationships overall (Crittenden et al., 2017). Additionally, babies with unsteady or insecure attachment commonly grow into adults categorized with a struggle to understand their own emotions and the feelings of others, making it unfeasible for them to put up with, let alone form healthy and well relationships. And so, it can be said that the quality of relationships made during childhood has enormous power on the relationships and emotional issues that cover an individual's adulthood.

Identity

Youngsters are confused today like never before particularly because of all the information prevailing in the media and just how society has formed unhealthy practices and values. It is extremely sad how the so-called "role models" negatively influence your children's lives. In our day and age, negative behaviour is being classified as good and good as bad. As parents, it is our due responsibility to educate our children and teach them not to get fully locked in the fantasy world of those around them. Parents are the first role models for their children. They come way before the media. Each individual is unique in their own way. Thus, trying to follow some other individual's pathway brings a lot of confusion to your mind.

All these mental health issues, which have become an epidemic, are mostly due to identity. I am much aware of biological problems relating to mental health issues, but the most common is the complications young people face regarding their gender. Various factors influence aggression during adolescence and emerging adulthood that include gender roles, social norms, type of school, parental manner, and conflict resolution skills. Sex, life phases, identity development, low self-confidence, and self-control were all explored in this research. The central beliefs of puberty and growing adulthood circle around identity formation (Duell & Steinberg 2019). Identity formation is considered to be the most important developmental issue for youth and emerging adults.

The low self-control theory has been used in several kinds of research to be aware of crime and violence in a better way. Mostly, impulsive behaviour, risk-taking aims, inclination towards physical activities rather than mental activities, and becoming self-centred are all instances of low self-control (Duell & Steinberg 2019). Studies have shown that low self-control is a strong indicator of aggression, defiance, and violence. According to Mamayek et al. (2017), childhood experiences affect the self-will of a child, which is then shifted to the later periods of their life.

Emotion

The teenage years come with an improved quest for independence and an inclination to spend more time with friends than family. Usually, adolescents begin relying emotionally less on their caregivers at this stage, but this emotional liberation comes after a period of pressure and sharp negative emotion experience. Negative affect is way more common in teenagers than in younger kids. However, it usually weakens by the time they get to high school. On the other hand, women also have an extended duration of negative affect in comparison with boys (Chervonsky and Hunt 2017).

Even in response to the same occurrence, teenagers are more likely to undergo intense feelings, both negative and positive, than their parents. Bad psychological results in young people, for example, anxiety, depression, and suicidality have been connected to greater intensity and regularity of positive sentiments, low concentration and frequency of negative feelings, variability of negative as well as positive emotions, and considerably low levels of emotional precision

(Chervonsky and Hunt 2017). The current review's analysis of normative trends of teenage emotional growth will perfectly lead to a better understanding of pathological emotional experience, clinical practice, and guiding treatment scrutiny. These adverse outcomes influence the emotional coordination during adulthood, displaying the need to manage youths' emotional experiences.

Conclusion

The mental and emotional characteristics of children and teenagers hugely impact their later life. In specific, kids and youngsters who display atypical traits, for instance, violence, unease, and depression, are more likely to go through challenging adulthood. Moreover, youths who live through traumatic events or display signs of aggression are at a greater risk of developing into adults having mental health issues, including hypertension or suicidal thoughts. We know through the attachment theory that insecure attachments are linked with difficult adulthood, with most of them exhibiting mental health issues. Additionally, poor identity and emotional development give rise to problems, including depression and dejection later during adulthood.

In case you are struggling with parenting issues at the moment or know somebody who is going through it, a wide range of support, care, and guidance is available at:

http://www.nhs.uk/Conditions/pregnancy-and-baby/Pages/services-support-for-parents.aspx.

https://www.nursingtimes.net/clinical-archive/neurology/brain-tests-may-predict-children-at-riskof-becoming-social-burdens-20-12-2016/#Peerreview

https://www.nursingtimes.net/clinical-archive/neurology/brain-tests-may-predict-children-at-riskof-becoming-social-burdens-20-12-2016/#Prospectivestudy

https://www.nhs.uk/conditions/baby/support-and-services/services-and-support-for-parents/